THE COMPLETE BOOK OF MIDDLEWARE

OTHER AUERBACH PUBLICATIONS

ABCs of IP Addressing
Gilbert Held
ISBN: 0-8493-1144-6

Application Servers for E-Business
Lisa M. Lindgren
ISBN: 0-8493-0827-5

Architectures for E-Business Systems
Sanjiv Purba, Editor
ISBN: 0-8493-1161-6

A Technical Guide to IPSec Virtual Private Networks
James S. Tiller
ISBN: 0-8493-0876-3

Building an Information Security Awareness Program
Mark B. Desman
ISBN: 0-8493-0116-5

Computer Telephony Integration
William Yarberry, Jr.
ISBN: 0-8493-9995-5

Cyber Crime Investigator's Field Guide
Bruce Middleton
ISBN: 0-8493-1192-6

Cyber Forensics: A Field Manual for Collecting, Examining, and Preserving Evidence of Computer Crimes
Albert J. Marcella and Robert S. Greenfield, Editors
ISBN: 0-8493-0955-7

Information Security Architecture
Jan Killmeyer Tudor
ISBN: 0-8493-9988-2

Information Security Management Handbook, 4th Edition, Volume 1
Harold F. Tipton and Micki Krause, Editors
ISBN: 0-8493-9829-0

Information Security Management Handbook, 4th Edition, Volume 2
Harold F. Tipton and Micki Krause, Editors
ISBN: 0-8493-0800-3

Information Security Management Handbook, 4th Edition, Volume 3
Harold F. Tipton and Micki Krause, Editors
ISBN: 0-8493-1127-6

Information Security Policies, Procedures, and Standards: Guidelines for Effective Information Security Management
Thomas Peltier
ISBN: 0-8493-1137-3

Information Security Risk Analysis
Thomas Peltier
ISBN: 0-8493-0880-1

Information Technology Control and Audit
Frederick Gallegos, Sandra Allen-Senft, and Daniel P. Manson
ISBN: 0-8493-9994-7

New Directions in Internet Management
Sanjiv Purba, Editor
ISBN: 0-8493-1160-8

New Directions in Project Management
Paul C. Tinnirello, Editor
ISBN: 0-8493-1190-X

A Practical Guide to Security Engineering and Information Assurance
Debra Herrmann
ISBN: 0-8493-1163-2

The Privacy Papers: Managing Technology and Consumers, Employee, and Legislative Action
Rebecca Herold
ISBN: 0-8493-1248-5

Secure Internet Practices: Best Practices for Securing Systems in the Internet and e-Business Age
Patrick McBride, Joday Patilla, Craig Robinson, Peter Thermos, and Edward P. Moser
ISBN: 0-8493-1239-6

Securing and Controlling Cisco Routers
Peter T. Davis
ISBN: 0-8493-1290-6

Securing E-Business Applications and Communications
Jonathan S. Held and John R. Bowers
ISBN: 0-8493-0963-8

Securing Windows NT/2000: From Policies to Firewalls
Michael A. Simonyi
ISBN: 0-8493-1261-2

TCP/IP Professional Reference Guide
Gilbert Held
ISBN: 0-8493-0824-0

AUERBACH PUBLICATIONS

www.auerbach-publications.com
To Order Call: 1-800-272-7737 • Fax: 1-800-374-3401
E-mail: orders@crcpress.com

THE COMPLETE BOOK OF MIDDLEWARE

JUDITH M. MYERSON

AUERBACH PUBLICATIONS

A CRC Press Company
Boca Raton   London   New York   Washington, D.C.

Library of Congress Cataloging-in-Publication Data

Myerson, Judith M.
    The complete book of Middleware / Judith M. Myerson.
        p. cm.
    ISBN 0-8493-1272-8 (alk. paper)
    1. Middleware. 2. Electronic data processing—Distributed processing. I. Title.

QA76.76.A65 M94 2002
005.7′13—dc21
                                            2002016475
                                                     CIP

Visit the Auerbach Web site at www.auerbach-publications.com

© 2002 by CRC Press LLC
Auerbach is an imprint of CRC Press LLC

No claim to original U.S. Government works
International Standard Book Number 0-8493-1272-8
Library of Congress Card Number 2002016475
Printed in the United States of America 1 2 3 4 5 6 7 8 9 0
Printed on acid-free paper

Contents

Introduction xv

1 Distributed Transaction and Messaging Middleware 1

   Remote Procedure Call 1

      RPC Model 1

      Port Mapper 2

      RPC Layers 2

      RPC Features 3

      XML-RPC 4

      Microsoft RPC Facility 5

      The Stubs 6

      OSF Standards for RPC 7

      Microsoft RPC Components 7

   Microsoft Messaging Queuing 8

      Writing Applications 8

      MSMQ Features 9

      Microsoft Queued Components 10

      When the Network Goes Down 12

   Distributed Processing Middleware 12

      Unisys' Distributed Processing Middleware 13

      BEA Tuxedo 15

      BEA Tuxedo/Q Component 18

   IBM MQSeries 19

      MQSeries Family 20

      Application Programs and Messaging 22

      Queue Managers 23

      Commercial Messaging 24

      MQSeries Internet Pass-Thru 25

      CICS and MQSeries 26

      MQSeries JMS Support 26

2 Object-Oriented Middleware: CORBA 3 29
    Introduction 29
    CORBA Release Summary 30
    Organizational Structure 31
    What Is New? CORBA 3 32
        Improved Integration with Java and the Internet 33
        Quality of Service Control 35
        The CORBA Component Model 36
        CCM Development Stages 37
        CCM Extensions to OMG IDL 37
        Component Usage Patterns 38
        Container Programming Model 39
        Integration with Enterprise JavaBeans 39
    CORBA Object Services 40
        Accessing Object Services 40
        OpenORB 43
    Other Supporting Facilities 44
    OMG Technology Committee 44
    Work-in-Progress Status 46
    Modeling Specifications 46
        MDA Inner Core 51
        MDA Middle Core 52
        MDA Outer Core 53
        UML Profiles, PIM, and PSMs 54
        Additional Specifications 55
        IDL Specified Models 55
        Bridging Platforms 56
        Extensions to IDL 56

3 Microsoft's Stuff 57
    Introduction 57
    .NET Architecture 58
        Multi-Platform Development 59
        What .NET Is Not 59
        Some Advantages 60
        Web Services 61
        .NET Architecture 61
        Building the .NET Platform 62
        .NET Enterprise Servers 63
        Microsoft Content Management Server 2001 63
        .NET Framework Security Policy 65
            Evidence-Based Security 66
            Role-Based Security 67
            Authentication and Authorization 67

Isolated Storage 68
Cryptography 68
Benefits to Users and Developers 69
Open.NET 69
SOAP 69
Microsoft Transaction Server 73
MSMQ in Windows XP 74
Windows 2000 Datacenter 76
Windows Clustering 76
Enterprise Memory Architecture 77
Winsock Direct 78
Windows 2000 Advanced Server 78
Increasing Server Performance 79
Increasing Server Availability 79
SMP and Advanced Memory Management 79
Windows 2000 Clustering Technologies 80
Cluster Service 80
Network Load Balancing 81
Windows 2000 Family Management Services 82
Microsoft Management Strategy 83

4   Ever-Expanding Java World 85
Introduction 85
Enterprise JavaBeans 85
Inside Enterprise Beans 86
The Container 87
Enterprise Bean Types 88
Passivation and Activation 90
CORBA Component Model 90
AlphaBean Examples 91
OpenEJB and CVS 91
Java 2 Enterprise Edition 92
Integration with Legacy, ERP, CRM, and SCM Applications 92
Oracle9i AS Containers for J2EE 95
Configuring and Assembling J2EE Applications 96
Enterprise Servlets with J2EE 98
J2EE Security Model for OC4J 99
RMI and Tunneling Services 100
Java Messaging Service 100
Messaging Domains 100
Point-to-Point 101
Publish/Subscribe 102
EJB 2.0: Message-Driven Beans 102
OpenJMS 103

Java Naming and Directory Interface 103
    Naming Systems and Services 104
        DNS 104
        CORBA and RMI 104
        Directory Services 104
    JNDI Architecture 105
    The Naming Package 106
    The Directory Package 106
    JNDI 1.2 107
Java Media Framework 107
Java APIs: XML Messaging, XML Parsing, and Data Binding 108
    The Java API for XML Messaging 108
    The Java API for XML Parsing 109
    The Java API for Data Binding 109
JXTA Project 109
JavaSpaces and Jini Technologies 110

5   Web Services: Hot Stuff 113
    Introduction 113
    Web Services 114
        Defining or Describing Web Services 114
        Comparing Definitions or Descriptions 116
        Web Services Stack 117
        Web Services Architecture (Narrative) 122
            Microsoft .NET Web Services 122
            Sun's ONE Web Services 122
            Oracle Web Services 123
            BEA Web Services 124
            Hewlett-Packard Web Services 124
            Borland Web Services 125
        Emerging Stack Layers 125
        UDDI Registration 126
        UDDI Registrars and Services 129
        Web Services Brokerage 129
        Workflow Processes 131
        Versioning of Web Services 133
    Third-Party Tools 134
        The Grand Central 134
        Cape Clear 134
        Silverstream 135
        IONA Technologies 136
            Interoperability Test Web Service Description 137
            Broker and Supplier Web Service Description 138
            Postal Rate Calculator Web Service Description 138

Finance Web Service Description 138
Electricity Web Service Description 138

6 Database Middleware and Other Stuff 157
Introduction 157
Data-Level Integration 157
WebFOCUS Business Intelligence Suite 158
Integration with Microsoft Tools 158
Scalability 159
Multi-Analytic Viewpoints 159
Java-Based Report Distribution 159
Wireless Capabilities 159
ISO 9000 Certification 159
Legacy–Web–ERP Integration 159
Development Tools 160
Components and Services 160
iWay Software: EAI Solutions 160
iWay Software: E-Business Integration 160
iWay Software: Mobile E-Business Integration 162
iWay Software: B2B Integration 163
iWay Software: E-Commerce Integration 163
DBMS/SQL Middleware 164
Pervasive.SQL Middleware 164
MERANT Data Connectivity 165
XML Database Middleware 165
Commercial Products 166
ActiveX Data Object (ADO): Microsoft 166
Allora: HiT Software 166
ASP2XML: Stonebroom 167
Attunity Connect 167
DB-X: Swift, Inc. 167
DB/XML Vision and xPower Transform:
BDI Systems, Inc. (acquired by DataMirror Corp.) 168
Delphi: Borland 168
PerXML Smart Transformation System: PerCurrence 168
XML-DB Link: Rogue Wave Software 168
XML Junction and Data Junction Suite 169
XMLShark: infoShark 169
XML SQL Utility for Java (Oracle8i Application) 169
Net.Data: IBM 170
Evaluation-Only Products 170
DatabaseDom: IBM 170
DataCraft: IBM 171
Java-Based Database Middleware 171

Business Sight Framework: Objectmatter 172
CocoBase (Free, Lite, Enterprise): Thought Inc. 172
CocoBase Enterprise Object to Relational Mapping:
Thought Inc. 173
DataDirect SequeLink: MERANT 173
DB2 Universal Database: IBM 173
dbANYWHERE Server: Symantec 173
DbGen Professional Edition: 2Link Consulting, Inc. 174
Enterprise Component Broker: Information Builders, Inc. 174
ExpressLane: XDB Systems 174
FastForward: Connect Software 174
Fresco: Infoscape Inc. 175
HiT JDBC/400: HiT Software, Inc. 175
HiT JDBC/DB2: HiT Software, Inc. 175
IDS Server: IDS Software 176
Jaguar CTS: Sybase Inc. 176
Javabase/400: Telasoft Data Corporation 176
jConnect for JDBC: Sybase Inc. 176
JDBC Developer: Recital Corporation 177
JDBC Lite: Software Synergy 177
JdbCache: Caribou Lake Software Inc. 177
jdbcKona: BEA Systems, WebXpress Division 177
JDX: Software Tree 178
JRB — Java Relational Binding: Ardent Software, Inc. 178
JSQL: Caribou Lake Software Inc. 178
Jsvr: Caribou Lake Software Inc. 178
JYD Object Database: JYD Software Engineering Pty Ltd. 179
ObjectStore PSE for Java: Object Design Inc. 179
ObjectStore DBMS: Object Design Inc. 179
OpenLink Data Access Drivers for JDBC:
OpenLink Software Inc. 179
Oracle Lite: Oracle Corporation 180
POET Object Server Suite: POET Software Corporation 180
PRO/Enable: Black & White Software Inc. 180
Relational Object Framework: Watershed Technologies 180
RmiJdbc: GIE Dyade 181
SCO SQL-Retriever: SCO 181
SOLID JDBC Driver: Solid Information Technology Ltd. 181
SOLID Server: Solid Information Technology Ltd. 181
Versant ODBMS: Versant Object Technology 182
VisiChannel (JDBC) Visigenic Software Inc. 182
XML-Enabled Databases 182
DB2 XML Extender and DB2 Text Extender: IBM 183

      Informix: IBM 183

      Microsoft SQL Server 2000 183

      Microsoft Access 2002 184

      Oracle8*i*/9*i* Application Servers 184

   Web Services-Enabled Database Middleware 185

   Windows Telephony with TAPI 185

   HTTPR 188

7 Bridging the Gap 191

   Introduction 191

   Bridging COBOL to Enterprise Java Beans 192

      Application Mining 192

      Accessing Legacy COBOL Assets from Java 192

      Calling Legacy COBOL from Java 192

         Java Considerations 193

         COBOL Considerations 193

      Calling Java from COBOL 194

      Calling COBOL Classes from Java 195

      COBOL Enterprise JavaBeans 196

      Enterprise JavaBeans Deployment Descriptor 196

      Deploying COBOL Enterprise JavaBeans Application 197

      Combination ActiveX/Java Classes 198

   Wireless Access Protocol: Accessing Oracle 198

      WAP Application 199

      Dialogue Scenarios 199

         Scenario One 200

         Scenario Two 200

         Scenario Three 200

      Database Table 201

      ASP Script: Connecting to Database 201

      XML Syntax 202

      XML Script 203

      Dialogues 204

      Conclusion 204

   XML: Its Role in TCP/IP Presentation Layer (Layer 6) 204

      Breaking the Barrier 204

      Product Integration 206

      Translating for All Browsers 206

      Dynamic XML Servers 207

      XML Mapping 208

      Natural Language Dialogue 208

      Universal XML 209

      Conclusion 209

XML Schemas 209
    Comparing XML Schema and DTD 210
    Strong Typing Advantage 211
    True Key Representation Advantage 212

8   Middleware Performance 217
Introduction 217
IP Traffic Performance 217
    Case Study 219
    Bandwidth Managers 220
    Traffic Shapers 221
        Changing Rates 222
        Moving Applications 222
    Content Delivery Networks 224
    Caching 225
    Load Balancing 227
Service Level Management 227
Communications Paradigms and Tools 228
    Comparing Paradigms 228
    Trade-Offs 229
    XML-RPC 231
Other Performance Tools 232
    Managing EJB and Java Performance 232
    Database 232
    Microsoft Operations Manager 2000 233
    Internet Security and Acceleration Server 2000 233
Middleware Selection 233
    Communications Middleware 234
    Database Middleware 235
    Systems Middleware 236
    E-Commerce Middleware 237
        Enterprise Connector Middleware 237
        Application Servers 238
        Messaging Middleware 238
    Java-Based Middleware 238
    Web Services Technology 239
    Middleware Interoperability 240
    Development Middleware 240

9   What Lies Ahead? 243
Introduction 243
    Evolutionary Paths 244
    Competing Paradigms 245
Middleware Hierarchy 245
    Database Middleware 246

Web Services 247
Emerging Internet Standards 248
   User Interface 248
   Security 248
   Workflow Standard 249
Interoperability 251
   SOAP Protocol 251
   J2EE and .NET Platform 253
Performance Tools 254
Service Levels 256

10 Glossary 259

About the Author 269

Index 271

Introduction

The wave of recent corporate mergers and growth of business on the Internet have boosted enterprise systems integration's profile in both IT and business. All these factors have contributed to enterprise integration's importance, but the marketplace conditions of today's open, collaborative-based economy are still the major reasons why companies choose an integrated solution. Companies that can provide information when it is needed, or that can quickly devise and roll out new products and services, are today's leading organizations. The source of information can be broad — from disparate systems connected to one another through middleware products of all sorts. Middleware technology enables a company to rapidly meet the demands of a changing market.

The Complete Book of Middleware brings together the perspectives, knowledge, and information on major and emerging middleware technologies. Each chapter examines an issue or technology relevant to today's enterprise. Collectively, these chapters span the range of industrial, emerging, and open middleware technologies, architectures, products, services, and standards. All attempt or aim at making cross-platform integration possible in varying degrees using XML-based technologies and standards. The integration between Java 2 Enterprise Edition (J2EE) and the .NET platform began in Summer 2001. J2EE runs on multiple platforms using the Enterprise JavaBeans (EJBs) capability of encapsulating objects, components, and Web services. The .NET platform will run on non-Microsoft operating systems after a standardization body approves the key parts of the technology for implementation and deployment. The interoperability for the third platform — Common Object Request Broker Architecture/Internet Inter-ORB Protocol (CORBA/IIOP) — will increase to a certain extent and will be more so when CORBA 3 is implemented and deployed, as the core of this version, the CORBA Component Model (CCM), has been virtually matched feature-for-feature with EJBs.

Still, middleware for Enterprise Application Integration (EAI) and Internet-based systems does not make up the full picture of today's enterprise. Middleware for legacy systems, E-commerce, and other Web-based systems, client/server applications, networks and communication systems, data warehousing, and integrated databases fills out the picture. The overriding goal of this book is to provide a comprehensive picture of middleware technologies and architectures.

To meet this goal, the book features the following chapters:

- Distributed Transaction and Messaging Middleware
- Object-Oriented Middleware: CORBA 3
- Microsoft's Stuff
- Ever-Expanding Java World
- Web Services
- Database Middleware
- Bridging the Gap
- Middleware Performance

Each chapter looks at these technologies from an enterprise perspective. An important part of this perspective is how each technology works within the entire organization, and each chapter covers integration through middleware technologies, products, services, and standards into the overall enterprise.

An organization can create new and innovative ways to service customers or to do business with suppliers and make itself a leader in its field. This capability relies on a successful strategy that gives the business insight and the technological know-how to ensure a successful systems integration strategy via creation or installation and deployment of middleware technologies.

The following gives a brief overview of each chapter.

Chapter 1, "Distributed Transaction and Messaging Middleware," focuses on the Remote Procedure Call (RPC), Microsoft Messaging Queuing, Distributed Transaction Processing, MQ Series, and their associated technologies. Related to the RPC are the XML-RPC and the Microsoft RPC facility. The XML-RPC is a specification that allows software running on disparate operating systems while the Microsoft RPC facility is compatible with the Open Group's Distributed Computing Environment (DCE) specification for remote procedure calls.

Applications can use MSMQ to send messages and continue processing regardless of whether the receiving application is running or reachable over the network. The MQSeries Integrator Agent for CICS is capable of accepting MQSeries messages and enables them to be processed within the CICS environment, and allows application to be run outside CICS on, for example, an IMS system.

Chapter 2, "Object-Oriented Middleware: CORBA 3," discusses CORBA's background, Java-to-XML mapping, and associated object services. It also covers the OMG Technology Committee and latest modeling specifications. The original CORBA focused on the development of an Interface Definition Language (IDL) that is independent of any programming language while CORBA 2.0 added Inter-ORB standards to ensure communication among ORBs provided by different suppliers. Along with IDL and Inter-ORB standards, this CORBA version includes common Object Services Specifications.

Considered by many to be the core of CORBA 3, the CORBA Component Model (CCM) packages up transactionality, persistence, event-handling security, and Portable Object Adapter (POA)-based server resource control into a development and runtime package that business programmers can handle. This model is intentionally matched feature-for-feature with EJBs. For this reason, CORBA 3 applications are intended to be broad and varied as well as friendly to loosely coupled interoperating systems characteristic of the business-to-business (B2B) applications. This is in contrast to CORBA 2 where it integrates distributed objects into a tightly coupled application.

The CCM was adopted by OMG in late 1999 and is scheduled for formal release prior to the end of 2001 as the numbered release CORBA 3. Also included are CORBA Scripting, Real-Time CORBA, and Minimal CORBA (for mobile applications).

Chapter 2 also describes seven phases of a CCM Development Project: analysis design phase, component declaration, component implementation, component packaging, component assembly, component deployment and installation, and runtime: component instance activation.

Chapter 3, "Microsoft's Stuff," focuses on the .NET platform on which Web services can be built. This platform represents an evolution of Component Object Model (COM). To allow .NET to run on non-Microsoft operating systems, Microsoft submitted key parts of the technology for standardization to ECMA,[1] an international standardization body, in late 2000.

The advantages of using .NET are that it offers remoting options, does not require registry of the interfaces, and skips the need for an interface language. Another major advantage is that the Web services components are just like any other middle-tier, business-rules objects through a Web server. This means that the same consistent functionality offered would be available at anytime, from anywhere in the world, using any device that can access the Internet.

Chapter 4, "Ever-Expanding Java World," covers EJB, J2EE, Java Messaging Service (JMS), Java Naming and Directory Interface (JNDI), Java Media Framework (JMF), and other Java technologies. They are used to build distributed applications for integration with Enterprise Resource Planning (ERP), Customer Relationship Management (CRM), Supply Chain Management (SCM), and other EAI systems, as well as non-EAI legacy and wireless applications.

Chapter 5, "Web Services: Hot Stuff," discusses Web services and related technologies (front-end, back-end) and standards. It covers how various vendors and organizations define Web services and present Web services architectures. The chapter also looks at the Universal Description, Discovery and Integration (UDDI) technology, Web service brokerage, and some third-party tools, gives workflow process examples, and briefly discusses versioning of Web services.

Also included is a short discussion on Bowstreet's jUDDI as free, open-source, Java-based software that has been architected to allow it to act as the UDDI front-end on top of existing directories and databases. jUDDI-enabled applications can look up services in the UDDI registry and then proceed to "call" those Web services directly.

Chapter 6, "Database Middleware and Other Stuff," covers mostly relational databases — data-level integration, SQL, XML databases, Java-based databases, XML-enabled databases and Web services-enabled databases — as the middleware. Java-based database middleware is the most popular, with at least 35 products, followed by XML database middleware with at least 12 products. Next in line is the XML-enabled database middleware from major vendors: DB2 XML Extender, Informix, MS SQL Server 2000, MS Access 2002, and Oracle8*i*/9*i* Application Server. Emerging is the Web service-enabled database middleware that will grow in popularity when the market for Web services reaches its full potential by late 2002 or 2003.

Chapter 7, "Bridging the Gap," discusses how middleware such as EJBs and markup languages can be used to bridge the gap in an enterprisewide system, what role XML has played in TCP/IP presentation layer, and what XML schemas are. It looks at how a legacy COBOL system is connected to EJBs and what the advantages of using XML schemas are in connecting E-commerce applications.

In view of the fact that the demand for mixing COBOL and Java is ever increasing, this chapter explains in detail how to bridge COBOL with EJBs. The existing (or legacy) COBOL applications contained within enterprises represent the result of a huge investment over many years, embodying the core of the business practices within COBOL business logic. The last thing you want to do is throw that all away and rewrite everything in Java.

Chapter 8, "Middleware Performance," discusses various performance considerations as they apply to middleware and its associated technologies. They include traffic performance, service levels, communications middleware paradigms, performance tools, and middleware selection. Each section of this chapter presents a different topic.

Chapter 9 discusses "What Lies Ahead?" for middleware technologies. It looks at evolutionary paths the technologies have taken and at competing paradigms between the .NET initiative and the J2EE platform. The chapter then proceeds to a middleware hierarchy that can be expanded to incorporate new technologies we have not dreamed of. Also included are the emerging Internet standards, innovative interoperability technologies, better performance tools, and improved service levels.

Note

1. ECMA is an international industry association founded in 1961 and dedicated to the standardization of information and communication systems.

Chapter 1

Distributed Transaction and Messaging Middleware

This chapter discusses various transaction and messaging middleware tools. They include the Remote Procedure Call, Microsoft Messaging Queuing, Distributed Transaction Processing, MQSeries, and their associated technologies.

Remote Procedure Call

In the early days of computing, a program was written as a large monolithic chunk, filled with goto statements. Each had to manage its own input and output to different hardware devices. As the programming discipline matured, this monolithic code was organized into procedures, with the commonly used procedures packed in libraries for sharing and reuse. Today, Remote Procedure Call (RPC) takes the next step in the development of procedure libraries. Now, procedure libraries can run on other remote computers. Some assume the role as a middleware in connecting the Enterprise Integration Systems (EIS)[1] Tier and the Clients Tier.

RPC Model

Remote Procedure Call (RPC) is a protocol that provides the high-level communications paradigm used in the operating system. The RPC model is similar to a local procedure call model in which the caller places arguments to a procedure in a specified location such as a result register. Then, the caller transfers control to the procedure. The caller eventually regains control, extracts the results of the procedure, and continues execution.

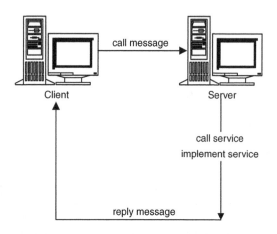

Exhibit 1. Simple RPC

The RPC presumes the existence of a low-level transport protocol, such as Transmission Control Protocol/Internet Protocol (TCP/IP) or User Datagram Protocol (UDP), for carrying the message data between communicating programs. It implements a logical client-to-server communications system designed specifically for the support of network applications.

In the RPC model, a client sends a call message (a procedural call) to a server (see Exhibit 1). When the message arrives, the server calls a dispatch routine, performs whatever network service is requested. Each network service is a collection of remote programs. A remote program implements remote procedures. The procedures, their parameters, and the results are all documented in the specific program's protocol. When the server is done, it sends a reply message that the procedural call is returning to the client.

Port Mapper

Typically, a server program based on an RPC library gets a port number at runtime by calling an RPC library procedure. The port-to-program mappings, which are maintained by the port mapper server, are called a *portmap*. The port mapper is started automatically whenever a machine is booted. Both the server programs and the client programs call port mapper procedures.

Every port mapper on every host is associated with port number 111. The port mapper is the only network service that must have a dedicated port. Other network services can be assigned port numbers either statically or dynamically, as long as the services register their ports with their host's port mapper.

RPC Layers

Programmers can take advantage of three RPC layers: highest, intermediate, and lowest. They write remote procedure calls to make the highest layer of RPC available to other users through a simple C language front-end routine that entirely hides the networking.

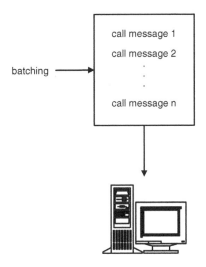

Exhibit 2.   Batching Calls

The intermediate layer containing RPC routines is used for most applications. It is sometimes overlooked in programming due to its simplicity and lack of flexibility. At this level, RPC does not allow timeout specifications, choice of transport, or process control in case of errors. And the intermediate layer of RPC does not support multiple types of call authentication.

For the higher layers, RPC takes care of many details automatically. However, the lowest layer of the RPC library allows the programmer to change the default values for these details.

RPC Features

The RPC features include:

- Batching calls
- Broadcasting calls
- Callback procedures
- The `select` subroutine

Batching allows a client to send an arbitrarily large sequence of call messages to a server (see Exhibit 2). Broadcasting permits a client to send a data packet to the network and wait for numerous replies (see Exhibit 3). The main differences between broadcast RPC and normal RPC are as follows:

- Normal RPC expects only one answer, while broadcast RPC expects one or more answers from each responding machine.
- The implementation of broadcast RPC treats unsuccessful responses as garbage by filtering them out. Therefore, if there is a version mismatch between the broadcaster and a remote service, the user of broadcast RPC might never know.

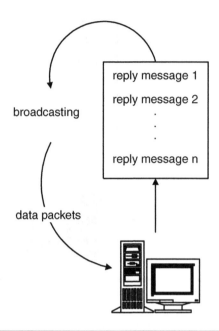

Exhibit 3.   Broadcasting Calls

- All broadcast messages are sent to the port-mapping port. As a result, only services that register themselves with their port mapper are accessible through the broadcast RPC mechanism.
- Broadcast requests are limited in size to the maximum transfer unit (MTU) of the local network. For the Ethernet system, the MTU is 1500 bytes.
- Broadcast RPC is supported only by packet-oriented (connectionless) transport protocols such as UPD/IP.

Occasionally, the server may need to become a client by making an RPC callback to the client's process. To make an RPC callback, the user needs a program number on which to make the call.

The `select` subroutine examines the I/O descriptor sets whose addresses are passed in the *readfds*, *writefds*, and *exceptfds* parameters to see if some of their descriptors are ready for reading or writing, or have an exceptional condition pending. It then returns the total number of ready descriptors in all the sets.

XML-RPC

XML-RPC is a specification and a set of implementations that allow software running on disparate operating systems, and in different environments, to make procedure calls over the Internet. As a remote procedure, it makes the calls using HTTP as the transport and XML as the encoding. XML-RPC is designed to permit complex data structures to be transmitted, processed, and returned.

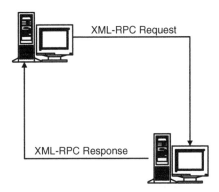

Exhibit 4.   XML-RPC Conversation

XML-RPC works by encoding the RPC requests into XML and sending them over a standard HTTP connection to a server, or listener piece. The listener decodes the XML, executes the requested procedure, and then packages up the results in XML and sends them back over the wire to the client. The client decodes the XML, converts the results into standard language datatypes, and continues executing. Exhibit 4 is a diagram showing an actual XML-RPC conversation between a client (requesting customer information) and a listener who is returning the results of that procedure.

There are two important aspects of this protocol that one should keep in mind when building middleware. XML-RPC is built on HTTP and, similar to ordinary Web traffic, its stateless conversations are of the request and response variety. There is no built-in support for transactions or encryption.

Microsoft RPC Facility

The Microsoft RPC facility is compatible with the Open Group's Distributed Computing Environment (DCE) specification for remote procedure calls and is interoperable with other DCE-based RPC systems, such as those for HP-UX and IBM AIX UNIX-based operating systems. The RPC facility is compatible with the Open Group specification.

The Microsoft RPC mechanism is unique in that it uses other RPC mechanisms, such as named pipes, NetBIOS, or Winsock, to establish communications between the client and the server. With the RPC facility, essential program logic and related procedure code can exist on different computers, which is important for distributed applications.

RPC is based on the concepts used for creating structured programs, which can be viewed as having a backbone to which a series of ribs can be attached. The backbone is the mainstream logic of the program that rarely changes. The ribs are the procedures that the backbone calls upon to do work or perform functions. In traditional programs, these ribs are statically linked to the backbone and stored in the same executable file. RPC places the backbone and the ribs on different computers.

Exhibit 5.   RPC Components

RPC Stub	Part of an application executable file or a DLL that is generated by the Microsoft Interface Description Language (MIDL) compiler specifically for each interface
Remote Procedure Call APIs	A series of protocol-independent APIs responsible for establishing connections and security as well as registering servers, naming, and endpoint resolution
Datagram Runtime	A connectionless RPC protocol engine that transmits and receives requests using connectionless protocols, such as UDP
Connection-Oriented Runtime	A connection-oriented RPC protocol engine that transmits and receives requests using connection-oriented protocols such as TCP
Local Runtime	A local RPC protocol engine that transmits and receives RPC requests between processes on the local computer

Windows 2000 uses dynamic link libraries (DLLs) to provide procedure code and backbone code. This enables the DLLs to be modified or updated without changing or redistributing the backbone portion.

Client applications are developed with specially compiled stub libraries provided by the application program. In reality, these stubs transfer the data and the function to the RPC runtime module. This module is responsible for finding the server that can satisfy the RPC command. Once found, the function and data are sent to the server, where they are picked up by the RPC runtime component on the server. The server builds the appropriate data structure and calls the function.

Microsoft RPC allows a process running in one address space to make a procedure call that is executed in another address space. The call looks like a standard local procedure call but is actually made to a stub that interacts with the runtime library and performs all the steps necessary to execute the call in the remote address space.

Exhibit 5 lists the components of RPC.

The Stubs

The client application calls a local stub procedure instead of the actual code implementing the procedure. Stubs are placeholder functions that make the calls to the runtime library functions, which manage the remote procedure call. They are compiled and linked with the client application. Instead of containing the actual code that implements the remote procedure, the client stub code is used. First, this stub retrieves the required parameters from the client address space and then translates the parameters as needed into a standard network data representation (NDR) format for transmission over the network. Next, it calls functions in the RPC client runtime library to send the request and its parameters to the server.

The server performs the server RPC runtime library functions to accept the request and call the server stub procedure. It then retrieves the parameters from the network buffer and converts them from the network transmission format to the format the server needs. After this, the server stub calls the actual procedure on the server.

The remote procedure runs, possibly generating output parameters and a return value. When complete, a similar sequence of steps returns the data to the client. The remote procedure first returns its data to the server stub. The server stub then converts output parameters to the format required for transmission over the network and returns them to the RPC runtime library functions. After this, the server RPC runtime library functions transmit the data on the network to the client computer.

The client completes the process by accepting the data over the network and returning it to the calling function. First, the client RPC runtime library receives the remote-procedure return values and returns them to the client stub. Then, the client stub converts the data from its network data representation to the format used by the client computer. The stub writes data into the client memory and returns the result to the calling program on the client. As the next step, the calling procedure continues as if the procedure had been called on the same computer.

OSF Standards for RPC

The design and technology behind Microsoft RPC is just one part of a complete environment for distributed computing defined by the Open Software Foundation (OSF),[2] a consortium of companies formed to define that environment. The OSF requests proposals for standards, accepts comments on the proposals, votes on whether to accept the standards, and then promulgates them.

The OSF-DCE remote procedure call standards define not only the overall approach, but the language and the specific protocols to use for communications between computers as well, down to the format of data as it is transmitted over the network.

The Microsoft implementation of RPC is compatible with the OSF standard with some minor exceptions. Client or server applications written using Microsoft RPC will interoperate with any DCE RPC client or server whose runtime libraries run over a supported protocol.

Microsoft RPC Components

The Microsoft RPC product includes the following major components:

- MIDL compiler
- Runtime libraries and header files
- Transport interface modules
- Name service provider
- Endpoint supply service

In the RPC model, one can formally specify an interface to the remote procedures using a language designed for this purpose. This language is called the Interface Definition Language (IDL) and the Microsoft implementation of this language is called the MIDL.

After creating an interface, one must pass it through the MIDL compiler. This compiler generates the stubs that translate local procedure calls into remote procedure calls. The advantage of this approach is that the network becomes almost completely transparent to one's distributed application. The client program calls what appears to be local procedures; the work of turning them into remote calls is done automatically. All the code that translates data, accesses the network, and retrieves results is generated by the MIDL compiler and is invisible to one's application.

The RPC allows a process running in one address space to make a procedure call that is executed in another address space. The call looks like a standard local procedure call but is actually made to a stub that interacts with the runtime library and performs all the steps necessary to execute the call in the remote address space.

Microsoft Messaging Queuing

Many distributed applications need the ability to handle delays between a request and a response. This is because all the steps of a distributed application process may not need to or cannot be completed at one time. Microsoft Message Queuing (MSMQ) allows applications to use components that communicate with one another using queued messages. Like e-mail messages that sit in an inbox, messages can exist on dissimilar systems that may not even be directly connected to each other.

Writing Applications

With MSMQ, one can write applications that do not require immediate responses from either clients or servers, which provide one with the flexibility needed to handle routine pauses within business processes (see Exhibit 6). MSMQ complements the capabilities inherent in COM+ and the transaction services included with the Microsoft Windows 2000 Server and Windows XP operating system. COM+ lets one write distributed applications; transaction services provide these applications with the capability of creating transactions — that is, groups of actions that either all succeed and are posted, or that fail and are rejected.

COM+ support makes it easy to access MSMQ from Microsoft Transaction Service, Microsoft Internet Information Service (IIS), Active Server Pages (ASP), popular applications such as Microsoft Excel, and a wide range of popular programming languages such as the Microsoft Visual Basic and Visual C++ development systems and Microfocus COBOL.

When writing components that take advantage of MSMQ, one's application can send messages to another application without waiting for a response.

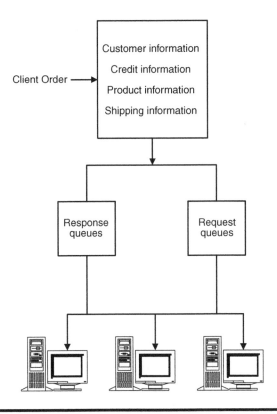

Exhibit 6.   MSMQ in Processing Client Order

Those messages are sent into a queue, where they are stored until a receiving application removes them. If a response is expected, the sending application can check a response queue when convenient.

For example, one can use MSMQ to write an application that will let customers submit orders over the Internet, even when the receiving Web server is not available (see Exhibit 7). The shipping department does not have to receive the customer order before the rest of the transaction can be completed. Using MSMQ, the order entry application can continue running even if the shipping application is not available.

MSMQ Features

MSMQ features generally include:

- COM-based access
- Integration with transactions
- Automatic message journaling
- Automatic notification
- Built-in data integrity, data privacy, and digital signature services
- Message priority support
- Simplified application integration
- Network protocol independence

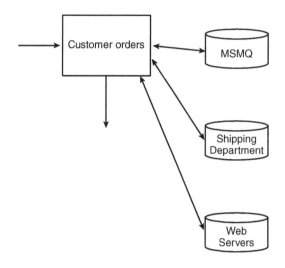

Exhibit 7.   Simple Order–Shipping Scenario

Exhibit 8.   Messaging Queuing 3.0 for Windows XP

Internet Messaging	HTTP as optional transport protocol; XML-formatted messages using SRMP (SOAP Reliable Messaging Protocol); support for Web farms and perimeter networks (firewalls)
Sending Messages to Multiple Destinations	IP multicast: Message Queuing support for the PGM "reliable multicast" protocol; multiple-element format names; distribution lists hosted in AD (Active Directory)
Improved Management/ Deployment	Message stores can grow beyond 2G; Message Queuing clients use LDAP to access AD; no need for a Message Queuing server on a domain controller
Triggers	Improved and integrated into the core product
Microsoft Management Console (MMC) Support	Message Queuing is now administered more completely using snap-ins hosted in an MMC console
Message Lookup	Retrieving a specific message without using cursors

Exhibit 8 gives a list of new features in Message Queuing 3.0 for Windows XP. Exhibit 9 indicates what features of Messaging Queuing 2.0 have been added to Windows 2000.

Microsoft Queued Components

Microsoft Queued Components (QC) extend the familiar COM programming model to situations in which applications might need to run asynchronously, such as when servers are disconnected or temporarily unavailable. QC accomplishes this by placing the method parameters passed to an object in an MSMQ message using a COM+ component called the Recorder (see Exhibit 10). The COM+ Player component then reads the message and runs it on Windows

Exhibit 9. Messaging Queuing 2.0 for Windows 2000

Full integration with Active Directory	Message Queuing 2.0 publishes all Message Queuing configuration objects through Microsoft Active Directory, allowing the configuration objects to be distributed and discovered throughout the entire Windows 2000 forest.
Windows 2000 security integration	In addition to providing support for access control, auditing, encryption, and authentication, Message Queuing also takes advantage of the new security features built into Microsoft Windows 2000, such as the Kerberos V5 security protocol. The U.S. version of Message Queuing now supports 128-bit encryption as well as 40-bit encryption.
Setup through Add/Remove in Control Panel	Message Queuing 2.0 now allows one to use the Control Panel to install Message Queuing clients with any supporting Message Queuing server.
Workgroup mode	Message Queuing installed in a workgroup can later join a domain, and then separate from the domain again.
Administration through the Microsoft Management Console	Message Queuing 2.0 now allows administration through MMC snap-ins.
Active/active cluster support	Message Queuing 2.0 fully supports active/active operation, which means that Message Queuing can run on all nodes in a server cluster simultaneously.

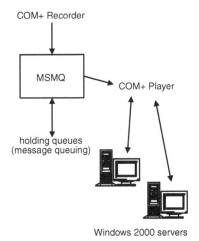

Exhibit 10. Queued Components

2000 Server located on a remote machine. Because QC uses MSMQ but does not require the programmer to write code for the MSMQ application programming interface (API), using QC may speed development time.

MSMQ implements asynchronous communications by enabling applications to send messages to, and receive messages from, other applications. These applications may be running on the same machine or on separate machines connected by a network. When an application receives a request message, it processes the request by reading the contents of the message and acting accordingly. If required, the receiving application can send a response message back to the original requester.

While in transit between senders and receivers, MSMQ keeps messages in holding areas called "queues" — hence the name "message queuing." MSMQ queues protect messages from being lost in transit and provide a place for receivers to look for messages when the receivers are ready to receive them.

When the Network Goes Down

Applications can use MSMQ to send messages and continue processing regardless of whether the receiving application is running or reachable over the network. The receiving application may be unreachable because of a network problem, or because of natural disconnection as in the case of mobile users who only connect to the network periodically. When applications use the transactional delivery mode in MSMQ, MSMQ also makes sure that messages are delivered exactly on time, and that messages are delivered in the order that they were sent.

MSMQ enables applications to send messages with delivery guarantees that can be applied on a message-by-message basis. When networks go down, receiving applications are offline, or machines containing message queues fail, MSMQ will ensure that messages get delivered as soon as connections are restored or applications and machines are restarted. MSMQ implements these guarantees using disk-based storage mechanisms and log-based recovery techniques. Using guaranteed delivery options, developers can focus on business logic and not on sophisticated communications and error-recovery programming.

MSMQ delivers messages using the lowest-cost route currently available. When networks fail, MSMQ automatically uses the next-lowest-cost route to deliver messages. Administrators define costs for each network connection between machines using the MSMQ Explorer. Administrators can also designate MSMQ servers as communication concentrators to handle all message traffic between two sites. Routing eliminates single points of failure, improves performance, and provides resiliency to communication environments.

MSMQ supports Internetwork Packet Exchange (IPX) and TCP/IP networking protocols (see Exhibit 11). MSMQ handles all protocol bridging requirements automatically.

Distributed Processing Middleware

The Open Group has published the Distributed Transaction Processing (DTP) model version 3 (G504), a software architecture that allows multiple application programs to share resources provided by multiple resource managers, and

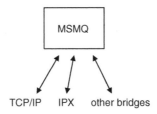

Exhibit 11.   MSMQ Network Support

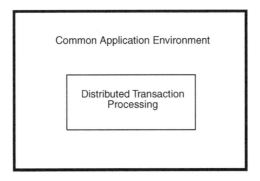

Exhibit 12.   Common Application Environment

allows their work to be coordinated into global transactions. It describes the use of the DTP model within the Common Application Environment (CAE) (see Exhibit 12) and is a prerequisite to other Open Group documents that address DTP. This document has been updated to account for CPI-C, Version 2 (C419), and the introduction of the X/Open High-level Transaction Language (HTL) (see Structured Transaction Definition Language (STDL), C611).

With the boom of Web commerce and Web-related technologies, businesses are streamlining back-end business applications and processes, making that infrastructure available to front-end users. However, greater demands on transaction processing, as well as advances in technology, are creating a requirement for businesses to move to an E-transaction processing environment.

In the OLTP model, many different people and points of intervention are required to coordinate work flow and individual tasks along the path of a complete business transaction. In an E-transaction processing model, separate tasks are now integrated into a streamlined process with less manual intervention.

While the evolution to E-transaction processing is taking place, let us take a quick look at how Unisys and BEA Systems have built their systems based on the DTP model.

Unisys' Distributed Processing Middleware

Unisys e-@ction Distributed Processing Middleware for ClearPath Servers provides several different interoperability and integration technologies. It establishes an implementation environment for today's systems that require techniques such as distributed transaction, message queuing, open data access, and multi-server integration.

A major feature of the ClearPath Server Integrated Operating Environment is X/Open-compliant software that enables applications to participate in distributed transactions. The Unisys Open/OLTP implementation is based on the industry-standard DTP model defined by X/Open. This implementation provides transaction processing protocols defined by ISO OSI standards.

The following are X/Open-compliant software for ClearPath Servers: Unisys Open Transaction Integrator, Unisys Open/OLTP, BEA Tuxedo, and MQSeries for ClearPath OS2200.

1. *Unisys Open Transaction Integrator (OpenTI)*. This enables one to integrate a variety of existing DTP services with the Microsoft Transaction Server (MTS) infrastructure. Specifically, OpenTI gives one the ability to provide Windows clients with access to existing applications and data on one's current transaction processing systems such as Unisys Open/OLTP and BEA Tuxedo, and to provide one's current transaction processing systems with access to other resources controlled by MTS. With OpenTI, one can expand the scope of existing solutions (e.g., Web-enabling services). Open Transaction Integrator Release 3.0 runs on the Windows 2000 platform and integrates seamlessly with COM+. It also provides a convenient development environment for creating and enhancing Microsoft Component Object Model (COM) applications. Developers can use any tools that support COM — Visual Basic, Visual C++, Visual J++, Sybase PowerBuilder, Borland Delphi, MicroFocus COBOL, Oracle Object for OLE, etc.

2. *Univsys Open/OLTP*. This software lets ClearPath Server applications participate in client/server transactions based on the industry standard DTP model. This implementation provides transaction processing protocols defined by OSI standards.

3. *BEA Tuxedo*. Client applications written in X/Open-compliant environments can access services that reside in any of the heterogeneous multi-processing (HMP) environments, as well as other UNIX, UNIXWare, or Windows NT servers that support the DTP model, such as Unisys Open/OLTP software or the optional, value-added TUXEDO product from BEA Systems, Inc.

4. *MQSeries for ClearPath OS2200*. This software is message-oriented middleware. It allows OS2200 applications to securely and reliably exchange messages with applications on a wide range of operating systems and platforms. This middleware is based on IBM MQSeries Version 5.0 and was developed by Unisys under license from IBM.

Additionally, MQSeries for ClearPath OS2200 can participate in X/Open DTP transactions as a supported X/Open resource manager. Using OLTP-TM2200 as the transaction manager in conjunction with MQSeries Syncpoint, an application developer can synchronize MQSeries messaging with Universal Data System (UDS) database updates as part of a global transaction. In this scenario, all messaging and database updates are committed (or rolled back) within the global transactional unit of work.

Exhibit 13. Tuxedo Core Subsystems

Transaction Manager
Workstation
Domains
DCE Integration
Queue Services

With the increase in the demand for E-transaction processing, UNISYS has built an E-business infrastructure. Among other things, it includes Web servers, Web browser access to transactions, Web-enabled transaction integration, and Web application development environment.

BEA Tuxedo

BEA Tuxedo is distributed transaction and messaging middleware. It features a high-level API for building distributed application components connected via message-based communications. Components execute in a managed server environment implemented by core BEA Tuxedo services. These services implement a sophisticated set of transaction and application management functions, and comprehensive distributed systems administration.

BEA Tuxedo applications range from single server systems with few clients and services, to large-scale distributed environments encompassing thousands of clients, hundreds of servers, and a large set of server components and services. They are specified by configuration files that translate into a tightly coupled set of runtime shared information bases. These shared bases (known as Bulletin Boards in the BEA Tuxedo world) reside on each participating server node.

The Transaction Manager is the core of BEA Tuxedo capabilities. It provides the unifying data structures and services for dynamic application processing. The Transaction Manager is supported by a group of subsystems providing advanced distributed functionality in the areas of client management, host connectivity, and enterprise application configuration. As shown in Exhibit 13, the core consists of five subsystems.

The Transaction Manager is the architectural hub of BEA Tuxedo. It is the core of each participating BEA Tuxedo server and provides the critical distributed application services: naming, message routing, load balancing, configuration management, transaction management, and security.

The Bulletin Board (BB) acts a name server for a BEA Tuxedo application and is replicated on participating nodes. To provide fast access, the name server exists as a structure in shared memory. The Transaction Manager uses the BB naming, configuration, and environmental statistics information to automatically load-balance service requests to available servers, route client requests based on data content, and prioritize service requests. Programmers code applications as function calls to logical entities called named services. The Transaction Manager maps these logical requests to specific service instances within the server node/server process environment.

Instead of coding the specific partitioning information into the application code accessing the accounts, one can use Transaction Manager routing. In effect, Transaction Manager looks at the specified data value, consults routing information stored in the BB, and dispatches the request to a service operating on the correct data partition. If one needs to change the database partitioning (migrating a partition to a new server, or changing the distribution of accounts across existing partition instances), one only needs to change the Transaction Manager routing information. The application code is not affected.

To ensure maximum application throughput, the Transaction Manager automatically performs load balancing and scheduling throughout the system. Using per-service load factors, the Transaction Manager delivers a particular request to the server that can process the request most quickly. The Transaction Manager determines the load on a given server by totaling the load factors for the currently enqueued requests.

Request prioritization is another core capability offered by the Transaction Manager. Certain service requests often need to have a higher priority than others. For example, an airline seat cancellation needs a higher priority than a reservation: canceled seats must be rebooked as soon as possible for most airlines.

The Transaction Manager includes many features supporting application availability, including process availability checks, timeout checks, automatic server restart and recovery procedures, and user-definable recovery procedures. The Transaction Manager not only controls the flow of activity in the application and but also ensures smooth efficient operations.

The Transaction Manager provides application service authentication, authorization, and access control through an architected security interface. The interface abstracts the Kerberos security model and allows Kerberos, or similar end-user authentication schemes, to be integrated with the application. One can use access control lists to protect services, queues, or events from unauthorized access.

The DTP capability guarantees the integrity of data accessed across several sites or managed by different database products. The Transaction Manager coordinates distributed transactions to enable multi-site updates against heterogeneous databases on networked computers. It tracks transaction participants using global transactions and supervises a two-phase commit protocol. This ensures that transaction commit and rollback are properly handled at each site.

The Transaction Manager also coordinates the recovery of global transactions in the event of site failure, network failure, or global resource deadlocks. The Transaction Manager uses the Open Group's X/Open XA interface for communication with the various resource managers.

BEA Tuxedo provides a simple, optional mechanism for enqueuing and dequeuing application requests and replies. Its Queue Services enables the following:

- Work in progress and workflow applications
- Guaranteed transaction submittal and completion

Exhibit 14. Tuxedo Queue Servers

Message queuing server	Enqueue and dequeue messages on behalf of clients and servers. This allows for transparent enqueuing and dequeuing of messages, whether or not the process is local to the queue.
Forwarding server	Dequeue queued messages and forwards them for processing. This allows for transparent processing of enqueued messages by existing Transaction Manager servers that do not know if the incoming message was sent as a request/response message or from a queue of stored requests.

- Time-sensitive request submittal
- Integration with the BEA Tuxedo MIB and GUI
- Transaction control for enqueuing requests
- Software fault resilience through easy mirroring of services and data

Queue Services provides applications with facilities for batch and time-delayed transactions. The option provides maximum flexibility for controlling application flow by maintaining LIFO, FIFO, or user-defined dequeuing and all original ATMI invocation properties, such as request priority or data-dependent routing.

The administrative functions of the queue option provide the system administrator with a great deal of flexibility in managing Queue Services servers. They enable the system administrator to configure the two servers briefly described in Exhibit 14. A response by the server is automatically enqueued to the associated reply queue for the message.

BEA Tuxedo incorporates and is the basis for the Open Group's X/Open TX interface standard for defining and managing transactions. The TX interface is based on the Transaction Manager's ATMI, and the two interfaces provide near-identical functionality.

Specifically, the TX interface enables programmers to define transaction boundaries within their application so the work performed by services can be treated as an atomic unit. Within a single Transaction Manager transaction, the work performed in various services, accessing various databases across many computers, is either committed or rolled back as a single atomic unit of work. This keeps all the databases synchronized, even if there are machine failures. The ATMI was selected by X/Open as the reference technology for OLTP application programming and renamed XATMI.

The COBOL API, available on both Transaction Manager and Workstation configurations, provides the ability to:

1. Have the COBOL API available on workstations and coexist with the DLL versions of Workstation for MS Windows and OS/2
2. Write clients and application service routines in the COBOL programming language

3. Interface to Transaction Manager primitives using subroutine linkage mechanisms familiar to COBOL programmers
4. Build application clients and servers using the familiar subroutine linkage mechanisms and integrate these clients and servers into an existing or new Transaction Manager application (the application can mix processes, using non-COBOL clients and servers)
5. Be compliant with ANSI X3.23-1985, and is based on Micro Focus COBOL

The internationalization feature enables BEA Tuxedo to furnish diagnostic and system messages in a language appropriate to the locale. All output messages are stored in catalogs so they can be easily translated and modified as needed. As a result, one can customize representations to conform to the date, time, and currency conventions of one's country. The Transaction Manager implementation conforms to The Open Group's internationalization XPG guidelines.

BEA Tuxedo/Q Component

The BEA Tuxedo/Q component allows messages to be queued to persistent storage (disk) or to nonpersistent storage (memory) for later processing or retrieval. The BEA Tuxedo ATMI provides functions that allow messages to be added to or read from queues. Reply messages and error messages can be queued for later return to client programs. An administrative command interpreter is provided for creating, listing, and modifying the queues. Servers are provided to accept requests to enqueue and dequeue messages, to forward messages from the queue for processing, and to manage the transactions that involve the queues.

BEA Tuxedo/Q provides other features to BEA Tuxedo application programmers and administrators. The application program or the administrator can control the ordering of messages on the queue. Control is via the sort criteria, which may be based on message availability time, expiration time, priority, LIFO, FIFO, or a combination of these criteria. The application can override the ordering to place the message at the queue top or ahead of a specific message that is already queued.

In addition, a BEA Tuxedo server is provided to enqueue and dequeue messages on behalf of, possibly remote, clients and servers. The administrator decides how many copies of the server should be configured. It is also provided to dequeue queued messages and forward them to services for execution. This server allows for existing servers to handle queued requests without modification. Each forwarding server can be configured to handle one or more queues. Transactions are used to guarantee "exactly once" processing. The administrator controls how many forwarding servers are configured.

There are many application paradigms in which queued messages can be used. This feature can be used to queue requests when a machine, server, or resource is unavailable or unreliable (e.g., in the case of wide-area or wireless

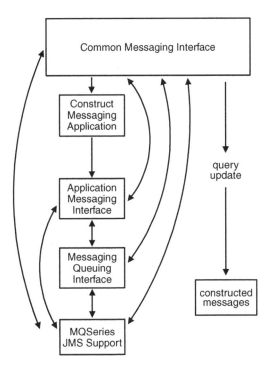

Exhibit 15. MQSeries APIs

networks). This feature can also be used for workflow provisioning where each step generates a queued request to do the next step in the process. Yet another use is for batch processing of potentially long-running transactions, such that the initiator does not have to wait for completion but is assured that the message will eventually be processed. This facility can also be used to provide a data pipe between two otherwise unrelated applications in a peer-to-peer relationship.

IBM MQSeries

With IBM's MQSeries,[3] one receives a family of four APIs (see Exhibit 15) designed to make programming straightforward for any messaging task — from the simple to the most advanced. IBM specified and developed these APIs. These APIs can be used for exchanging messages as indicated in Exhibit 16.

The CMI will provide programming support for both language-dependent and language-independent data structures in a consistent manner. It will handle tagged value data such as XML, and language-dependent structures found in C and Java, used in conjunction with the message dictionary support provided in MQSeries Integrator.

Exhibit 16. Describing MQSeries APIs

MQI (Messaging Queuing Interface)	API that provides full access to the underlying messaging implementation, available for all key languages and environments
JMS (Java Message Service)	Java standard that provides much of the function available through the MQI (see Chapter 4)
AMI (Application Messaging Interface[a,b,c])	API that provides the handling of messages with a higher level of abstraction that moves message-handling logic from the application into the middleware; the AMI has been adopted by the Open Applications Group as its Open Application Middleware API Specification (OAMAS)[d]
CMI (Common Messaging Interface)	Simplifies the creation of message content. All four APIs can interoperate. (One can construct a messaging application with the CMI, in conjunction with a message delivery API, like the MQI, the AMI, or MQSeries Support for JMS. One can also query and update constructed messages regardless of their physical representation.)

[a] The JMS is an API defined for the Java environment, with a number of vendors providing implementations. The AMI is an API adopted by the Open Applications Group that supports C, C++, COBOL, and Java. Both APIs support point-to-point and publish/subscribe styles of communication. Both APIs allow destinations or services to be defined outside the application. The AMI uses policies to indicate how messages should be sent or received and can be extended, using policy handlers.

[b] AMI V1.2 (WIN32, including Windows 2000, AIX, Solaris, HP-UX, OS/400) is available via the Web as a product extension. It provides additional functions, such as:
— Pluggable policy handlers providing a framework that allows customers and vendors to extend the function of the AMI. One could use this simply to write an audit log, to define error-handling policies, or even use it to implement AMI running over non-MQSeries transports. A set of sample policy handlers is provided.
— Directory support, storing the AMI service and policy definitions in an LDAP directory.
— National Language translation.

[c] The AMI supports C, C++, and Java on all platforms except OS/390. C and COBOL are supported on OS/390.

[d] OAMAS supports a number of application communication patterns, including datagrams, request/response, file transfer, and publish/subscribe, and communicates with message brokers such as MQSeries Integrator.

MQSeries Family

The MQSeries family forms the key integration layer in the IBM Application Framework for E-business, as shown in Exhibit 17. An additional release (Version 5.2.1) MQSeries for Windows NT and Windows 2000 includes new usability enhancements (MSI Install, Active Directory, and built-in authentication) and has achieved Microsoft certification for Windows 2000 Server. Compaq users can now participate in business process management with MQSeries for Compaq NonStop Kernel V5.1 and MQSeries for Compaq OpenVMS Alpha

Exhibit 17.   MQSeries Family

MQSeries Integrator
MQSeries Workflow

MQSeries Adapter Offering
MQSeries Everyplace for Multi-Platforms

WebSphere Business Integrator
WebSphere Partner Agreement Manager
WebSphere Adapters

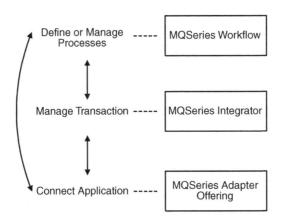

Exhibit 18.   MQSeries Integration Example

V5.1. Another important new product, MQSeries link for R/3 for OS/390 connects SAP R3 applications on an OS/390, or eserver zSeries to other applications (including SAP R/3, SAP R/2, and non-SAP) across both IBM and non-IBM platforms.

The following is a list of MQSeries products that can be integrated with one another, depending on organizational and technical requirements. Exhibit 18 shows a simple integration example.

1. The *MQSeries Integrator* improves business effectiveness. It uses enterprise-defined transformations and intelligent routing to automatically select and distribute information to the applications and people who need it. The latest release extends support for existing AIX, Sun Solaris, and Windows NT and 2000 platforms, to include HP-UX and a solution for eserver iSeries.

2. The *MQSeries Workflow* (available on AIX, HP-UX, Sun Solaris, Windows, and z/OS) is the process engine for business process management (BPM) from IBM. It is now enriched with a fully supported Web client, a rapid user interface wizard, support for Oracle8, and improved performance. Like other members of the MQSeries family, it is open and standards-based, and supports Web services.

3. The *Adapter Offering* works with MQSeries messaging to reduce the risk, complexity, and cost of point-to-point application integration. It provides the framework and tools to build adapters to a wide range of applications, making it easier and quicker to manage the integration of business processes. The latest release extends support for Windows and enhances the offering for the Java environment.

4. The *MQSeries Everyplace for MultiPlatforms* provides mobile workers and remote systems with dependable and secure access to business processes. The latest release sees the introduction of an input node to MQSeries Integrator, as well as a Retail Edition, and direct support for Linux and HP-UX.

5. The *WebSphere Business Integrator* runs on Windows NT/2000 and delivers a cohesive platform with integrated tooling for the design, development and deployment of adaptive end-to-end business process solutions across diverse applications and enterprises. It builds upon tried and tested products from the IBM portfolio, packaged together with a common installation tool.

6. The *WebSphere Partner Agreement Manager* enables an organization to automate interactions with suppliers, business partners, customers, and E-markets to improve supply chain efficiency and effectiveness. It now supports closer integration with the WebSphere family, including WebSphere Business Integrator.

7. The *WebSphere Adapters* use open standards to connect WebSphere Application Servers or MQSeries applications to popular packaged software from J.D. Edwards, Oracle, PeopleSoft, and SAP more quickly and easily. This significantly enhances integration opportunities with some of today's leading E-business products.

Application Programs and Messaging

The IBM MQSeries range of products provides application programming services that enable application programs to communicate with each other using messages and queues. This form of communication is referred to as asynchronous messaging. It provides assured, once-only delivery of messages. Using MQSeries means that one can separate application programs, so that the program sending a message can continue processing without having to wait for a reply from the receiver. If the receiver, or the communication channel to it, is temporarily unavailable, the message can be forwarded at a later time. MQSeries also provides mechanisms for generating acknowledgments of messages received.

The programs that comprise an MQSeries application can be running on different computers, on different operating systems, and at different locations. The applications are written using a MQI so that applications developed on one platform can be transferred to another.

Exhibit 19 shows that when two applications communicate using messages and queues, one application puts a message on a queue and the other application gets that message from the queue.

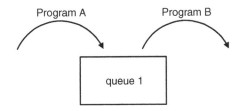

Exhibit 19.   Programs Connected to Same Queue

Queue Managers

In MQSeries, queues are managed by a component called a queue manager that provides messaging services for the applications and processes the MQI calls they issue. The queue manager ensures that messages are put on the correct queue or that they are routed to another queue manager.

Before applications can send any messages, one must create a queue manager and some queues. MQSeries provides the utilities to help do this and to create any other MQSeries objects needed for one's applications.

Any MQSeries application must make a successful connection to a queue manager before it can make any other MQI calls. When the application successfully makes the connection, the queue manager returns a connection handle. This is an identifier that the application must specify each time it issues an MQI call. An application can connect to only one queue manager at a time; thus, only one connection handle is valid (for that particular application) at a time. When the application has connected to a queue manager, all the MQI calls it issues are processed by that queue manager until it issues another MQI call to disconnect from that queue manager.

Before an application can use a queue for messaging, it must open the queue. In putting a message on a queue, the application must open the queue for putting. Similarly, if getting a message from a queue, the application must open the queue for getting. One can specify that a queue is opened for both getting and putting, if required. The queue manager returns an object handle if the open request is successful. The application specifies this handle, together with the connection handle, when it issues a put or a get call. This ensures that the request is carried out on the correct queue.

When the open request is confirmed, the application can put a message on the queue. To do this, it uses another MQI call on which one must specify a number of parameters and data structures. These define all the information about the message one is putting, including the message type, its destination, which options are set, etc. The message data (i.e., the application-specific contents of the message the application is sending) is defined in a buffer, which is specified in the MQI call. When the queue manager processes the call, it adds a message descriptor that contains the information needed to ensure that the message can be delivered properly. The message descriptor is in a format defined by MQSeries; the message data is defined by the application (this is what one puts into the message data buffer in the application code).

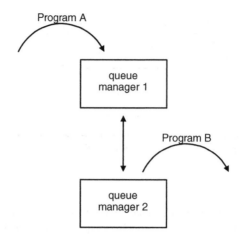

Exhibit 20. Programs Connected to Different Queue Managers

The program that gets the messages from the queue must first open the queue for getting messages. It must then issue another MQI call to get the message from the queue. On this call, one must specify which message one wants to get.

Exhibit 20 shows how messaging works when the program putting the message and the program getting the message are on the different computers and connected to different queue managers.

Commercial Messaging

For true commercial messaging, middleware needs to provide more than assured delivery. MQSeries is designed to meet the requirements of real business systems. It supports transactional messaging, which means that operations on messages can be grouped into "units of work." A unit of work is either committed in its entirety, or backed-out, so that it is as if none of the operations took place. This means that data is always in a consistent state.

For example, an application gets a message off a queue, processes the data in the message, and creates five further messages to be sent to other applications, all within one unit of work. If the output queue for the last of the five messages is temporarily full, then the application can back out the entire unit of work, so the input message that it got from the queue will be returned to the queue, and the first four messages that were put onto output queues will be removed. After the back out, it is as if the application never got the message in the first place. The application can then try the processing again at a later time.

MQSeries can also coordinate units of messaging work with other transactional work (e.g., database updates) so that message data and database data remain completely in-sync at all times.

Security is one of the most important aspects of a distributed system and MQSeries provides a flexible security framework that allows the appropriate security architecture to be implemented to meet one's specific requirements.

There are several aspects to the MQSeries security model:

1. *MQSeries Administration Commands.* Administration of MQSeries is performed using a number of commands. For example, create queue manager; start queue manager. Control of individual user's access to these commands is via normal operating system controls, such as access control lists.

2. *Access to Queue Manager Objects.* MQSeries allows one to control application access to queue manager objects, such as the queue manager itself, and its queues. MQSeries on MVS conforms to the SAF interface and thus one can use an external security manager, such as RACF or TopSecret, to control application access to a queue manager. MQSeries on most other platforms provides a security manager that allows one to specify access controls for queue manager objects. If the security manager does not do exactly what is needed, then one can write one's own, because MQSeries provides a documented interface for security management.

3. *Channel Security.* To protect the information flowing between MQSeries queue managers, MQSeries supports exit points into which one can link security modules. For example, when two queue managers initiate communications via an MQSeries channel, each queue manager can verify the identity of the other before exchanging any data. Similarly, during message transmission, data can be encrypted before it is sent over the network and decrypted when it arrives at the receiving end.

4. *Application Security.* The MQI programming interface provides facilities for applications to identify themselves, both by platform and application, and by principle (or user identifier). This information is propagated with the message, and only privileged applications can change it. Applications can therefore use this information to make extra security checks on messages that they receive.

The asynchronous nature of message queuing may mean that applications are idle for periods of time when there are no messages to process. To avoid having idle processes consume system resources while there is no work to do, MQSeries provides a mechanism to "trigger" applications to start when certain conditions are met.

Triggering works by defining a specific condition for an application's queue, which, when met, will cause the queue manager to send a trigger message to an MQSeries queue called an "initiation queue." The trigger message is processed by a special application called a trigger monitor, which reads the trigger message from the initiation queue and uses the information in the message to decide which application to start to process the messages on the application's queue.

By using a trigger monitor one can have a single process that initiates many application processes to handle messages arriving on many different queues, as required.

MQSeries Internet Pass-Thru

The following new features have been added to MQSeries Internet Pass-Thru (MQIPT):

- Support added for AIX, HP-UX, and Microsoft Windows 2000 platforms
- Use of an HTTP proxy for outbound connections
- SSL support
- Use of a SOCKS proxy for outbound connections
- An Administration GUI for managing one or more MQIPT servers
- Support for the IBM Network Dispatcher

MQIPT provides a single point of control over the access to multiple queue managers and supports Java and Windows 2000. It allows the passage of MQSeries messages through firewalls without additional administrative overhead for firewall administrators. It can operate as a stand-alone service, receiving and forwarding MQSeries message flows. Using MQIPT, existing MQSeries applications can pass data through the firewall without the need to change them.

MQIPT does not store any MQSeries message data on disk. MQSeries message data only passes through the memory of the MQIPT application. It is possible to run more than one MQIPT on the same machine, but only one can be run as a system service.

CICS and MQSeries

CICS is an application server that provides E-business online transaction processing and transaction management for mission-critical applications on OS/390 servers as well as other platforms The MQSeries Integrator Agent for CICS is capable of accepting MQSeries messages and enables them to be processed within the CICS environment and allows an application to be run outside CICS on, for example, an IMS system. One can use a browser to direct access to CICS without the need for intermediate gateways or Web servers or to connect to CICS through the IBM WebSphere Application Server for OS/390. One can access CICS transactions through standard CORBA clients using standard IIOP protocols for distributed object programming.

Exhibit 21 displays a quick look at what CICS products IBM currently offers.

Browsers can access servlets running in WebSphere Application Server. These servlets use JavaBeans, which in turn use the Common Connector Framework (CCF) to access CICS applications. The CCF provides a common way for Java application to connect to subsystems such as CICS, SAP, and IMS, among others. For connecting to CICS, the CCF is based on the CICS Transaction Gateway (CTG) Java classes provided with CICS TS V1.3. The CCF connector will be replaced with the J2EE connector.

MQSeries JMS Support

IBM's SupportPacs MA88 contains MQSeries classes for Java and MQSeries classes for Java Message Service. It provides support for developing MQSeries applications in Java (for deployment on MQSeries V5.1 and V5.2) through the following Java-based APIs: MQSeries classes for Java V5.2.0 and MQSeries

Exhibit 21. CICS Offerings

CICS Transaction Server V2.1 for z/OS and OS/390	Extend CICS applications with Enterprise Java E-business technology; run mixed application types and workloads within a single CICS system; and use existing DB2, IMS DB, and VSAM data from Enterprise JavaBean (EJB) applications.
CICS Transaction Server for OS/390, V1.3	Includes CICS Transaction Gateway V3, among others. This gateway uses the latest technologies, both HTTP and Java based, to link the open, object-oriented world of Web browsers on the Internet or an intranet to CICS enterprise computing. It is also available for CICS Transaction Server for VSE/ESA and CICS for VSE/ESA. CICSPlex System Manager, an integral part of CICS Transaction Server, is IBM's System-390 management product for CICS networks.
CICS Transaction Gateway V4.0	Includes support for the Java Developer's Toolkit (JDK) Version 1.3 as well as support for Windows 2000, the HP-UX 11.00, and Linux on OS/390 platforms. It also allows one to connect their J2EE architectures to enterprise CICS programs and data. This gateway is the prime CICS connector to address the requirements to extend CICS applications with Enterprise Java E-business technology to J2EE environments,

Note: Effective December 31, 2002, CICS for MVS/ESA will be withdrawn.

classes for Java Message Service (JMS) V5.2.00. It is available on the following platforms: AIX, HP-UX, iSeries, Linux for Intel, Linux for OS/390, Microsoft Windows, Sun Solaria, and OS/390 V2R9 or higher (including z/OS).

MQSeries classes for Java Message Service (JMS) is a set of Java classes that implement Sun Microsystem's Java Message Service specification. A JMS application can use the classes to send MQSeries messages to either existing MQSeries or new JMS applications. An application can be configured to connect as an MQSeries client using TCP/IP, or directly using the Java Native Interface (JNI). If the client-style connection is used, no additional MQSeries code is required on the client machine. In addition to asynchronous message delivery, MQSeries JMS also provides support for XA transactions via the XA Resource interface (not available for iSeries, OS/390, or z/OS).

Notes

1. An EIS generally comprises Enterprise Resource Planning (ERP) systems and application servers (database, client, and Web).
2. In selecting the RPC standard, the OSF cited the following rationale:
   a. The three most important properties of a remote procedure call are simplicity, transparency, and performance.
   b. The selected RPC model adheres to the local procedure model as closely as possible. This requirement minimizes the amount of time developers spend learning the new environment.

      c. The selected RPC model permits interoperability; its core protocol is well-defined and cannot be modified by the user.

      d. The selected RPC model allows applications to remain independent of the transport and protocol on which they run, while supporting a variety of other transports and protocols.

      e. The selected RPC model can be easily integrated with other components of the DCE.

3. As of August 2001, IBM announced that the following MQSeries products are to be renamed as part of the consolidation of IBM's middleware product portfolio:

      a. MQSeries to WebSphere MQ

      b. MQSeries Integrator to WeSphere MQ Integrator

      c. MQSeries Workflow to WebSphere Process Manager

      d. MQe to WebSphere MQ Everyplace

      e. WS BtoBi PAM to WebSphere Partner Agreement Manager

Chapter 2

Object-Oriented Middleware: CORBA 3

This chapter discusses the new CORBA 3 and its background and associated object services. It also covers the OMG Technology Committee and latest modeling specifications.

Introduction

CORBA (the acronym for Common Object Request Broker Architecture) relies on a protocol called the Internet Inter-ORB Protocol (IIOP) for remoting objects. It will not work without the protocol. Everything in the CORBA architecture is built upon the foundation of Object Request Broker (ORB) over which each CORBA object interacts transparently with other CORBA objects in a heterogonous, distributed environment. Each object interfaces with others via a set of methods.

The ORB itself is represented as a pipeline with supporting facilities of four kinds (see Exhibit 1):

1. *Common Object Services* provide a long list of standard services needed to distribute objects successfully (see the section entitled "CORBA Object Services").
2. *Common Frameworks* are collections of objects to provide comprehensive services for application deployment which cut across many application domains such as printing, compound documents, meta objects, and agents. They are often constructed out of underlying Common Object Services.
3. *Domain Objects* are business objects that represent and model specific domains, such as telecommunications, shipping, utilities, and medical businesses. They similarly utilize Common Frameworks and Object Services to provide their functionalities.

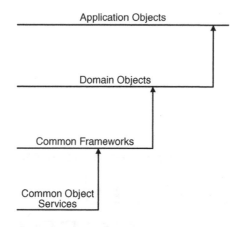

Exhibit 1.   Visual View of Facilities

4. *Application Objects* express their functionality of the particular application under development. They can be constructed out of all categories of CORBA Objects.

To request a service, a CORBA client acquires an object reference to a CORBA server object. The client calls on the object reference as if the CORBA server object resided in the client's address space. When the ORB finds a CORBA object's implementation, the system prepares it to receive requests, communicate requests to it, and carry the reply back to the client.

A CORBA object interacts with the ORB either through the ORB interface or through an object adapter — either a Basic Object Adapter (BOA) or a Portable Object Adapter (POA). CORBA can be used on diverse operating system platforms from mainframes to UNIX boxes to Windows machines to handheld and mobile devices as long as there is an ORB implementation for that platform.

CORBA Release Summary

We have come a long way to CORBA 3 since CORBA 1 was first released in 1991. CORBA 1 focused on the development of an Interface Definition Language (IDL) that is independent of any programming language. This IDL provided a beginning point for ORB developers while CORBA 2.0 added Inter-ORB standards to ensure communication among ORBs provided by different suppliers. Along with IDL and Inter-ORB standards, this CORBA version includes common Object Services Specifications (for more information, see section entitled "What Is New? CORBA 3").

Then the OMG preannounced CORBA 3 with a suite of ten specifications in a September 1998 press release. According to Exhibit 2, not all specifications were adopted and issued as CORBA 3. Most were spread over three point releases CORBA 2.2, 2.3, and 2.4, while the major release 3.0 was released in early 2001. The table shows the release number, the date it was published, the included specifications, and the date it was originally accepted.

Exhibit 2.   CORBA Release Summary

Release	Date	Included Specification	Originally Adopted
CORBA 2.2	February 1998	POA	June 1997
		IDL-to-Java Mapping	July 1998
CORBA 2.3	June 1999	Valuetypes	May 1998
		Java-to-IDL Mapping	August 1998
CORBA 2.4	Late 2000	Messaging	September 1998
		Interoperable Naming Service	March 1999
CORBA 3.0	Early 2001	CORBA Component Model	Late 1999
		CORBA Scripting	May 1999
		Real-Time CORBA	May 1999
		Minimal CORBA	November 1998

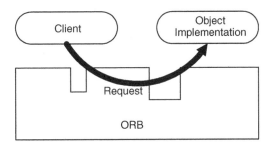

Exhibit 3.   Client Sending Request to Object Implementation

CORBA 2.4 originally included several Quality of Service (QoS) specifications such as Asynchronous Messaging, Minimum CORBA, and Real-Time CORBA specifications, as well as revisions made by several RTFs and FTFs, including those responsible for the Interoperable Naming Service, Components, Notification Service, and Firewall specifications. Minimum CORBA (for embedded systems) and Real-Time CORBA (for real-time operating systems) eventually became part of CORBA 3.

As it now stands, CORBA 3 comprises three components on integration with Java and the Internet, quality control and a component model, each of which is further explained in the section entitled "What Is New? CORBA 3."

Organizational Structure

CORBA is structured to allow integration of a wide variety of object systems. We start with a client sending a request to an object implementation (see Exhibit 3). The ORB provides for all mechanisms to find the object implementation for the request, to prepare the implementation to receive the request, and to communicate the data making up the request. To make the request, the client can use the dynamic invocation interface (DII).

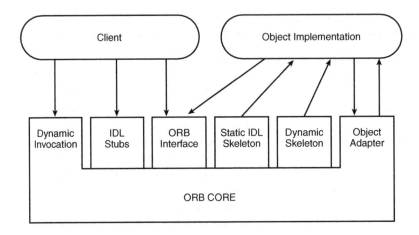

Exhibit 4.   Structure of Object Request Interfaces

The DII allows the dynamic construction of object invocations, rather than calling a stub routine that is specific to a particular operation on a particular object. This allows a client to specify the object to be invoked, the operation to be performed, and the set of parameters for the operation through a call or sequence of calls.

Another way of making the request is to use an OMG IDL stub (depending on the interface of the target object). Object-oriented programming languages such as C++ and Smalltalk do not require stub interfaces. The client can also directly interact with the ORB for some functions.

The request goes to the object implementation to receive it as an up-call interface either through the OMG IDL skeleton or through a dynamic skeleton (see Exhibit 4). The existence of a skeleton does not imply the existence of a corresponding client stub. The up-call interface allows object implementations to write routines that conform to the interface and is identical for all ORB implementations and there can be multiple object adapters. With the normal-call interface, each object has stubs and a skeleton.

The dynamic skeleton interface (DSI) is analogous to the client's side's DII. Rather than being accessed through a skeleton specific to a particular operation, an object's implementation is reached through an interface that provides access to the operation name and parameters. The object implementation can call the object adapter and the ORB while processing a request.

There are a wide variety of ORB implementations possible with CORBA. An ORB can support multiple options and protocols for communication. The options are listed in Exhibit 5.

What Is New? CORBA 3

Considered by many to be the core of CORBA 3, the CORBA Component Model (CCM) packages up transactionality, persistence, event-handling security, and POA-based server resource control into a development and runtime

Exhibit 5.   ORB Examples

Client and implementation-resident ORB	If there is a suitable communication mechanism, an ORB can be implemented in routines resident in the clients and implementation.
Server-based ORB	To centralize the management of the ORB, all clients and implementations can communicate with one or more servers that route requests from clients to implementations.
System-based ORB	To enhance security and performance, the ORB could be provided as a basic service of the underlying operating system.
Library-based ORB	For objects that are lightweight and whose implementation can be shared, the implementation might actually be in a library.

package that business programmers can handle. Intentionally matched feature-for-feature with EJBs, the CCM fulfills the last promise made by the Java and Internet integration theme that started the three categories. The CCM was adopted by OMG in late 1999 and is scheduled for formal release before the end of 2001 as the numbered release CORBA 3. A brief description of CORBA scripting languages is included.

This section looks at major parts of CORBA 3, CCM development stages, CCM extension to IDL, component usage patterns, the container programming model, and integration with Enterprise JavaBeans. In addition to the CORBA Component Model, CORBA 3 consists of two other parts: improved integration with Java and the Internet and Quality of Service control.

Improved Integration with Java and the Internet

The first major part of CORBA 3 is improved integration with increasingly popular Java over the Internet. This became more important as the environments of servers became outnumbered by client machines by many orders of magnitude. Computers built for homes and offices have a lot of power, and downloadable code removes many of the system administration obstacles. One can now download, for example, various codes (IDL templates) for CORBA applications under development for wired or wireless offices. The OMG has published a standard protocol for CORBA over wireless.

This section briefly looks at the status of CORBA's `valuetypes`, Java-to-XML mapping, XML/Value mapping, the Naming Service, the CORBA Firewall specification, and the DCE/Internetworking specification. Readers should review the section on Work-In-Progress Status of various groups of the OMG Technology Committee for any other specifications of interest. Check the OMG Web site for any updates.

Java and CORBA work well together. Java, like CORBA, is object-oriented and has a distribution facility, Remote Method Invocation (RMI), with parallels to CORBA. Both run over the Internet. Java is the only language with a reverse mapping from its object interfaces to IDL. CORBA's `valuetype` aligns with

Java's `serializable`. The basic level of the CORBA component is aligned with its Enterprise Java Beans (EJB) specification. On the other hand, CORBA is a multi-language environment, while Java is a single-language environment evenly distributed through RMI. Additionally, Java has a larger programmer base than CORBA.

The `valuetype` and the reverse Java-to-IDL mapping are building blocks for XML/Value Mapping, asynchronous invocations, and the CCM. The `valuetype` allows an object to be passable with values. It gives CORBA programmers an alternative construct that passes by value, rather than by reference. The way the `valuetype` was defined gives CORBA a construct that parallels Java's `serializable`. In other words, one can pass values between Java and CORBA programs. The `valuetype` was formally released as part of CORBA 2.3.

When coding a CORBA program, one defines the interface to each object type by writing it to IDL, and then uses an IDL compiler to convert it to the language of choice: C, C++, Java, Smalltalk, Ada, COBOL, Lisp, PL/1, Python, etc. To reverse the mapping to IDL, one needs Java's `serializable` and CORBA's `valuetype`. Without them, one will not be able to do so. This mapping allows Java RMI objects to interoperate over the network like CORBA objects. The Java-to-IDL mapping was formally released as part of CORBA 2.3.

The Java-to-IDL mapping serves as building blocks for XML/Value Mapping (and the CCM). Although the role that XML plays in building Internet commerce is significant, the original CORBA 3 press release did not cover the topic of mapping XML to CORBA `valuetypes`. What it does is present an XML document as a collection of native CORBA types — in a standard way.

The specification lets one take advantage of a data type definition (DTD) if there is one, but works perfectly well for DTD-less XML documents if there is no DTD. XML documents that come with DTDs have a static structure. Those without DTDs give a flavor of dynamic structure. The static mapping takes advantage of the extra information in the DTD. Although more applications use static rather than dynamic mapping, one is better off with dynamic mapping especially in developing Internet commerce applications. For the less sophisticated, static mapping is easier to work with and analyze.

The XML/Value specification maps the DOM interfaces to CORBA `valuetypes`. Not presented in the DOM specification are the methods to parse from an XML document to a node tree and serialize from a node tree to XML documents. A new DOM version is needed to make the XML/Value Mapping work. As of July 2001, Microsoft had not formally announced this version and the work-in-progress status of the XML/Value FTF (in the category of PTC Revision Task Forces) indicates that submission deadlines have not been set. It has not yet been issued as part of a numbered CORBA release. Check the OMG site for status changes.

The *CORBA Firewall Traversal specification* allows firewalls to be configured for CORBA, passing IIOP traffic when they are supposed to and keeping it out when they are not. As of July 2001, the work-in-progress status of the CORBA Firewall Traversal RTF (in the ORB and Object Services Platform Task Force category) indicates that initial submissions have been received. Proposals called for specification of IDL interfaces, mechanisms, and conventions that will permit IIOP to traverse inter-network firewalls or similar specifications for any other OMG inter-ORB protocols. Check the OMG Web site for status changes.

The Interoperable *Naming Service* is divided into three parts. The first part defines human-readable object references, while the second part enhances the ORB's handling of object references for standard services of start-up. The third part standardizes the textual representation of an object's name. In short, this service is key to allowing newly discovered CORBA objects to be invoked over the Internet. All of the provisions of this service were added to the CORBA core in release 2.4.

Although the DCE/CORBA Internetworking specification passed the OMG PTC vote in September 1998, the marketplace did not fully embrace it. As a result, this specification was not fully adopted.

Quality of Service Control

Quality of Service control allows one to control the characteristics of an environment or select and tune a specialized version of CORBA. It includes CORBA Messaging, Invocation Quality of Service, Real-Time CORBA, Fault-Tolerant CORBA, Minimum CORBA, and Smart Transducers. Each is briefly discussed.

- *CORBA Messaging* encompasses both asynchronous and messaging mode invocations. This specification was added to CORBA 2.4 and appears as Chapter 22.
- *Invocation Quality of Service* pertains to both asynchronous and synchronous invocations. Under CORBA 3, one can prioritize invocations, set timeouts, and control other characteristics when environments become overloaded.
- *Real-Time CORBA,* the first of the three specialized versions of CORBA, extends the CORBA architecture to give real-time applications the resource control they need to guarantee end-to-end predictability for distributed applications built on real-time operating systems. This specification was added to CORBA 2.4 and appears as Chapter 24.
- *Fault-Tolerant CORBA,* the second of the three specialized versions, standardizes redundancy software configurations and systems to provide the Enterprise applications with more reliable performance.
- *Minimum CORBA,* the last of the specifications, is aimed at embedded and card-based systems. This specification defines a small-footprint CORBA configuration by omitting dynamic features (DII, interface repository). This specification was added to CORBA 2.4 as Chapter 23.

CORBA 3 applications are broad, varied, and friendly to loosely coupled interoperating systems characteristic of the business-to-business (B2B) applications. This is in contrast to CORBA 2 where it integrates distributed objects into a tightly coupled application. B2B and some business-to-consumer (B2C) applications must be loosely coupled, meaning that services are available when needed. These services can wait for a response. This can be partially accomplished with CORBA's ability to transmit requests in XML.

Many applications require that invocations complete within a certain time. This is particularly true for Internet commerce applications. If invocations are not completed on time, an enterprise can lose many customers. This is where Real-Time CORBA plays a significant role in time-critical applications. It is being used today in many systems, from military to flight and space control. This leads us in two directions: Fault-Tolerant and Minimum CORBA. The first provides extra reliability in systems while the second makes the software as small as possible to fit into embedded systems, such as those found in TV or VCR.

The OMG has already gone beyond Minimum CORBA with Smart Transducers RTF (in the category of ORB and Object Services Platform Task Force). For those who do not know, smart transducers are systems-on-the-chip. The task force suggests that three levels of interfaces are required: a real-time service interface to deliver the data, a diagnostic and maintenance interface to query log data, and a configuration interface for initial configuration and updates. As of July 2001, current status shows that initial submissions have been received.

The CORBA Component Model

The CORBA component model (CCM) is the most interesting specification of CORBA 3. It combines the key services, with the POA's servant handling capability for scalable servers, and wraps these tools with higher-level interfaces. CCM applications are very compact and are easy to code. Codes are automatically generated from declarations in new languages built upon OMG IDL.

CCM applications are modular and can be assembled from CCM components — commercial or in-house programmed. CCM components and EJBs can be combined in a single application. In addition, CCM applications can scale to enterprise and Internet usage levels.

The CCM consists of a number of interlocking pieces that comprise the complete server computing architecture. These pieces include:

- The components themselves, including:
  - An abstract component model, as extensions to IDL and the object model
  - A component implementation framework, using the new Component Implementation Definition Language (CIDL)
- The component container programming model expressed alternatively as the component implementer and client view and the container provider view
- Integration with Persistence, Transactions, and Events Services
- Component packaging and deployment
- Interworking with EJB 1.1
- Component MetaData Model — Interface Repository and Meta-Object Facility (MOF) extensions

CCM Development Stages

Here are the steps in a CCM development project.

1. *Analysis design phase.* This step includes all the modeling analysis work that happens before a developer is ready to start designing CORBA components. It produces a Unified Modeling Language (UML) model of the application in several parts, including architecture, a set of use cases, and others. One can construct a UML model and use it for one's CORBA or CMM application. One will have to subset UML to CORBA because CCM has not been fully standardized.

2. *Component declaration.* This step requires one to declare CORBA component's methods and home in OMC IDL, using the component extensions. Then use CORBA 3 IDL to compile it. Server-side products include skeletons and an XML component description.

3. *Component implementation.* The first part of the implementation step is to declare each component's persistent state in Persistent Definition Language (PSDL, an extension of OMG IDL) and some behavior in CIDL. One can use PSDL directly in one's programming language. The Persistent State Service (PSS) automates storage and retrieval of a servant's persistent state and is the last of the building blocks. The PSS is implemented with the CCM container that connects to an implementation of the PSS to provide persistence. Compilation of the CIDL generates component skeletons that one fills in with business logic in the chosen programming language.

4. *Component packaging.* This step generates a component descriptor: a file, in XML, that tells the CCM runtime how to connect to and manage the implementation. It tells how to package the implementation and the component descriptor into a component archive file (the file extension of `.car`).

5. *Component assembly.* In this optional step, one can configure each component in the assembly, describe how it connects to the other included components, and tell how the different component types will be partitioned among a set of computers. One can do this if the installation is designed for a multi-machine execution environment for load-balancing.

6. *Component deployment and installation.* CCM product vendors must provide a runtime that supports transactions, security, and event handling. These systems may support persistence as well, although the CMM specification allows a runtime to rely on a separate compliant PSS implementation.

7. *Runtime: component instance activation.* At runtime, components are activated by the container POA using the subset of modes available, and are invoked by clients via their IDL interfaces. Once deployed and installed, the component factories are available to be activated and used via the standard CORBA ORB mechanisms.

CCM Extensions to OMG IDL

A component is a new basic metatype in CORBA. A component is not the same thing as an interface. The various stubs and skeletons a component bears are referred to as ports. Four types have special names:

Exhibit 6.   CCM Component Categories

Component Category	CORBA Usage Model	Container API Type	Primary Key	EJB Bean Type
Service	Stateless	Session	No	—
Session	Conversational	Session	No	Session
Process	Durable	Entity	No	—
Entity	Durable	Entity	No	Entity

1. *Facets* are the potentially multiple interfaces that a component provides to its clients.
2. *Receptacles* are the client stubs that a component uses to invoke other components, as described in its configuration file.
3. *Event sources* are the named connection points that emit events of specified type to one or more interested consumers, or to an event channel.
4. *Event sinks* are the named connection points into which events of a specified type can be pushed by a supplier or an event channel.

Both event types constitute a CCM event model that is based on publish/subscribe. This model supports a subset of the semantics of the CORBA Notification Service, using simplified interfaces.

A component may also incorporate client stubs used to invoke other CORBA objects — the naming or trader service, for example.

Other new features of the model include:

- *Primary keys:* values that components that have persistent state expose to their clients to help identify themselves (a customer account number or social security number might be a primary key)
- *Attributes and configuration:* named values exposed through accessors and mutators primarily used for component configuration
- *Home interfaces:* provide standard factory and finder operations

Component Usage Patterns

There are seven categories, four supported by the CCM, two by EJB, and an "empty" category that you can declare and support yourself. Every component type that you define (using IDL, PSDL, and CIDL) must have a category in its composition CIDL.

The component category is built up from a CORBA usage model and a Container API type. The four component categories are (see also Exhibit 6):

1. *Service components* have no state and no identity. The usage model is stateless. The Container API type is Session.
2. *Session components* have transient state and non-persistent identity. The usage model is conversational. Both the Container API and EJB Bean types are Session. What this means is that the object reference is transient. It

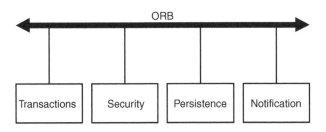

Exhibit 7. Container-Provided Services

will not survive from one session to another and, having no persistent state, it cannot have a primary key.

3. *Process components* have persistent identity and state that may span sessions, but no key is visible to the client. The usage model is durable. The Container API Type is Entity. It does not have an EJB Bean type.

4. *Entity components* have persistent state and identity, visible to the client through a primary key. Both Container API and EJB Bean types are Entity.

Container Programming Model

This model is the programming environment that CCM gives us. The container is the server's runtime environment for a CORBA component implementation, offering CCM services to the components it serves. The POA forms the basis for scalable CORBA servers. The CCM Container is a specialized POA and uses the PSS to store the state of persistent objects when executing code is deactivated between calls. Replacing the now-deprecated Persistent Object Service, the PSS is used by the CCM Container to store the state of persistent objects when executing code is deactivated between calls. The PSS was adopted in late 1999, and is scheduled for inclusion in a formal CORBAservices release before the end of 2001, intentionally synchronized with the formal release of the CCM as part of CORBA 3.

There are two types of interfaces that CCM uses:

- *External API types:* These are the APIs that clients use to invoke operations on the component or its home.
- *Container API types:* These are local interfaces that allow either component-to-container or container-to-component invocations. Component-to-container invocations request the container-provided services (see Exhibit 7), such as Transactions, Security, Persistence, and Notification). Container-to-component invocations primarily concern activation/deactivation and informing the servant of its primary key so that it can restore the required state.

Integration with Enterprise JavaBeans

The required programming API for Java CORBA Components is EJB 1.1. The EJB 2.0 specification, released after the CCM, requires that EJBs interoperate

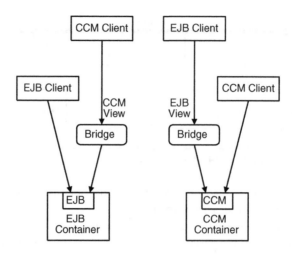

Exhibit 8.   Interoperability Between CORBA Components and EJBs

over the network using OMG's protocol IIOP using equivalent IDL generated from Java objects via the reverse Java-to-IDL mapping.

Building on this foundation, the CCM specification includes a comprehensive forward and reverse mapping of EJB operations to CCM operations. The correspondence is extremely close; a thin bridge can span the gap (see Exhibit 8). It encompasses not only method invocations, but also container, factory, finder, and other infrastructure operations. With suitable bridges in place, an EJB running in a CORBA EJB container can look like a CCM component, and a CCM component running in a CCM container can look like an EJB.

The CCM architecture allows a component to bear multiple interfaces, and Component Home type provides class-like operations. Four pre-coded selectable resource allocation patterns, selected from over 200 provided by the POA, simplify server-side programming while preserving flexibility.

CORBA Object Services

This section looks at what object services are available and provides a brief discussion on OpenORB.

Accessing Object Services

The implementation of business objects will often involve access to standard CORBA object services (see Exhibit 9). Other services, such as the Change Management Service will be added over time as they are agreed to by the OMG.

1. *Collection Service* supports the grouping of objects and support operations for the manipulation of the objects as a group. Common collection types are queues, sets, maps, etc. Collections can guarantee the uniqueness of

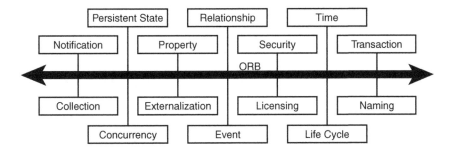

Exhibit 9. CORBA Object Services

elements, while others allow multiple occurrences of elements. A user chooses a collection type that matches the application requirements based on manipulation capabilities.

2. *Concurrency Service* provides the locking mechanisms that enable sharing of business object state between active clients and integrates this mechanism with the underlying application/database functions. It ensures that the consistency of the object is not compromised when accessed by multiple users, applications, or other types of concurrently executing computations. This service is used with Persistence Service and Transaction Service.

3. *Event Service* supports the asynchronous mechanism for passing messages on events between business objects that may not know about another and for automatic notification of changes from one object to another. It decouples the communication between objects and defines two roles for objects: the supplier role and the consumer role. *Suppliers* produce event data and *consumers* process event data. Event data is communicated between suppliers and consumers by issuing standard CORBA requests. This communication model contrasts with method calls.

4. *Externalization Service* uses a special streaming mechanism for moving or copying the contents of business objects to an external medium. To externalize an object is to record the object's data in a stream of data. Objects can be externalized to a stream (in memory, on a disk file, across the network, and between hoses) and subsequently be internalized into a new object in the same or a different process. The Externalization Service is related to the Relationship Service. It also parallels the Life Cycle Service in defining externalization protocols for simple objects, for arbitrarily related objects, and for graphs of related objects that support compound operations.

5. *Licensing Service* provides a mechanism for producers to control the user of their intellectual property in a manner determined by their business and customer needs. It includes three objects: Licensing Service Manager, Producer Licensing Service, and Licensing Systems.

6. *Life Cycle Service* defines services and conventions for creating, deleting, copying, and moving objects. Because CORBA-based environments support distributed objects, the Life Cycle Service defines conventions that allow clients to perform life cycle operation on objects in different locations. This service may vary from vendor to vendor in the way developers are

allowed to have some measure of control over physical aspects of the objects.

7. *Naming Service* supports the use of human-readable and user-friendly names for business objects and the grouping together of conceptually related objects within a network. A naming graph allows more complex names to reference an object.

8. *Notification Service* describes a CORBA-based notification service, a service that extends the existing Event Service. New capabilities include the ability to transmit events, the ability for clients to specify when events they are interested in receiving, the ability to transmit events in the form of a well-defined data structure, and the ability for the event types offered by suppliers to an event channel to be discovered by consumers of that channel so that consumers can subscribe to new event types as they become available.

9. *Persistence State Service* provides the mapping (IDL) between business object state and external persistent datastores and describes how objects are stored uniformly in various repositories. It works well with the Transaction Service and the POA. (Note that Persistent State Service replaces Persistent Object Service.)

10. *Property Service* is concerned with an object supporting an interface that consists of operations and attributes. Two objects are of the same type if they support the same interface. Properties are types, names values dynamically associated with an object, outside the type system. One example is a particular document declared as important must be read by the end of the month. Another example is an online service download utility that increments a counter every time an object is downloaded by a user.

11. *Query Service* provides query operations on collections of objects and can be used to access server objects or the data in external databases using keys and the query engine the service provides. The queries are predicate based and may return collections of objects. They can be specified using object derivatives of SQL or other styles of object query languages, including direct manipulation query languages.

12. *Relationship Service* concerns distributed objects that are frequently used to model entities in the real world. They do not exist in isolation and are related to one another. One example of real-world entities and relationships is that a company employs one or more persons; and a person is employed by one or more companies. Another example of several relationships is employment relationships between companies and people.

13. *Security Service* provides authentication checks for clients wishing to access business objects or components and authorization checks at the class, instance, or method level. It is also designed to allow implementations to provide protection against the following: security controls being bypassed; tampering with communication between objects — modifying, inserting, and deleting items; and lack of accountability due, for example, to inadequate identification of users.

14. *Time Service* involves time service requirements on representation of time and source of time. The service should also provide the following facilities: ascertain the order in which "events" occurred, generate time-based events based on timers and alarms, and compute the interval between two events.

Exhibit 10. Reference Model

Object Request Broker	Enables objects to transparently make and receive requests and responses in a distributed environment.
Object Services	A collection of services (interfaces and objects) that support basic functions for using and implementing objects. Services are necessary to construct any distributed application and are always independent of application domains.
Common Facilities	A collection of services that many applications may share, but which are not as fundamental as the Object Services. For example, a system management or electronic mail facility could be classified as a common facility. The Object Request Broker (ORB), then, is the core of the Reference Model. Nevertheless, it alone cannot enable interoperability at the application semantic level. An ORB is like a telephone exchange: it provides the basic mechanism for making and receiving calls but does not ensure meaningful communication between subscribers. Meaningful, productive communication depends on additional interfaces, protocols, and policies that are agreed upon outside the telephone system, such as telephones, modems, and directory services. This is equivalent to the role of Object Services.

15. *Trading Object Service* facilitates the offering and the discovery of instances of services of particular types. A trader is an object that supports the trading object service in a distributed environment. It can be viewed as an object through which other objects can advertise their capabilities and match their needs against advertised capabilities. Advertising a capability or offering a service is called "export." Matching against needs or discovering services is called "import." Export and import facilitate dynamic discovery of, and late binding to, services.

16. *Transaction Service* defines interfaces that allow multiple, distributed objects to cooperate to provide atomicity. These interfaces enable the objects to either commit all changes together or to rollback all changes together, even in the presence of (noncatastrophic) failure. This ensures that transactional actions affecting many objects are indivisible.

To understand how Object Services benefit all computer vendors and users, it is helpful to know that the key to understanding the structure of the architecture is the Reference Model, as shown in the Exhibit 10.

OpenORB

OpenORB Enterprise Suite includes an ORB designed for large scalability, compliance, interoperability, and improved performance, and provides CORBA Services and Extensions. It now includes Notification Service and a new configuration system that allows the configuration and IDL files to be embedded in the JAR files. OpenORB Enterprise Suite is well suited for distributed

Exhibit 11. Domain Specifications

Specifications	Interfaces
OMG Financial	Concurrency
	General Ledger
	Party Membership Facility
OMG Healthcare	Clinical Observations Access Service
	Lexicon Query Service
	Person Identification Service
	Resource Access Decision
OMG Manufacturing	Distributed Simulation Systems
	Product Data Management Enablers
OMG Transportation	Air Traffic Control
OMG Utilities	Utility Management System (UMS) Data Access Facility
OMG Security	Common Secure Interoperatility V2 (CSIv2)
	Security Service
	Resource Access Decision (RAD)
	Enterprise Security with EJB and CORBA

Java applications developed with CORBA. As of May 2001, OpenORB Enterprise Suite 1.1.0 is available at http://openorb.exolab.org/.

Other Supporting Facilities

In addition to CORBA Object Services, other supporting facilities include CORBA facilities and several domain specifications. The CORBAfacilities are services that many applications share but which are not as fundamental as CORBAservices. Available are four specifications: Internationalization and Time, Mobile Agent Facility, Task and Session, and Workflow Management.

As shown in Exhibit 11, each domain provides OMG-compliant specifications according to the goals of the specification.

OMG Technology Committee

OMG's Technology Committee's organizational structure is composed of the Platform Technology Committee (ptc@omg.org), Domain Technology Committee (dtc@omg.org), and Architectural Board. As of July 2001, groups in Exhibits 12, 13, and 14 comprise the Platform Technology Committee, while groups in Exhibits 15, 16, and 17 make up the Domain Technology Committee. Exhibit 18 gives groups with the Architectural Board. (Source: *OMG In Motion* Newsletter, June 2001).

OMG will add or reorganize groups as needed or requested. Not all groups for both committees have any activities. Some of those with work-in-progress status directly or indirectly pertain to CORBA.

Exhibit 12.   Platform Technology RTFs and FTFs

CWM RTF	XMI 1.2 RTF
UML 1.4 RTF	MOF 1.4 RTF
UML Profile for CORBA FTF	Core RTF
Security 1.8 RTF	C++ Mapping RTF
Interop RTF	OTS RTF
Java-to-IDL Mapping RTF	C Language Mapping RTF
Components FTF	PSS FTF
Clock Service & Executor FTF	Portable Interceptors RTF
IDL-to-Java RTF	Relationship Services RTF
IDL Script RTF	CSIv2 FTF
Additional Structures for OTS FTF	Security 1.9 RTF
Object Reference Template FTF	XML Value FTF

Exhibit 13.   Platform Technology SIGs (PSIGs)

Agents PSIG (agents@omg.org)
  Process WG
  CWM WG
  BOI WG
  UML 2.0 WG
Benchmarking PSIG (benchmark@omg.org)
Digital Asset Management PSIG (docman@omg.org)
Internet PSIG (internet@omg.org)
Japan PSIG (jsig@omg.org)
Product Standard Definition SC (psdef@omg.org)
Realtime PSIG (realtime@omg.org)
  RT Analysis & Design WG
  RT High Performance CORBA WG
  Embedded Systems WG
  Publish/Subscribe WG
  Online Upgrades WG
  Safety Critical WG
  MicroCORBA WG
  Realtime Java WG

Exhibit 14.   Platform Technology Task Force

ORB and Object Services Platform Task Force (orbos@omg.org)
  Wrappers WG

Exhibit 15. Domain Technology RTFs and FTFs

Public Key Infrastructure FTF	Genomic Maps FTF
PDM RTF 1.4	CORBA-FTAM/FTP Interworking FTF
Telecom Wireless FTF	Organizational Structures FTF
Macromolecular Structure FTF	Bibliographic Query Service FTF
Telecom Service Access and Subscription FTF	

Exhibit 16. Domain Technology SIGs (DSIGs)

Analytical Data Management DSIG (statistics@omg.org)
Autonomous Decentralized Service System DSIG (adss@omg.org)
CORBAgis DSIG (corbagis@omg.org)
Distributed Simulation DSIG (simsig@omg.org)
Enterprise Application Integration DSIG (eai@omg.org)
Human Resources DSIG (hr@omg.org)
Super Distributed Objects DSIG (sdo@omd.org)
SWradio DSIG (swradio@omg.org)

Work-in-Progress Status

As of July 2001, the status of each group is provided in Exhibit 19. To obtain more information, go to http://www.omg.org/schedule and click on the group of interest.

Modeling Specifications

This section discusses various modeling specifications, particularly the Model-Driven Architecture (MDA). We begin with a brief discussion of IT system life cycles, move to more details about the three cores of MDA, and then look at related topics.

IT systems have historically been developed, managed, and integrated using a range of methodologies, tools, and middleware and there appears to be no end to this innovation. What we have seen in the last few years, especially as a result of efforts at OMG and W3C, is a gradual move to more complete semantic models as well as data representation interchange standards. OMG contributions include CORBA, UML, XML Meta Interchange (XMI), MOF, and CWM. W3C contributions include XML, the XML Schema, and the ongoing work of XML-PC working group. These technologies can be used to more completely integrate the value chain (or life cycle) when it comes to developing and deploying component-based applications for various target software architectures.

The life cycle of an application can vary dramatically, depending on whether one is building a new application from scratch or just surgically

Exhibit 17. Domain Technology Task Force

Command, Control, Computing, Communications and Intelligence DTF
 (c4i@omg.org)
   C4I Roadmap WG
Common Enterprise Model Domain Task Force (bomsig@omg.org)
   IT Asset Management WG
   Organizational Structure Evaluation WG
Electronic Commerce Domain Task Force (ec@omg.org)
   Brokerage WG
   Object Oriented Electronic Data Interchange WG
   Reference Architecture WG
   EC Roadmap WG
   EC eCataloguing WG
Finance Domain Task Force (finance@omg.org)
   Insurance WG
   Accounting WG
   Postal Authorities WG
Healthcare Domain Task Force (healthcare@omg.org)
   CORBAmed Roadmap WG
Life Sciences Research Domain Task Force (lifesciences@omg.org)
   LECIS
   MAPS
   Gene Expression
Management Group (wask@omg.org)
   Cheminformatics
   Bibliographic Services
   Clinical Trials
   Macromolecular Structures
   Architecture & Roadmap
   Sequence Analysis
   Visualization & UI
   Web Pages WG
Manufacturing Domain Task Force (mfg@omg.org)
   Workflow WG
   Product and Process Engineering WG
   Common Business Objects WG
   Manufacturing Execution Systems/Machine Control WG
   People Who Like People WG
Space Domain Task Force (space@omg.org)
Telecommunications Domain Task Force (telecom@omg.org)
   Wireless CORBA WG
   Open Service Market WG
   Network Management WG
Transportation Domain Task Force (transport@omg.org)
   Rail Transport WG
   Air Transport WG
   Highways WG
Utilities Domain Task Force (utilities@omg.org)

Exhibit 18.   Architectural Board

Liaison Subcommittee (liaison@omg.org)
Object & Reference Model Subcommittee (ormsc@omg.org)
   ORM WG
Security SIG (secsig@omg.org)
Testing & Validation SIG (test@omg.org)

Exhibit 19.   Work-In-Progress Status

ORB and Object Services Platform Task Force
Security Domain Membership RFP (Status: Revised submissions have been received.)
Unreliable Multicast RFP (Status: Revised submissions have been received.)
Dynamic Scheduling RFP (Status: Revised submissions have been received.)
Parallel Processing RFP (Status: Revised submissions have been received.)
RT Notification RFP (Status: Initial submissions have been received.)
CORBA Firewall Traversal RFP (Status: Initial submissions have been received.)
CORBA/SOAP RFP (Status: Initial submissions have been received.)
Extensible Frameworks RFP (Status: Initial submissions have been received.)
WAP WMLScript Mapping RFP (Status: Initial submissions have been received.)
Online Upgrades RFI (Status: RFI has been issued; responses pending.)
ATLAS RFP (Status: The Technology Adoption vote has completed.)
GIOP SCTP Mapping RFP (Status: Initial submissions have been received.)
Smart Transducers RFP (Status: Initial submissions have been received.)
Load Balancing RFP (Status: Letters of Intent have been received.)
C Mapping RFP (Status: RFP has been issued; responses pending.)

PTC Revision Task Forces
Core December 2000 RTF (Status: No deadlines have passed.)
Security 1.8 RTF (Status: Technology Adoption vote is underway.)
Security(1.9) December 2000 RTF (Status: No deadlines have passed.)
C++ December 2000 RTF (Status: No deadlines have passed.)
OTS December 2000 RTF (Status: No deadlines have passed.)
IDL-to-Java December 2000 RTF (Status: No deadlines have passed.)
Interop December 2000 RTF (Status: No deadlines have passed.)
XMI 1.2 RTF (Status: No deadlines have passed.)
UML RTF January 2001 (Status: No deadlines have passed.)
MOF 1.4 RTF (Status: No deadlines have passed.)
Java-to-IDL December 2000 RTF (Status: No deadlines have passed.)
Components FTF (Status: The Technology Adoption vote has completed.)
Components December 2000 FTF (Status: No deadlines have passed.)
PSS December 2000 FTF (Status: No deadlines have passed.)
IDLscript December 2000 RTF (Status: No deadlines have passed.)
Python Mapping 1.1 RTF (Status: RTF Revision is complete.)
Portable Interceptors RTF (Status: No deadlines have passed.)
Clock Service and Executor FTF (Status: No deadlines have passed.)
UML Profile for CORBA FTF (Status: The Technology Adoption vote has completed.)
Relationship Services RTF (Status: No deadlines have passed.)

Exhibit 19. Work-In-Progress Status (Continued)

Additional Structures for OTS FTF (Status: No deadlines have passed.)
CSIv2 FTF (Status: No deadlines have passed.)
PL/1 FTF (Status: The Technology Adoption vote has completed.)
Object Reference Template FTF (Status: No deadlines have passed.)
XML/Value FTF (Status: No deadlines have passed.)
CWM RTF (Status: No deadlines have passed.)

Analysis and Design Platform Task Force

Action Semantics for UML RFP (Status: Initial submissions have been received.)
UML Profile for EDOC RFP (Status: Revised submissions have been received.)
UML Textual Notation RFP (Status: Letters of Intent have been received.)
UML Profile for Scheduling RFP (Status: Revised submissions have been received.)
SPE Management RFP (Status: Revised submissions have been received.)
XMI Prod. of XML Schema RFP (Status: Revised submissions have been received.)
UML Profile for EAI RFP (Status: Initial submissions have been received.)
UML 2.0 Infrastructure RFP (Status: Letters of Intent have been received.)
UML 2.0 Superstructure RFP (Status: Letters of Intent have been received.)
UML 2.0 OCL RFP (Status: Letters of Intent have been received.)
UML 2.0 Diagram Interchange RFP (Status: RFP has been issued; responses pending.)
CWM MIP RFP (Status: Letters of Intent have been received.)
CWM Web Services RFP (Status: Letters of Intent have been received.)
UML Testing Profile RFP (Status: RFP has been issued; responses pending.)

Real-Time PSIG

Safety Critical RFI (Status: RFI has been issued; responses pending.)

Common Enterprise Models Domain Task Force

Doc. Repository Integration RFP (Status: Revised submissions have been received.)
Workflow RAI RFP (Status: Letters of Intent have been received.)
Workflow Process Definition RFP (Status: RFP has been issued; responses pending.)
Software Portfolio Mgmt. RFP (Status: Initial submissions have been received.)
Competency RFP (Status: RFP has been issued; responses pending.)
Knowledge Mgmt. RFI (Status: Responses have been received.)

Manufacturing Domain Task Force

PDM Enablers V2.0 RFP (Status: Revised submissions have been received.)
CAD Services RFP (Status: Revised submissions have been received.)
Distributed Simulation V2.0 RFP (Status: Letters of Intent have been received.)

Electronic Commerce Domain Task Force

Registration & Discovery RFP (Status: Revised submissions have been received.)

Telecommunications Domain Task Force

Telecom Distrib. Accounting RFP (Status: Letters of Intent have been received.)

Financial Domain Task Force

Product & Agreement Mgmt. RFP (Status: RFP has been issued; responses pending.)
Payroll Facility RFP (Status: RFP has been issued; responses pending.)
AR/AP Facility RFP (Status: RFP has been issued; responses pending.)

Healthcare Domain Task Force

Healthcare Data Interpretation RFP (Status: Revised submissions have been received.)
Order Entry/Tracking RFP (Status: Letters of Intent have been received.)
HILS RFP (Status: Revised submissions have been received.)

Exhibit 19.   Work-In-Progress Status (Continued)

Transportation Domain Task Force

Surveillance RFP (Status: Revised submissions have been received.)

ITS Center to Center RFI (Status: Responses have been received.)

Flight Planning RFI (Status: Responses have been received.)

Interoperability for Rail RFI (Status: Responses have been received.)

Lifesciences Domain Task Force

Entity Identification Service RFP (Status: Revised submissions have been received.)

Gene Expression RFP (Status: Revised submissions have been received.)

Chemical Structure RFP (Status: Initial submissions have been received.)

LECIS RFP (Status: Revised submissions have been received.)

BSANE RFP (Status: Initial submissions have been received.)

Lifesciences RFI 8 (Status: RFI has been issued; responses pending.)

Chemical Sample Mgmt. RFI (Status: RFI has been issued; responses pending.)

C4I Domain Task Force

Generic Sonar Interface RFI (Status: RFI has been issued; responses pending.)

Super Distributed Objects DSIG

Super Distributed Objects RFI (Status: Responses have been received.)

DTC Revision Task Forces

Genomic Maps FTF (Status: No deadlines have passed.)

PDM RTF 1.4 (Status: RTF Revision is complete.)

TSAS FTF (Status: No deadlines have passed.)

CORBA-FTAM/FTP FTF (Status: No deadlines have passed.)

Public Key Infrastructure FTF (Status: No deadlines have passed.)

Bibliographic Query Service FTF (Status: No deadlines have passed.)

Macromolecular Structure FTF (Status: No deadlines have passed.)

Organizational Structure FTF (Status: No deadlines have passed.)

Telecom Wireless FTF (Status: No deadlines have passed.)

adding a wrapper to an existing application. The cost of enhancement and maintenance of an application as well as the cost of integrating new applications, with existing applications, far exceeds the cost of initial development.

In addition, the application life cycle itself can be quite complex, involving several vendors in each of the life cycle phases. Hence, the need for information interchange and interoperability between tools and middleware provided by different vendors (a very common situation in enterprises today) is critical.

Like the life cycles for IT systems, the MDA supports many of the commonly used steps in model-driven, component-based development and deployment. A key aspect of MDA is that it addresses the complete life-cycle analysis and design, programming aspects (testing, component build, or component assembly), as well as deployment and management aspects. Exhibit 20 depicts a high-level representation of how the various pieces fit together in MDA. As one can see, the model has three cores: inner, middle, and outer. The inner core consists of the UML, Component Warehouse Modeling (CWM), and MOF, while the middle core focuses on CORBA, XMI/XML, .NET, and Java — the

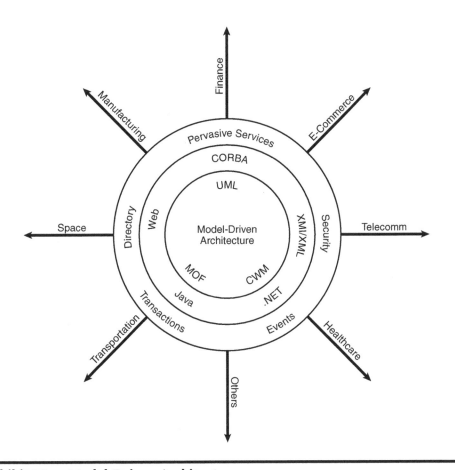

Exhibit 20.   Model-Driven Architecture

middleware. The outermost core is composed of Directory, Pervasive Services, Security, Events, and Transactions. Obviously, the inner core maps to the middle core, which in turn, utilizes the outer core to build a Model-Driven Architecture.

MDA Inner Core

The UML, CWM, and MOF comprise the inner core. In September 2000, OMG members started work on the Release 2.0 major revision of the UML specification. The new release will be tailored to MDA requirements. This work is being done in four parts:

- ■ UML 2.0 Infrastructure scheduled to complete early 2002
- ■ UML 2.0 Superstructure scheduled to complete mid-2002
- ■ UML 2.0 OCL scheduled to complete early 2002
- ■ UML 2.0 Diagram Interchange scheduled to complete by mid-2002

UML addresses the modeling of architecture, objects, interactions between objects, data modeling aspects of the application life cycle, as well as the design aspects of component-based development, including construction and assembly. Note that UML is powerful enough that it can be used to represent artifacts of legacy systems. Artifacts captured in UML models (Classes, Interfaces, Use Cases, Activity Graphs, etc.) can be easily exported to other tools in the life-cycle chain using XMI.

MOF provides the standard modeling and interchange constructs used in MDA. These constructs are a subset of the UML modeling constructs. Other standard OMG models, including UML and CWM, are defined in terms of MOF constructs.

This common foundation provides the basis for model/metadata interchange and interoperability, and is the mechanism through which models are analyzed in XMI. MOF also defines programmatic interfaces for manipulating models and their instances spanning the application life cycle. These are defined in IDL and are being extended to Java.

By defining the common meta-model for all of OMG's modeling specifications, the MOF allows derived specifications to work together in a natural way. The MOF also defines a standard repository for meta-models and, therefore, models (because a meta-model is just a special case of a model).

CWM is the OMG data warehouse standard. It covers the full life cycle of designing, building, and managing data warehouse applications and supports management of the life cycle. It is probably the best example to date of applying the MDA paradigm to an application area.

The CWM standardizes a complete, comprehensive meta-model that enables data mining across database boundaries at an enterprise and goes well beyond. Like a UML profile but in data space instead of application space, it forms the MDA mapping to database schemas. The product of a cooperative effort between OMG and the Meta-Data Coalition (MDC), the CWM does for data modeling what UML does for application modeling.

Two related adoption efforts will extend CWM to the Internet. They are:

- CWM Web Services
- CWM Metadata Interchange Patterns (MIP)

CWM Web Services will enable CWM-based metadata interchange over the Internet by specifying the syntax and semantics of CWM metadata interchange using a CWM Web Services API and loosely coupled communications. The interaction patterns, standardized by the separate MIP RFP, will be general enough to be used elsewhere.

MDA Middle Core

The middle core focuses on CORBA, XMI/XML, .NET, and Java. Historically, the integration between the development tools and the deployment into the middleware framework has been weak. This is now beginning to change by using key elements of the MDA — specific models and XML DTDs and Schemas that span the life cycle, and profiles that provide mappings between the models used in various life-cycle phases.

XMI, which marries the world of modeling (UML), metadata (MOF and XML), and middleware (UML profiles for Java, EJB, IDL, Enterprise Distributed Object Computing (EDOC)), plays a pivotal role in the OMG's use of XML at the core of the MDA. It also provides developers focused on implementation in Java, VB, HTML, etc., with a natural way to take advantage of the software platform and engineering discipline when a more formal development process is desired.

XMI is a standard interchange mechanism used between various tools, repositories, and middleware. XMI can also be used to automatically produce XML DTDs and XML Schemas from UML and MOF models, providing an XML serialization mechanism for these artifacts. XMI has been used to render UML artifacts (using the UML XMI DTD), data warehouse and database artifacts (using the CWM XMI DTD), CORBA interface definitions (using the IDL DTD), and Java interfaces and Classes (using a Java DTD).

MDA Outer Core

OMG Domain Task Forces, after years of writing specifications in only CORBA, are moving quickly to write base specifications in the MDA. OMG recognizes (based on analogy to the CORBA-based Object Management Architecture) three levels of MDA-based specifications: The Pervasive Services, The Domain Facilities, and MDA Specifications.

The Pervasive Services include enterprise necessities such as Directory Services, Transactions, Security, and Event Handling (Notification). Additional Pervasive Services may be defined, either from the list of CORBA services already standardized by OMG or from other suggestions from OMG members.

The Domain Facilities include industries such as healthcare, manufacturing, telecommunications, biotechnology, etc. Although MDA-based standards have yet to emerge, OMG Domain Task Forces have started to work in MDA to realize the many benefits of this architecture. OMG's Life Science Research Domain Task Force, working in biotechnology, has modified its Mission and Goals Statement to reflect its work in MDA.

In mid-2000, even before MDA, OMG's Healthcare Domain Task Force (formerly known by its nickname CORBAmed) published its Clinical Image Access Service (CIAS), including a non-normative UML model that describes the normative specification written in OMG IDL. One can examine this document to get an idea of what a future MDA specification might look like. In a true MDA specification, the UML model will be normative and fully developed, defining all interfaces and operations, including parameters and types, and specifying pre- and post-conditions in Object Constraint Language.

MDA Applications themselves perhaps created and maintained by a software vendor or end-user company or enterprise using MDA tools to run an MDA-based methodology, are not standardized by OMG. MDA-based development tools will be widely available and enterprises around the world will start their application development by building a PIM instead of writing code.

Exhibit 21.   Other UML Profiles

The UML Profile for EDOC	Define a profile for component-based systems. This profile will be used to define core PIMs.
The UML Profile for EAI	Define a profile for loosely coupled systems; that is, those that communicate using either asynchronous or messaging-based methods. These modes are typically used in Enterprise Application Integration, but are used elsewhere as well. This specification is expected to complete by the end of 2001.
A UML Profile for Scheduling	Will support precise modeling of predictable — that is, real-time — systems, precisely enough to enable quantitative analysis of their schedulability, performance, and timeliness characteristics. This specification is scheduled to complete soon.

Several companies have already developed applications using tools that are close enough to the MDA (although MDA was not formally defined when the work was done) to be recognizable as model-driven development.

UML Profiles, PIM, and PSMs

Technically speaking, applications and frameworks (that is, parts of applications that perform a particular function) can all be defined in the MDA as a base Platform-Independent Model (PIM) that maps to one or more Platform Specific Models (PSMs) and implementations. Both levels of models will be defined in UML, making it the foundation of the MDA. OMG members are already taking the group's well-established CORBAservice specifications and mapping them back to PIMs where they can serve all platforms through the MDA development pathway.

That is, business experts can model exactly the business rules they want into the PIM. Once business experts have completed the PIM, it can be implemented on *virtually any* platform, or on multiple platforms with interoperability among them, to meet the needs of the industry and companies that use it.

In the MDA, both PIMs and PSMs will be defined using UML profiles. Eventually, OMG will define a suite of profiles that span the entire scope of MDA. *UML Profiles* tailor the language to particular areas of computing (such as EDOC) or particular platforms (such as EJB or CORBA).

For example, the UML Profile for CORBA defines the mapping from a PIM to a CORBA-specific PSM. The UML Profile for CORBA specification was designed to provide a standard means for expressing the semantics of CORBA IDL using UML notation and thus to support expressing these semantics with UML tools.

As of July 2001, OMG standards for other profiles are in process, as shown in Exhibit 21. These profiles are critical links that bridge the UML community (model based design and analysis) to the developer community (Java, VB, C++ developers), middleware community (CORBA, EJB, and SOAP developers).

Additional Specifications

Several additional specifications will help tailor the UML to support MDA. A new Action Semantics for UML specification, scheduled to complete in mid-2001, will enhance the language's representation of behavior. A human-readable UML Textual Notation will enable a new class of UML editor programs and enhance the way UML models can be manipulated. It will fit into the EDOC, Notation elements will map one-to-one to the more verbose XMI, but syntax will differ. This specification is scheduled to complete in late 2001.

Another specification of interest to the CORBA, UML, and MDA community is a standard Software Process Engineering Metamodel that will define a framework for describing methodologies in a standard way. This specification is scheduled to complete soon. It will not standardize any particular methodology, but will enhance interoperability from one methodology to another.

IDL Specified Models

IDL itself is not tied to any specific language environment or platform. This is what made it possible to have ISO adopt IDL as a standard without any specific reference to CORBA. Indeed, there are many systems in this world that use IDL to specify the syntactic model of the system but do not use CORBA as the underlying platform. While OMG has not standardized any such usage of IDL with alternative platforms, there are broadly deployed instances in the industry of such use. However, it should be noted that despite being platform and language environment independent, IDL specified models are restricted to expressing only the syntax of the interactions (i.e., operation signatures).

OMG has chosen to use IDL together with the CORBA platform (ORB and language mappings) as a reasonable package of facilities to standardize. This facilitates algorithmic construction of skeletons of portable components of the system for a specific language environment, from language-independent specifications, using an IDL compiler. The big win from this is *portability of specifications* from one language environment to another, as well as *portability of implementations* among different instances of the same language environment.

Additionally, given specifications of the exact syntax of interaction between objects that constitute the system, it is also possible to automatically generate the syntactic form that is carried on a wire that connects the two communicating objects. OMG has standardized on GIOP/IIOP as the standard means of conveying communication between IDL declared objects deployed on a CORBA platform. Again, IDL, and even the CORBA platform, do not preclude use of other means of communication between objects. Indeed, it is quite possible for two CORBA objects to communicate with each other using DCOM or SOAP on the wire. But the adoption of a single means of interoperation ensures *interoperability of implementations*.

Bridging Platforms

The general philosophy has been to adopt a single set of standards within a broader framework that allows alternatives if there is such a need. The standard interoperability framework recognizes such possibilities and explicitly defines domains and how bridges can be specified to enable objects in different domains to communicate with each other, thus making it possible to construct systems that span multiple domains.

This framework has been successfully used to specify bridges between the CORBA platform with GIOP/IIOP-based communication and the COM/DCOM platform and communication domain in an existing OMG standard. More recently, an inter-domain bridge between the CCM and the EJB Component Model has also been adopted as a standard.

The problem of bridging from one platform to another becomes considerably simpler if the two platforms in question share a common model at a higher level of abstraction. It is fortunate that most broadly deployed distributed computing environments happen to share such a common model, although never formally expressed as such, thus making construction of bridges among them feasible.

Extensions to IDL

Various attempts have been made to extend IDL to capture richer structural and behavioral information and to automatically generate implementation artifacts for a given platform that enforces the constraints as specified in the richer specification.

A recent example of this is the Components extension of IDL together with the XML-based deployment descriptors, which facilitates specification of entire systems in terms of its constituent components, their interactions, and deployment characteristics. However, it should be noted that all such extensions so far have been point solutions, without paying much attention to a general model for specifying such extensions.

A model defined in the UML Profile for CORBA provides an alternative representation of an IDL model. They are different representations of the same model. In fact, there is precisely one IDL representation that can be derived from a model represented using the UML Profile for CORBA. The UML model may, however, provide additional information (such as cardinality) that cannot be represented in an IDL model today.

Appropriate extensions to IDL that allow representation of these additional relevant concepts would make it possible to map a model expressed in the CORBA Profile of UML to an equivalent IDL model in a reversible fashion. That is, one would be able to reconstruct the corresponding UML from the equivalent IDL, without loss of information. This ability to "round-trip" the transformation in this way would allow designers and architects to work in the technology they are comfortable with (UML or IDL) and algorithmically generate the alternative representation for the specification.

Chapter 3

Microsoft's Stuff

This chapter discusses Microsoft's stuff that the world has come to know. They include the .NET platform architecture and associated technologies — Simple Object Access Protocol (SOAP), Windows 2000 operating systems, and Microsoft Transaction Server.

Introduction

The .NET platform represents an evolution of the Component Object Model (COM). The next generation of COM, COM+, is part of .NET Framework. In 1995, Microsoft and DEC[1] published the COM specification and it has been the keystone of development using Microsoft platforms ever since. In theory, COM is available on Macintosh and UNIX platforms. But COM requires a registry, which is built into Windows and is merely emulated on other systems. So, in practice, COM has become a Windows-only solution.

Creating a chart in Excel and pasting it into a Word document, using Outlook to send an e-mail, and developing an application in Visual Basic all require COM to provide interoperability among them. Another example of COM components includes ActiveX controls that can be embedded into a Windows or a Web page. There is a huge third-party market of controls providing functionality such as grids, graphs, calendars, 3-D viewers, sockets, etc.

Internet Explorer supports ActiveX controls because it is a Microsoft product. On the other hand, Netscape Navigator does not because of issues with cross-platform compatibility and security, among others. Consequently, the use of ActiveX controls is mostly limited to intranet and extranet sites where it is possible to mandate the browser type and operating system that visitors often use.

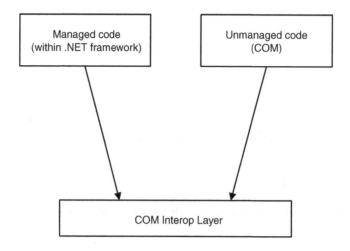

Exhibit 1. "COM InterOp" Layer

Distributed COM (DCOM) extends COM to allow components to be registered on one machine and called securely from a client program on another computer over the network. Previously called "Network OLE," DCOM is designed for use across multiple network transports, including Internet protocols such as HTTP. DCOM is based on the Open Software Foundation's DCE-RPC specification and works with both Java applets and ActiveX components through its use of the COM.

At the 1997 Professional Developers Conference in San Diego, California, Microsoft announced plans for COM+, an extension to the COM. COM+ builds on COM's integrated services and features, making it easier for developers to create and use software components in any language.

Because most COM components are written as Dynamic Link Libraries (DLLs), the components are usually hosted or run in either Microsoft Transaction Server (MTS)[2] on NT4 platforms or in COM+, which is built into all Windows 2000 platforms.

.NET Architecture

The .NET platform represents an evolution of COM. It is used to create software components that are completely object based. We will see "COM.NET" as the next step in COM evolution. Microsoft has already replaced ADO with ADO.NET, and ASP with ASP.NET.

.NET is designed to be able to interact with COM. It needs to do this anyway to provide support for COM+, which is considered part of the .NET framework, and may be used to host .NET as well as COM components.

This facility is provided by the .NET framework's "COM InterOp" layer (see Exhibit 1), which provides access between what .NET calls "managed" code

(code that is running within the .NET framework) and "unmanaged" code (such as COM). This is two-way access, so a COM client could also access a .NET component.

IS departments that want to sample the .NET development experience may choose to start by exploring ASP.NET because doing so only requires that the .NET platform be installed on a server machine. The code behind[3] the ASP.NET page accesses an existing COM component that is hosted in COM.

The existing COM component could be a production component because the ASP.NET page is treated as just another client. ASP.NET pages can be introduced onto an existing site without any disruption to the existing ASP pages. The Web server simply looks at the file extension of the requested page. If the extension is `.aspx`, the request is treated as an ASP.NET request.

Multi-Platform Development

Only some .NET facilities are Windows-specific. The Windows Forms framework is intended to replace the Windows graphical API and the graphical part of Microsoft foundation classes (for C++), and ASP.NET is implemented on top of Microsoft's Internet Information Server (IIS) Web server. Most of the rest of .NET could, in principle, be implemented on top of Linux, Solaris, or other systems.

One will see .NET on non-Microsoft operating systems. Although one currently needs Windows to use .NET, in late 2000 Microsoft submitted key parts of the technology for standardization to ECMA,[4] an international standardization body. The elements still under discussion include the common language runtime (CLR), Common Language Specification (CLS), Microsoft Intermediate Language (MSIL), C#, and more than 1000 components from the basic libraries. Microsoft is actively pushing to complete the work much faster than the usual time it takes for such standards processes.

The recently announced MONO effort (http://www.go-mono.net) is intended to develop an open-source implementation of .NET, based on the ECMA specifications and suitable for running on platforms such as Linux. Such efforts indicate that the transformation of .NET into a multi-platform development environment may happen faster than expected.

What .NET Is Not

In describing .NET, it is useful first to point out what it is not. It is neither an operating system nor a programming language. Microsoft operating systems continue their own evolution — Windows 2000, Me, XP, CE for embedded devices. As for programming languages, .NET has introduced a new one, C# (C-sharp), but it is not the focus of the technology.

Technically, C# looks very much like Java, with extensions similar to mechanisms found in Delphi and Microsoft's Visual J++. These extensions include "properties" — an attempt to remedy Java's information-hiding

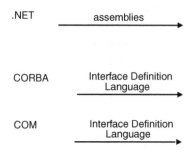

Exhibit 2. .NET vs. CORBA/COM

deficiencies — and an event-driven programming model using the notion of "delegates" — object wrappers around functions — that are appropriate for graphical user interface and Web applications.

While it is likely to become a serious competitor to Java, C# is not an attempt to replace it. Instead, a distinctive characteristic of .NET is its language neutrality. In addition to Microsoft-supported languages, .NET is open to many others, including COBOL, Eiffel, Fortran, Perl, Python, Smalltalk, and a host of research languages from ML to Haskell and Oberon.

Some Advantages

The advantages of using .NET are that it offers remoting options, does not require registry of the interfaces, and skips the need for an interface language. There are two ways of using the HTTP transport. One way is to use the SOAP formatter to convert the call into an industry-standard XML format for remote procedure calls. This format, SOAP, is primarily intended for use over HTTP because it is text based and it is unlikely to be blocked by corporate firewalls. Another way is to go through the Web server, which can host either an ASP.NET listener application or a Web service.

In addition, .NET classes are packaged in self-describing assemblies (DLL and .exe files). The assembly contains the program code and a description of what that code does — somewhat like an interface does in COM. The result is that there is no longer any need to register the interface, thus paving the way to running .NET on operating systems other than Windows.

.NET removes the distinction between a program element and a software component, providing significant benefits over technologies such as CORBA and COM (see Exhibit 2). Because an assembly provides a well-defined set of interfaces, other assemblies can use it directly. To turn a software element into a reusable component, CORBA and COM require writing an interface description in a special Interface Definition Language (IDL). .NET does not have anything similar to IDL. One can use a .NET assembly directly as a component without any further wrapping because it is already equipped with the necessary information. Meanwhile, two models must coexist; COM InterOp (see Exhibit 1) should ease the transition.

Frameworks and Libraries: ASP.NET, ADO.NET Windows Forms	
Interchange Standards: SOAP, WSDL	Common Development Tools: Visual Studio.NET
Component Model	
Object Model and Common Language Specification	
Common Language Runtime	

Exhibit 3.   .NET Layers

Web Services

Another major advantage of using the .NET platform are the Web services components that are just like any other middle-tier, business-rules objects through a Web server. This means that the same consistent functionality offered would be available anytime, from anywhere in the world, using any device that can access the Internet.

Imagine a company that processes credit card payments offering a Web service that allows the following data to be posted securely to its Web server: merchant ID, card number, expiration date, amount, customer name, and billing address. Upon receiving a client's call, the Web service validates the data and credits payment to the company's account based on the merchant ID. It then responds securely by returning a SOAP XML block containing the authorization code and a transaction number. Data is returned by such a Web service when the client asks for its Web Service Description Language (WSDL). WSDL, an XML-based standard that has been agreed upon by the industry, lists the methods available from the Web service with their arguments and return types. Web services are therefore self-describing.

Web services can be accessed by other Web services or accessed directly by user interfaces. Because the data is sent using Get or Post and XML, clients do not have to be Windows based or even .NET based. A client application for this service could be an E-commerce site, or it could be a handheld device with a card reader to swipe the credit card and a keypad to enter the amount.

Offering Web services either as a revenue stream or as a way of disseminating specific information — such as the information that would be held in a database — is a common goal for the 36 founding member companies of Universal Description, Discovery and Integration (UDDI) of Business for the Web. This organization is responsible for WSDL and two of the leading members, IBM and Microsoft, host UDDI Business Directories of available Web services. For more information on Web services, skip to Chapter 5.

.NET Architecture

Exhibit 3 shows that .NET architecture, Microsoft's Web development platform, consists of six layers from the user-visible Web services to the internal object model and CLR.

Exhibit 4.   Describing Each .NET Layer

Layer 1: Web Services	The top layer provides .NET users — persons and companies — with Web services for E-commerce and business-to-business applications.
Layer 2: Frameworks and libraries	The second layer consists of a set of frameworks and libraries including ASP.NET, and active server pages for developing smart Web sites and services; ADO.NET. Also included are an XML-based improvement to ActiveX Data Objects, for databases and object-relational processing, and Windows Forms for graphics.
Layer 3, first part: Interchange standards	XML-based interchange standards serve as a platform-independent means of exchanging objects, such as SOAP and WSDL.
Layer 3, second part: Development environment	The Visual Studio.NET is an outgrowth of Visual Studio extended with an application programming interface, not only supporting Microsoft-implemented languages such as Visual C++, Visual Basic, and C#, but also allowing third-party vendors to plug in tools and compilers for other languages.
Layer 4: Component model	Before .NET, there were already three major contenders for leadership in the field of models and standards for component-based development: CORBA from the Object Management Group, J2EE from Sun, and Microsoft's COM. .NET brings in one more model, based on object-oriented ideas: with .NET one can build "assemblies," each consisting of a number of classes with well-defined interfaces.
Layer 5: Object model	The object model provides the conceptual basis on which everything else rests, in particular, .NET's OO type system. The common language specification defines restrictions ensuring language operability.
Layer 6: Common language runtime	The CLR provides the basic set of mechanisms for executing .NET programs regardless of their language of origin: translation to machine code (judiciously incremental translation, or "jitting"), loading, security mechanisms, memory management (including garbage collection), version control, and interfacing with non-.NET code.

Exhibit 4 gives a brief description of each layer.

Building the .NET Platform

As shown in Exhibit 5, five areas where Microsoft is building the .NET platform are servers, tools, XML Services, Clients, and .NET Experience. XML Services have already been discussed in the section entitled "Web Services," while servers are covered separately in the section entitled ".NET Enterprise Servers." The remaining three areas are briefly discussed as follows.

Exhibit 5. Building the .NET Platform

- Servers
- Tools
- XML Services
- Clients
- .NET Experience

- *Tools.* Visual Studio.NET is Microsoft's multi-language development tool to help developers quickly build XML Web services and applications that scale easily, using the language of their choice. They include Visual Basic, Visual C++, and C#.
- *Clients.* They include PCs, laptops, workstations, phones, handheld computers, tablet PCs, game consoles, and other smart devices that can access XML Web services. Some of the .NET client software that Microsoft offers includes: Windows CE, Windows Embedded, Window 2000, and the upcoming Windows XP.
- *.NET Experience.* .NET Experiences are XML Web services that allow one to access information across the Internet and from stand-alone applications in an integrated way. In addition to Visual Studio .NET, one other product that Microsoft is transitioning into .NET Experiences is MSN bCentral.

.NET Enterprise Servers

The .NET Enterprise Servers, including the Windows 2000 server family, make up Microsoft .NET's server infrastructure for building on integrated business infastructure — from messaging and collaboration to database management, from E-commerce to mobile information access, and from content management to Web Services, as shown in Exhibit 6.

Microsoft Content Management Server 2001

A recent addition to .NET Enterprise Servers is Microsoft Content Management Server 2001, a rebranded version of the Ncompass Labs' Resolution that Microsoft acquired in May 2001. It fills a void in Mircosoft's E-commerce product lineup with content contribution and delivery, site development, and enterprise site management. It enables businesses to effectively create, deploy, and manage Internet, intranet, and extranet Web sites. In particular, it focuses on three areas: managing Web services (see Exhibit 7), dynamic content delivery (Exhibit 8), and rapid time-to-market for enterprise Web sites (Exhibit 9).

Unlike Resolution, which ran on both Windows NT and Windows 2000, Microsoft Content Management Server 2001 works only with Windows 2000. It can be used with, for example, Microsoft's Commerce Server 2000 and SQL

Exhibit 6.   .NET Enterprise Servers

Application Center 2000 Server	Deploy and manage highly available and scalable Web applications built on Windows 2000 operating systems
BizTalk Server 2000	Build XML-based business processes across applications and organizations
Commerce Server 2000	Build E-commerce solutions with feedback mechanisms and analytical capabilities
Content Management Server 2001	Manage content for E-business Web sites
Exchange Server 2000	Enable messaging and collaboration; support collaborative activities, including group scheduling, discussions groups, and team folders; provide Instant Messaging real-time data and video; conferencing
Host Integration Server 2000	Bridge to legacy systems by providing application, data, and network connectivity
Internet Security and Acceleration Server 2000	Enable secure, fast Internet connectivity with multi-layer enterprise firewall
Mobile Information 2001 Server	Enable application support by mobile devices
SharePoint Portal Server 2001	Share and publish business information
SQL Server 2000[a]	Provide Web-enabled database and data analysis package and support for structured XML data and the ability to query across the Internet
Windows 2000	Build on NT technology

[a] For details, see Chapter 6.

Exhibit 7.   Managing Web Services

In-context authoring templates	Build and contribute richly formatted content in easy-to-use templates without leaving the Web site
Real-time content updates	Publish content directly onto development
Revision tracking and page archiving	Compare changes of previous work with existing pages
Flexible workflow	Multiple levels of approval
Content scheduling	Use automated tools to schedule content publication and archival times
Extensible object properties	Create custom metadata properties on content objects and profile content as it is being created
Dynamic server clustering	Enable load-balanced environments that provide site scalability and server failover
Object caching	Caching of content objects in RAM and on the disk
SMP support	Support for multiple CPUs on Windows 2000 Advanced Server and Windows 2000 Datacenter Server

Exhibit 8. Dynamic Content Delivery

Dynamic page assembly	Content objects and templates are assembled as pages are requested from the Web server
Presentation templates	Site design and layout are controlled by presentation templates
Dynamic template switching	Change layout or design of the page in real-time
Object-based content repository	Stored in Microsoft SQL Server™ 2000 as reusable objects
Connected content pages	Publish contents through multiple presentation templates to multiple locations or Web sites
Language-specific content targeting	Target localized content objects to specific users based on individual language preferences

Exhibit 9. Rapid Time-to-Market Enterprise Web Sites

Sample templates and Web sites	Provides customization code
COM API	Share content with other systems using the Publishing API
Template and resource galleries	Ensure centralized control over corporate publishing and design standards
Dynamic site map	Generate site map and navigation
Site deployment manager	Move content and Web sites between servers
.NET suite integration	Integrate with Windows 2000 Advanced Server, Microsoft SQL Server 2000, Microsoft Commerce Server 2000, and FrontPage 2000
Windows Active Directory Services (ADS)	Use existing ADS and NT Domain directory services for security
XML	Publish content in XML format

Server 2000, both of which run only on Windows 2000. Microsoft's choice to limit the content management server to Windows 2000 allows potential users to take advantage of the operating system's built-in network load-balancing capabilities that make it easier to do the following:

- Load pages much faster
- Add servers or scale out as network traffic increases

Other Microsoft server products include BackOffice Server, Proxy Server, Site Server, Small Business Server, SNA Server, and Systems Management Server.

.NET Framework Security Policy

The .NET Framework Security solution is based on the concept of managed code, with security rules enforced by the CLR. Most managed code is verified

Exhibit 10.   .NET Framework Building Blocks

- Evidence-based security
- Role-based security
- Authentication and authorization
- Isolated storage
- Cryptography
- Extensibility

to ensure type safety, as well as the well-defined behavior of other properties. In verified code, a method declared as accepting a four-byte value, for example, will reject an attempted call with an eight-byte parameter as not type safe. Verification also ensures that execution flow transfers only to well-known locations, such as method entry points — a process that eliminates the ability to jump execution to an arbitrary location.

Verification prevents code that is not type safe from executing, and catches many common programming errors before they cause damage. Common vulnerabilities — such as buffer overruns, the reading of arbitrary memory or memory that has not been initialized, and arbitrary transfer of control — are no longer possible. This benefits end users because the code they run is checked before it executes.

The CLR also enables *unmanaged code* to run, but unmanaged code does not benefit from these security measures. Specific permissions are associated with the capability to call into unmanaged code, and a robust security policy will ensure that those permissions are conservatively granted. The migration from unmanaged code to managed code will, over time, reduce the frequency of calls to unmanaged code.

Now take a closer look at the building blocks of Microsoft .NET Framework Security. As shown in Exhibit 10, they are evidence-based security, role-based security, the concepts of authentication and authorization, as well as isolated storage, cryptography, and extensibility. Also included are the key benefits to developers, administrators, and end users of the .NET Framework Security policy.

Evidence-Based Security

The .NET Framework introduces the concept of *evidence-based* security. *Evidence* simply refers to inputs to the security policy about code. It is, in essence, the set of answers to questions[5] posed by the security policy:

- *From what site was the assembly obtained?* Assemblies are the building blocks of .NET Framework applications. They form the fundamental unit of deployment, version control, reuse, activation scoping, and security authorization. An application's assemblies are downloaded to the client from a Web site.
- *From what URL was the assembly obtained?* The security policy requires the specific address from which the assembly was downloaded.

- *From what zone was the assembly obtained?* Zones are descriptions of security criteria, such as Internet, intranet, local machine, etc., based on the location of the code.
- *What is the strong name of the assembly?* The *strong name* is a cryptographically strong identifier provided by the author of the assembly. While it does not provide any authentication of the author, it uniquely identifies the assembly and ensures that it has not been tampered with.

Once the policy has been completed, an initial set of permissions is created. Assemblies can fine-tune these grants by making specific requests in three areas:

- The first is to specify a minimal set of permissions that the assembly must have in order to operate. If these permissions are not present, the assembly will fail to load and an exception will be thrown.
- Next, an optional set of permissions can be specified. While the assembly would like any of these permissions, it will still load if they are not available.
- Finally, particularly well-behaved assemblies can actually refuse risky permissions that they do not need.

These three fine-tuning options are accomplished as load-time declarative statements.

Role-Based Security

Sometimes, it is appropriate for authorization decisions to be based on an authenticated identity or on the role associated with the context of the code's execution. For example, financial or business software may enforce policy through business logic that evaluates role information. The amount of a financial transaction may be limited based on the role of the user who is making the request. Bank tellers may be allowed to process requests up to a certain dollar amount, whereas anything more requires the role of a supervisor.

Authentication and Authorization

Authentication is the process of accepting credentials from a user and validating those credentials against some authority. If the credentials are valid, one speaks of having an authenticated identity. Authorization is the process of determining whether that authenticated identity has access to a given resource. Authentication can be accomplished by either system or business logic, and is available through a single API.

In ASP.NET forms authentication, the user provides credentials and submits the forms. If the application authenticates the request, the system issues a cookie that contains the credentials in some form or a key for reacquiring the identity. Subsequent requests are issued with the cookie in the request headers and they are authenticated and authorized by an ASP.NET handler using

Exhibit 11.   Cryptographic Objects

Supports:
- Encryption
- Digital signatures
- Hashing
- Random number generation

whatever validation method the application desires. If a request is not authenticated, HTTP client-side redirection is used to send that request to an authentication form, where the user can supply authentication credentials. Forms authentication is sometimes used for personalization — the customization of content for a known user. In some of these cases, identification rather than authentication is the issue, so a user's personalization information can be obtained simply by accessing the user name.

The purpose of authorization is to determine whether a requesting identity is granted access to a given resource. ASP.NET offers two types of authorization services: file authorization and URL authorization. File authorization determines which access control lists are consulted based on both the HTTP method being used and the identity making the request. URL authorization is a logical mapping between pieces of the URI namespace and various users or roles.

Isolated Storage

Isolated storage is a new set of types and methods supported by the .NET Framework for local storage. In essence, each assembly is given access to a segregated storage on disk. No access to other data is allowed, and isolated storage is available only to the specific assembly for which it was created.

Isolated storage might be used by an application to keep activity logs, save settings, or save state data to disk for later use. Because the location of isolated storage is predetermined, isolated storage provides a convenient way to specify unique space for storage without the need to determine file paths.

Code from the local intranet is similarly restricted, but less so, and can access a larger quota of isolated storage. Finally, code from the Restricted Sites zone (sites that are not trusted) gets no access to isolated storage.

Cryptography

The .NET Framework provides a set of cryptographic objects (see Exhibit 11) implemented through well-known algorithms, such as RSA, DSA, Rijndael/AES, Triple DES, DES, and RC2, as well as the MD5, SHA1, SHA-256, SHA-384, and SHA-512 hash algorithms. The XML Digital Signature specification, under development by the Internet Engineering Task Force (IETF) and the World Wide Web Consortium (W3C), is also supported. The .NET Framework uses cryptographic objects to support internal services. The objects are also available as managed code to developers who require cryptographic support.

Benefits to Users and Developers

.NET's security policy — a benefit to both users and developers — comprises four major techniques.

1. *Type verification.* The system verifies all .NET codes follow the object model's type system rules.
2. *Origin verification.* Any .NET assembly can and usually should be signed using 128-bit public key cryptography,[6] which prevents impersonating another software source.
3. *A fine-grained permission mechanisms.* Each assembly can specify the exact permissions that it requires its callers to have: file read, file read and write, DNS access, and others, and including new programmer-defined permissions.
4. *A notion of "principal."* Software elements can assume various roles during their lifetimes, with each role giving access to specific security levels.

For modifications to the runtime security behavior of an assembly, changes can be made as either *declarative* or *imperative* security, depending on the requirements of the programmer. Declarative security enables a programmer to specify security requirements for an assembly directly in the metadata of that assembly's code. Imperative security is implemented directly in code. Programmers take security actions programmatically, and the permission is either granted or denied, based on the state of the security stack.

Open.NET

Developers had planned by the end of 2000 to release open-source versions of key Microsoft .NET tools. If successful, enterprises would have an easier time integrating various operating systems that run online applications.

Developer of the popular Gnome user interface for Linux, Ximian leads the project, called MONO. The group is working on several open-source .NET projects. One is a version of the C# language, a competitor of Java. The other is the .NET CLI that runs programs written in C, C++, C#, COBOL, and Pascal. The developers are also building a set of class libraries, which are software components used in developing applications.

The primary goal for the project is to build a good set of tools for developing Web services for Linux. Applications using MONO will be interoperable with .NET services running on Windows; thus, for example, a Web storefront running on Linux would be able to call services for payment processing, user authentication, and inventory management running on Windows.

SOAP

On August 1, 2001, the World Wide Web Consortium released a public draft of SOAP v 1.2 designed to define messaging formats between different architectures.

It removes ambiguities on how messages are processed, provides more feedback in error messaging, and updates the XML Schema and name spacing.

In September 2000, the OMG's Platform Technology Committee (PTC) began work on a standard meant to integrate SOAP with OMG's CORBA. It allows SOAP clients to invoke CORBA servers, and CORBA clients and servers to interoperate using SOAP. The PTC also looked at efforts to standardize methods to transmit CORBA network packets through firewalls and to adapt real-time object request brokers to emit alternative protocols needed for telecommunications and other real-time applications.

The SOAP was born out of an idea for an XML-based RPC mechanism originally fostered by Dave Winer of Userland Software back in 1998. The idea evolved through a joint effort of Winer, Don Box at DevelopMentor, and Microsoft to publicly emerge as SOAP version 0.9 in the latter part of 1999. At that time, the reaction of the developer community was mixed.

IBM officially joined the SOAP development effort in May of 2000 by co-authoring the SOAP version 1.1 specification, co-submitting it as a W3C Note, officially signaling the start of the "Web services revolution." With IBM on board, developers on non-Microsoft development platforms stood up and took notice of SOAP for pretty much the first time.

From that point on, Microsoft and IBM took the lead in putting SOAP-enabled development tools into the hands of developers. Starting simple, IBM was the first to produce a Java-based toolkit for SOAP that was donated to the open-source Apache Software Foundation for further development. Microsoft released the first rendition of its SOAP Toolkit soon thereafter and announced their massive .NET Web services initiative the following July.

With industry support for SOAP growing rapidly, IBM and Microsoft next turned their attention to filling the various holes in the Web Services Architecture that was emerging. Namely, with the potential that SOAP-enabled applications would grow rapidly, there needed to be a mechanism for describing the capabilities of such services as well as a mechanism for locating services once they had been deployed. In September 2000, Microsoft, IBM, and Ariba jointly announced the UDDI. Then, just a matter of weeks later, the same three companies announced the WSDL, an XML grammar for describing the capabilities and technical details of SOAP-based Web services that compliments SOAP by allowing for dynamic cross-platform integration.

There are at least 39 different implementations of the SOAP Specification, with growing support for multiple operating systems and development languages. While each of these has its own level of capability, standards support, and quality control, they all share at least one thing in common: they all understand how to create and consume SOAP Envelopes. Regardless of how the tool was implemented, or where it is deployed, there exists the potential of seamless interoperability that would allow applications written in one language on one platform to consume the services of applications written in a completely different language on a completely different platform.

Exhibit 12 displays a side-by-side feature comparison of four of the most popular SOAP implementations available for the Java, Win32, and Perl environments. There are far more similarities between implementations than differences

Exhibit 12. SOAP Implementations

Feature	Choices	*Apache SOAP v2.1*	*SOAP::Lite for Perl*	*MS SOAP Toolkit* Beta 2
SOAP 1.1 Compliance				
Data Types				
Custom Encoding Styles	(Yes/No/Limited)	Yes	No	Limited
Arrays				
Single dimensional	(Yes/No/Limited)	Yes	Yes	Yes
Multi-dimensional	(Yes/No/Limited)	No	No	Yes
Partial	(Yes/No/Limited)	No	No	No
Sparse	(Yes/No/Limited)	No	No	No
Multi-references	(Yes/No/Limited)	Limited	Yes	Limited
Header/body cross-references	(Yes/No/Limited)	Limited	Yes	Limited
Circular references	(Yes/No/Limited)	No	Yes	No
Entity encoding	(Yes/No/Limited)	Yes	Yes	Yes
Fault				
Actor	(Yes/No/Limited)	Limited	Limited	Limited
Complex detail	(Yes/No/Limited)	Yes	Yes	Yes
XML Schema data types support	(Yes/No/Limited)	Yes	Yes	Yes
Attributes				
Must understand	(Yes/No/Limited)	Limited	No	Limited
Actor	(Yes/No/Limited)	Limited	Limited	Limited
Root	(Yes/No/Limited)	Yes	Limited	No
Id/href	(Yes/No/Limited)	Limited	Yes	Limited
HTTP				
M-POST	(Yes/No/Limited)	No	Yes	No
Object serialization	(Yes/No/Limited)	Yes	Yes	Yes
UTF8 support	(Yes/No/Limited)	Yes	Limited	Yes
Transports				
SMTP	(No/Full/Client/Server)	Yes	Client	No
POP3	(No/Full/Client/Server)	No	Server	No
FTP	(No/Full/Client/Server)	No	Client	No
TCP	(No/Full/Client/Server)	No	Full	No
HTTP	(No/Full/Client/Server)	Yes	Server	Yes
IO	(No/Full/Client/Server)	No	Full	No

Exhibit 12. SOAP Implementations (Continued)

Feature	Choices	Apache SOAP v2.1	SOAP::Lite for Perl	MS SOAP Toolkit Beta 2
Access to transport specific details (like cookie)	(Yes/No)	No	Yes	No
Extensions (i.e., compression or encryption)	(Yes/No) Name Extensions		Compression	
SOAP Attachments Support	(Yes/No/Limited)	Yes	Limited (Parsing Only)	No
Security				
SSL	(Yes/No/Limited)	Yes	Yes	Yes
Basic/digest authentication	(Yes/No/Limited)	No	Yes	Yes
Digital signatures	(Yes/No/Limited)	No	No	No
Administration and Configuration				
Logging	(Yes/No/Limited)	Limited	Yes	Yes
File-based configuration	(Yes/No/Limited)	Yes	No	Yes
Un/deployment (utility, Web-based access)	(Yes/No/Limited)	Yes	N/A	Yes
Messaging Patterns				
One-way messages	(Yes/No/Limited)	Yes	Yes	No
Asynchronous messages	(Yes/No/Limited)	No	No	No
Dispatching				
Namespace to class/ object	(Yes/No/Limited)	Yes	Yes	Yes
SOAP action	(Yes/No/Limited)	Yes	No	Yes
Other	(Name)			
Serialization Support				
Payload generation (from description/manually)	(Manual/From Description)	Both	Both	Both
Custom serialization	(Yes/No/Limited)	Yes	Yes	Yes
Custom deserialization	(Yes/No/Limited)	Yes	Yes	Yes
Service Description				
WSDL				
Can read	(Yes/No/Limited)	No	Yes	Yes
Can generate	(Yes/No/Limited)	No	No	Yes
Is optional/required	(Optional/Required)	N/A	Optional	Optional
Stub required (static/ dynamic)	(Static/Dynamic)	Static	Both, Optional	Dynamic
Complex types	(Yes/No/Limited)	N/A	No	Yes

Exhibit 12. SOAP Implementations (Continued)

Feature	Choices	Apache SOAP v2.1	SOAP::Lite for Perl	MS SOAP Toolkit Beta 2
Other	(Name)			Message encoding extension
Error handling	(Yes/No/Limited)	Yes	Yes	Yes

Source: James Snell, "Web Service Insider, Part 1: Reflections on SOAP," DeveloperWorks, Web Services, Web Services Articles (http://www-106.ibm.com/developerworks/webservices/library/ws-ref1.html, April 2001).

in specific SOAP or SOAP-related features that are supported. The differences that do exist, however, are, in some cases, significant enough to cause quite a few headaches.

Both Apache and Microsoft have worked around certain differences and limitations in implementing the SOAP specification. One can find instructions and sample codes at http://www.microsoft.com and http://www.ibm.com.

If one needs an XML to convert SOAP-based calls to traditional remote procedure calls, consider Software AG's middleware product, EntireX, for example. In addition, the company's integration product, Tamino X-Bridge, now works with user-defined rules to forward incoming XML documents to the right applications.

Microsoft Transaction Server

Every Windows desktop or server running Windows 98/NT/2000 is inherently a transaction-capable machine. Microsoft made entry into transaction computing, first with the Open Database Connectivity (ODBC) functionality and then with the MTS. Having installed Windows 2000, one no longer needs to install MTS with a separate package. It comes with the OS, queuing and asynchronous remote invocations to support any enterprise system — an online commerce system, a Web-enabled customer relationship management (CRM) system, or a supply-chain automation system based on transactional workflow.

Of course, distributed access and manipulation of data is not all there is to transaction processing. Issues concerning scaling to a large number of concurrent activities, as well as the control and management of resources, are also extremely important for transaction processing. Solutions that a decade ago were only available on mainframes were very expensive and much more primitive.

In addition to transaction servers, a short description of MTS can be the list of the main services it provides: object monitoring, transaction services, and security services. MTS builds upon COM and its communication-enabled version, DCOM. MTS, using the COM facilities, defines a set of interfaces and protocols that components can use to their own advantage.

In Windows 2000, concurrency control can be set at different levels for each component, allowing high-performance, carefully tuned components to execute unhindered by external thread control.

The functional unit used by MTS for administration, deployment, and execution time is the component package. Packages can be created and configured using the Package Wizard (renamed COM Application Wizard in Windows 2000). Once a package is created, components can be added using the Component Wizard to import them from DLL or by selecting them from among the ones that are already registered.

This process is very flexible because components can be grouped within packages in many ways. Components within a package share the execution process, and therefore the identity under which they execute; they share a more direct although less-secured access to each other, and they also share properties maintained by the Shared Property Manager. MTS is also capable of exporting packages from one machine to another, thus facilitating the build, stage, and deploy process.

MSMQ in Windows XP

Message Queuing is available on all Microsoft platforms from Windows CE 3.0 or higher to the Windows 2000 Server family, Windows XP Professional, and Windows .NET Server.

In Windows XP, the next version of MSMQ (Message Queuing 3.0) introduces several exciting new features designed to extend the application developer's set of tools to support new types of messaging-based applications. In particular, the four new areas that MSMQ 3.0 focuses on are one-to-many messaging, messaging over the Internet, programmable management, and message queuing triggers.

MSMQ is fully integrated with other Windows 2000 features such as Microsoft ComPlus Transactions (formerly known as MTS); Microsoft IIS, the built-in Windows 2000 Server Web server; Windows 2000 clustering services; and the Windows 2000 security environment. MSMQ offers seamless interoperability with the IBM MQSeries products through the Microsoft MSMQ-MQSeries Bridge and with other message queuing products through products from Level 8 Systems, Inc.

MSMQ technology enables applications running at different times to communicate across heterogeneous networks and systems that may be temporarily offline. Applications send messages to queues and read messages from queues. MSMQ provides guaranteed message delivery, efficient routing, security, and priority-based messaging. It can be used to implement solutions for both asynchronous and synchronous scenarios requiring high performance.

Consider the following scenario. A sending MSMQ application sends two messages that must arrive in order at a specific URL. The first message sent in the first HTTP session might be directed to server A in the Web farm, but the second message might be sent in a different HTTP session and might be directed to server B. The MSMQ service on server B will process the message

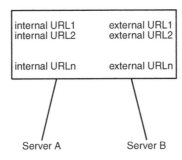

Exhibit 13. External–Internal URL Mapping

Exhibit 14. Real-Time Messaging Multicast

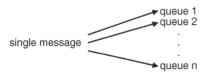

Exhibit 15. MSMQ Distribution Lists

but reject it because it does not know that the first message was delivered to server A.

To address this issue, MSMQ introduces a new concept: the MSMQ reverse message proxy server. Each reverse message proxy in the Web farm will maintain a mapping (see Exhibit 13) between the external URL and internal URL of a queue. For every incoming message arriving at a Web farm computer, MSMQ 3.0 will read the external URL address to which it was sent. If there is an entry in the map for that external URL, MSMQ 3.0 will forward the message to the internal URL associated with it.

MSMQ 3.0 offers several ways to implement the one-to-many model:

- *Real-time messaging multicast.* A single copy of the message is sent on the network that can be processed and distributed by numerous destination applications (see Exhibit 14).
- *Distribution lists and multiple element format names.* This allows a sending application to send a single message to a list of destination queues. Sending a message to a list of queues, however, uses more network resources than real-time message multicast, because multiple messages are sent on the network (see Exhibit 15).

MSMQ Triggers is a Message Queuing application that allows one to automatically associate incoming messages in a queue with functionality in a COM component or stand-alone .exe. With MSMQ Triggers, one can invoke business rules in response to incoming messages without any additional programming required. Likewise, MSMQ Triggers is a simple and scalable mechanism that exposes business logic in MTS packages via Message Queuing. By providing native support within Message Queuing for triggers, one can deploy standard mechanisms for invoking behavior at a queue level.

MSMQ 3.0 message storage is limited by disk space. In particular, MSMQ 3.0 has relaxed the 2 GB storage limit per machine. The theoretical capacity limit to persistent MSMQ 3.0 messages is 1TB (terabyte).

The following are features that are no longer relevant, useful, or have been superseded.

- The MSMQ Exchange connector is no longer supported in Windows XP. Otherwise, it continues to be available for previous versions of Windows (Windows NT 4.0 and Windows 2000).
- The IPX Protocol is no longer supported by MSMQ 3.0 in Windows XP.
- The MSMQ service is not available in the Windows XP Personal version. You can run DCOM-based applications on Windows XP Personal in order to access MSMQ.

Windows 2000 Datacenter

Windows 2000 Datacenter Server is the operating system for running mission-critical databases, enterprise resource planning (ERP) software, and high-volume real-time transaction processing. Datacenter is optimized for large data warehouses, econometric analysis, large-scale simulations in science and engineering, online transaction processing (OLTP), and server consolidation.

Designed to work in high-traffic computer networks, Datacenter supports up to 32-way symmetric multi-processing (SMP) and up to 64 gigabytes (GB) of physical memory. In addition to both four-node clustering and load-balancing services as standard features, it also provides the Internet and network operating system (NOS) services of all the versions of Windows 2000 Server.

New features include Physical Address Extension (PAE) to extend physical memory substantially; Winsock Direct to facilitate high-speed communications in a system area network (SAN); and the Process Control tool, a new job object management tool.

Windows Clustering

Windows Clustering is a feature of Windows 2000 Advanced Server and Windows 2000 Datacenter Server that provides multiple complementary clustering technologies. Network Load Balancing (NLB) clusters provide higher scalability and availability for TCP/IP-based services and applications by combining up to 32 servers running Windows 2000 Advanced Server or Windows 2000 Datacenter

Exhibit 16. Network Load Balancing Checklist

1. Read "Best Practices."
2. Read "Network Load Balancing System Requirements."
3. Read "Planning Your Network Load Balancing Cluster."
4. (Optional) Install a second network adapter.
5. Have ready the cluster's full Internet name.
6. Have ready the cluster's primary IP address.
7. Have ready the subnet mask for the cluster.
8. Have ready the current IP address for each host in the cluster.
9. Have ready the subnet mask for each host in the cluster.
10. Read "Cluster Parameters."
11. Carefully consider how *multicast support* should be configured.
12. Carefully consider how *remote password* should be configured.
13. Carefully consider how *confirm password* should be configured.
14. Carefully consider how *remote control* should be configured.
15. Read "Host Parameters."
16. Carefully consider how *priority (ID)* should be configured.
17. Carefully consider how *initial state* should be configured.
18. Read "Port Rules."
19. Carefully consider how *port range* should be configured.
20. Carefully consider how *protocols* should be configured.
21. Carefully consider how *filtering mode* should be configured.
22. Carefully consider how *affinity* should be configured.
23. Carefully consider how *load weight* should be configured.
24. Carefully consider how *equal load distribution* should be configured.
25. Carefully consider how *handling priority* should be configured.
26. Install NLB.

Server into a single cluster. They can also provide load balancing for servers running COM+ applications.

Before installing NLB, it is vital to review the checklist (see Exhibit 16), including the sections on cluster parameters, host parameters, and port rules. It will be impossible to properly configure NLB without a thorough understanding of these three topics.

Windows 2000 Datacenter Server supports up to four nodes in a cluster, while Windows 2000 Advanced Server is limited to two nodes. A server cluster cannot be made up of nodes running both Windows 2000 Advanced Server and Windows 2000 Datacenter Server. In a three-node or four-node server cluster, all nodes must run Windows 2000 Datacenter Server. Similarly, a two-node cluster must be made up of nodes running either Windows 2000 Advanced Server or Windows 2000 Datacenter Server, but not both.

Enterprise Memory Architecture

Using Enterprise Memory Architecture (EMA), one can run applications that take advantage of large amounts of physical memory on Windows 2000

Exhibit 17. Checklist: Enabling Application Memory Tuning

1. Review the concepts behind application memory tuning.
2. Read EMA hardware requirements.
3. Determine whether the computer supports application memory tuning by consulting the Microsoft Windows Hardware Compatibility List (HCL).
4. If hardware is unsupported, do one of the following:
   a. Update the hardware. If updating the hardware, back up the system first.
   b. Or, select different hardware on which to enable application memory tuning.

Exhibit 18. Checklist: Enabling Physical Address Extensions (PAE)

1. Enable application memory tuning.
2. Review the concepts behind Physical Address Extension.
3. Read EMA hardware requirements.
4. Determine whether the computer supports PAE by consulting the Microsoft HCL and contacting the vendor.
5. Determine whether the network and storage adapters support PAE by consulting the Microsoft Windows HCL.
6. If the hardware is unsupported, do one of the following:
   a. Update the hardware. If updating the hardware, back up the system first.
   b. Or, select different hardware on which to enable application memory tuning.
7. PAE X86.

Datacenter Server. EMA supports two types of memory enhancement: application memory tuning — also known as four-gigabyte tuning (4GT) — and PAE X86. Neither is enabled by default. Both application memory tuning and PAE must be manually enabled by editing the Boot.ini file.

Before enabling application memory tuning and PAE, one must use two checklists: enabling application memory tuning (see Exhibit 17) and enabling PAE X86 (see Exhibit 18).

Winsock Direct

Winsock Direct is an abstraction layer in the Windows 2000 Datacenter Server network architecture. It enables unmodified Windows Sockets (Winsock) applications that use TCP/IP to fully exploit the performance benefits of system area networks (SANs) for most communication within a SAN. One must use Checklist: Preparing the System Area Network for Winsock Direct (see Exhibit 19) before one begins using Winsock Direct with the system area network.

Windows 2000 Advanced Server

Windows 2000 Advanced Server is the server operating system for line-of-business applications and E-commerce. It includes all the features and application availability of Windows 2000 Server, with additional scalability and reliability

Exhibit 19.   Checklist: Preparing the System Area Network for Winsock Direct

1. Confirm that the hardware can support a SAN.
2. Install and configure the SAN hardware and software.
3. Review the concepts behind Winsock Direct.

features, such as clustering, designed to keep mission-critical business up and running and grow under heavy loads. It is well suited for departmental servers running applications such as networking, messaging, inventory and customer service systems, databases, and E-commerce Web sites.

Increasing Server Performance

Advanced Server lets one increase server performance and capacity by adding processors and memory. This approach to increasing network capacity is referred to as *scaling up*.

Just as a desktop computer has only one processor, many server PCs also have a single CPU. One can increase the performance of a server computer by adding processors that can work together, and many well-known server manufacturers offer multi-processor servers. Enhanced SMP support in Advanced Server lets one use multi-processor servers.

Another way to increase server performance is to add memory, which allows the computer to work with more information at once. Advanced Server includes enhanced memory capabilities that let one increase the memory available for server processing.

Increasing Server Availability

The two clustering technologies in Advanced Server let more than one server work together on a particular task. The first, called the Cluster service, is used to link individual servers so they can perform common tasks. If one server stops functioning, its workload is transferred to the other server.

The second clustering technology, called NLB, is used to make sure a server is always available to handle requests. NLB works by spreading incoming client requests among a number of servers that are linked together to support a particular application. A typical example is to use NLB to process incoming visitors to a Web site. As more visitors come to the site, one can incrementally increase capacity by adding servers. (This type of expansion is often referred to as software scaling or *scaling out*.) Major system vendors, including Dell, Compaq, IBM, Hewlett-Packard, Unisys, and Data General, offer solutions that take advantage of Cluster service.

SMP and Advanced Memory Management

Another feature of the Advanced Server is the support for enhanced SMP and large memory to increase availability and scalability. To let software use multi-

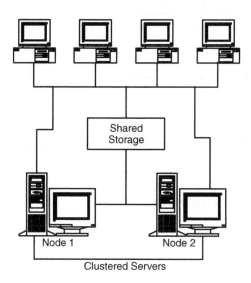

Exhibit 20.   Cluster Service: Single View of Multiple Servers

processor servers, Advanced Server supports up to eight-way SMP. Improvements in the implementation of the SMP code allow for improved scaling linearity, making Advanced Server a platform for business-critical applications, databases, and Web services. Existing Windows NT Server 4.0, Enterprise Edition servers with up to eight-way SMP can install this product.

Advanced Server also supports up to eight gigabytes (8 GB) of memory when used with processors supporting Intel's PAE. Combined with support for eight-way SMP, this enhanced large memory support ensures that memory- and processor-intensive applications can be run on the operating system.

Windows 2000 Clustering Technologies

The two Advanced Server clustering technologies are called Cluster service and NLB. They can be used independently or in combination and applied to the Datacenter Server.

A server cluster is a set of independent servers (referred to as nodes) and connected storage devices that are managed together. Advanced Server supports two-node clusters. Clustered servers are physically connected by cables and programmatically connected by cluster software. The servers do not have to be the same size or have the same configuration.

Cluster Service

Exhibit 20 shows that the cluster appears to be a single system to clients and applications in an environment of multiple servers. Cluster service is ideal for ensuring the availability of critical line-of-business and other back-end systems,

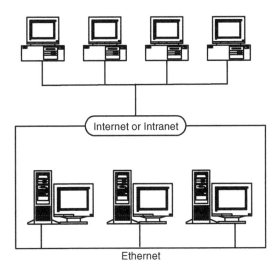

Exhibit 21. Network Load Balancing

such as Microsoft Exchange Server 2000 or a Microsoft SQL Server 2000 database acting as a data store for an E-commerce Web site. Should one server stop functioning, a process called *failover* automatically shifts its workload to another server in the cluster to provide continuous service.

Line-of-business applications are applications that are central to a company's operations, and include systems such as databases, messaging servers, ERP applications, and core file and print services. Cluster service in the Windows 2000 operating system ensures that these critical applications are online when needed by removing the physical server as a single point of failure. Doing so does not add complexity for users. Because the cluster appears as a single-system image to end users, applications, and the network, they can work with the cluster as if it were any other server.

Cluster service is supported by dozens of cluster-aware applications spanning a wide range of functions and vendors. Cluster-aware applications include databases such as Microsoft SQL Server 7.0, SQL Server 2000, and IBM DB2; messaging servers such as Microsoft Exchange Server 5.5, Exchange 2000 Server, and Lotus Domino; management tools such as NetIQ's AppManager; disaster recovery tools such as NSI Software's DoubleTake 3.0; and ERP applications including SAP, Baan, PeopleSoft, and JD Edwards. And one can now cluster such services as DHCP, WINS, SMTP, and NNTP.

Network Load Balancing

In addition to failover, some forms of clustering also employ load balancing, which distributes incoming requests across a group of servers. As shown in Exhibit 21, NLB complements Cluster service by supporting highly available and scalable clusters for front-end applications and services such as Internet

---

Exhibit 22. Management Services

- Group Policy
- Windows Management Instrumentation
- Windows Script Host
- Microsoft Management Console

---

and intranet sites, Web-based applications, media streaming, and Terminal Services.

Using both clustering technologies together, one can create an *n*-tier E-commerce application by deploying NLB across a front-end Web server farm, and clustering back-end line-of-business applications such as databases with Cluster service.

NLB load-balances incoming IP traffic across clusters of up to 32 nodes. NLB enhances both the availability and scalability of Internet server-based programs such as Web servers, streaming media servers, and Terminal Services.

By acting as the load-balancing infrastructure and providing control information to management applications built on top of Windows Management Instrumentation (WMI), NLB can readily integrate into existing Web server farm infrastructures.

NLB in both Windows 2000 Advanced Server and Datacenter Server, and its predecessor in Windows NT Server 4.0, Enterprise Edition, are in use on a range of popular Web destinations, including Dell.com, TV Guide Online, and Personable.com, as well as Microsoft Web properties including Microsoft.com, MSN network of Internet Services, and MSNBC.

Windows 2000 Advanced Server provides the features required to create highly available and scalable systems. It includes features to help ensure that one's systems are always available. It is well-suited to environments that require a high-performance server, and are capable of supporting multiple processors and larger amounts of memory than Windows 2000 Server.

Windows 2000 Family Management Services

The Windows 2000 Server family provides management services through infrastructure enhancements such as the Active Directory service, as well as tools built on the infrastructure, such as IntelliMirror management technologies. Windows 2000 Server — Advanced or Datacenter — help system administrators better manage servers, networks, and Windows-based desktops. As shown in Exhibit 22, they include:

- *Group Policy,* based on the Active Directory, is a key component of the IntelliMirror. Group Policy helps one control user access to desktop settings and applications by group rather than by individual user and computer. Group Policy lets one define and control the amount of access users have to data, applications, and other network resources.

- *Windows Management Instrumentation (WMI)* provides unified access and event services, allowing one to control and monitor Windows-based environments, Simple Network Management Protocol (SNMP) devices, and all host environments that support the Web-Based Enterprise Management (WBEM) standards initiative of the Distributed Management Task Force (DMTF).[7]
- *Windows Script Host (WSH)* allows one to automate and integrate common tasks using a variety of scripting environments, including Microsoft Visual Basic, Scripting Edition (VBScript), Microsoft Jscript, and Perl. This feature includes direct scripting to Active Directory and WMI.
- *Microsoft Management Console (MMC)* provides a common user interface presentation tool where one can integrate all the necessary Windows-based and Web-based administration components needed to fulfill a specific task.

Microsoft Management Strategy

Microsoft Operations Manager 2000 complements the capabilities of two other management solutions from Microsoft: Systems Management Server and Application Center 2000. While Systems Management Server delivers change and configuration management for desktops and servers, Microsoft Operations Manager 2000 handles the operational management of servers and applications. Most enterprises will need both products, and will benefit from their complementary operations.

Application Center 2000 also serves a different purpose than Microsoft Operations Manager. It is designed specifically for those enterprises that deploy and manage high-availability Web- and component-based applications built on the Windows 2000 operating system.

While each of these products addresses a different area of IT systems management, they are not mutually exclusive. When taken together — and added to the management technologies built into the Windows 2000 operating system — Microsoft Operations Manager, Systems Management Server, and Application Center comprise a complete set of management solutions for Windows 2000-based environments of all sizes.

Notes

1. Now part of Compaq.
2. Now known as Microsoft ComPlus Transactions, an integrated feature of Windows 2000 operating systems.
3. "Code behind" is a Microsoft term used to describe the language page that coexists with the HTML page. It can be written in any of the .NET languages, including C# and VB.NET.
4. ECMA is an international industry association founded in 1961 and dedicated to the standardization of information and communication systems.
5. These questions could be incorporated into a security questionnaire as part of risk assessment of .NET Framework-based systems.

6. The U.S. Department of Commerce requires a company to qualify before buying the 128-bit SSL encryption software separately or included with a package. The U.S. Government determines the categories of companies that can implement the 128-bit SSL encryption technology outside the United States and across U.S. borders. Any company or organization around the world can purchase an ID encrypted with 128 bits, with the following exceptions.

— Persons listed on the U.S. Government's Denied Person's List

— Customers located in the following countries: Afghanistan, Cuba, Iran, Iraq, Libya, North Korea, Serbia, Sudan, and Syria.

7. Formerly Desktop Management Task Force.

Chapter 4

Ever-Expanding Java World

This chapter covers Enterprise JavaBeans (EJB), Java 2 Platform Enterprise Edition (J2EE), Java Messaging Service (JMS), Java Naming and Directory Interface (JNDI), Java Media Framework (JMF), and other Java technologies. They are used to build distributed applications for integration with Enterprise Resource Planning (ERP), Customer Relationship Management (CRM), Supply Chain Management (SCM), and other Enterprise Application Integration (EAI) systems, and non-EAI legacy and wireless applications as well.

Introduction

In 1995, Java technology was incorporated into Netscape Navigator, the world portal to the Internet. As the Internet was becoming popular as a way of moving media content using HTML, Java technology was designed to move it across networks of heterogeneous devices.

Meanwhile, the availability of cheaper computing power and increased network bandwidth gave rise to distributed-based computing applications. A distributed application is a configuration of services provided by different application components running on physically independent computers that appear to the users of the system as a single application running on a phsycial machine.

To connect applications requiring operating systems across the Internet, platform developers and enterprise development teams use various middleware products, such as EJB, J2EE, and associated server-side technologies. All aim to simplify the development of middleware components.

Enterprise JavaBeans

Enterprise JavaBeans (EJB) servers provide a transaction processing (TP) monitor-like environment for distributed components. The TP monitor characteristics of the EJB platform allow developers to streamline development by

Exhibit 1.   Logical View of EJB's Three-Tier Architecture

Tier	Coverage
Presentation	Java clients accessing enterprise beans using JNDI and Java RMI-IIOP. Examples include desktop Java applications, Java servlets, or other enterprise beans.
Middle	Enterprise JavaBeans
Resource	Database

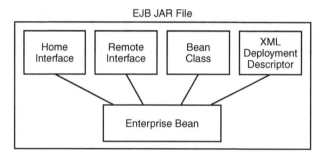

Exhibit 2.   EJB Components

automatically managing the entire application environment, including transactions, security, concurrency, persistence, load balancing, and failover. The distributed-component characteristics of the EJB permit them to assemble applications from flexible and reusable components.

The distributed components used in EJB are called *enterprise beans (beans)*. Enterprise beans are written in Java and are used to model the business logic of an organization. When a bean is developed, it can be assembled with other beans into applications and deployed into an EJB server.

Component developers write business components (enterprise beans) according to the programming model defined in the EJB specification, making the enterprise beans more portable across all EJB servers. This architecture could be expanded to *n*-tiers to suit specific requirements of an ERP,[1] CRM, and SCM system or subsystem under development.

Exhibit 1 shows how EJB logically fits into a three-tier architecture and what each tier covers.

Inside Enterprise Beans

As shown in Exhibit 2, an enterprise bean comprises at least four parts: home interface, remote interface, bean class, and XML deployment descriptor. Home interface, the most important part, declares factory methods that are used by Java clients to create new enterprise beans, locate existing beans, and destroy them. Clients are not necessarily only people or workstations; they may be servers, other beans, or anything else.

The benefits of using the home interface is that in CORBA and RMI applications, a factory would have to be developer-defined and implemented completely. In EJB, however, the developer defines the home interface but does not have to implement the home class, which is generated by a tool provided by the EJB vendor.

Remote interface declares the business methods of the enterprise bean that are used by Java clients at runtime. This interface, for example, advertises the business methods, such as adding an item for purchase to a shopping cart. Bean class encapsulates the application logic of the bean and implements the business methods defined in the remote interface, while the XML deployment descriptor is an XML configuration file that describes the enterprise bean and its runtime attributes to the EJB server when it is deployed.

The bean developer must create all four parts and package them — all at once — into a JAR[2] file for deployment. One part at a time cannot be packaged. To read configurations in the XML deployment descriptor, get the tools from the EJB servers to open a JAR file.

The Container

Once created, the enterprise bean is deployed into a *container*[3] that is responsible for managing transactions, security, concurrency, persistence, and resources the enterprise bean uses at runtime. In addition, the container generates two distributed component proxies:

- *EJBHome* implements the enterprise bean's home interface. There is only one EJBHome for every enterprise bean deployment.
- *EJBObject* implements the enterprise bean's remote interfaces. There is one EJBObject for every remote reference to an enterprise bean. As shown in Exhibit 3, there can be several EJBObjects for an EJBHome.

To get to an enterprise bean's EJBHome, use JNDI[4] on a Java client on the presentation tier (first tier) to obtain a remote reference (proxy) to an enterprise bean's EJBHome. EJB servers must use some kind of JNDI-compatible naming or directory service to provide access to the EJBHome. Some EJB servers use third-party naming or directory services while others provide their own. Without a directory of some sort, one cannot get to the EJBHome.

The client uses the EJBHome to create or find specific enterprise beans in the EJB container. When it does, it receives a remote reference to an EJBObject. The EJBObject implements the enterprise bean's remote interface and delegates calls made by the client to instances of the bean.

Java clients access enterprise beans through their EJBHome and EJBObject remote proxies, rather than directly. The EJB container intercepts every method invocation made on the remote proxies. When it does so, it can manage the bean's runtime environment associated with the invocation. Exhibit 4 shows the results of method invocations on EJBHome and EJBObjects.

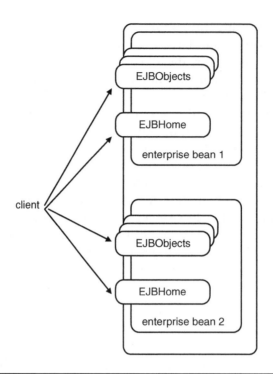

Exhibit 3.   EJBHome and EJBObject Proxies

Exhibit 4.   Method Invocations

Component Proxies	Method Invocations
EJBHome	Cause the enterprise bean's container to create or locate enterprise beans and provide EJBObject proxies to the client
EJBObject	Delegated to an instance of the enterprise bean class, which contains the business logic needed to service the request

The EJB container can use many instances of the enterprise bean class to support many clients. This allows the EJB server to scale, so that it can handle very large client loads.

Enterprise Bean Types

An enterprise bean comprises three types: *session, entity*, and *message-driven*. While the message-driven bean is new in EJB 2.0, the session and entity beans were introduced in Enterprise JavaBeans 1.0 in 1998. Session and entity beans are similar to typical distributed components; they reside in the middle tier and handle synchronous remote method calls made by clients (see Exhibit 5), while a message-driven bean processes asynchronous messages delivered via JMS.[5] This bean is not like a distributed component.

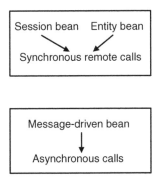

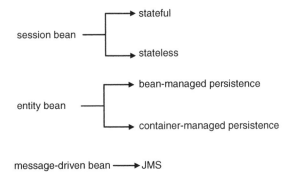

Exhibit 5. Synchronous/Asynchronous Calls

Exhibit 6. Enterprise Bean Types

Exhibit 7. Bean Examples

Bean Type	Example
Stateful session	Flight, hotel, car-rental reservations
Stateless session	Credit-card processing, financial calculations, and library searches
Entity	Bank account

A *session bean* can be stateful or stateless (see Exhibit 6). A stateful session bean is dedicated to the Java client that created it. Its class defines instance variables that can hold session data from one method invocation to the next, making methods interdependent. This trait allows the bean to act as an extension of the client, maintaining session data on the EJB server and executing tasks for the client. Stateful session beans are used to model business concepts that represent agents or roles that perform tasks on a client's behalf. Examples of such beans may include a bank teller who processes monetary transactions, a shopping cart used in online commerce, or a travel agent who makes flight, hotel, and car-rental reservations (see Exhibit 7).

Stateless session beans are not dedicated to a single client; they are shared by many. This sharing makes stateless session instances more scalable, but also prohibits them from maintaining session data. Stateless session beans behave more like an API, where method invocations are not interdependent. Each invocation is effectively stateless and is analogous to static methods in Java classes. Stateless session beans are used to model stateless services such as credit-card processing, financial calculations, and library searches.

Entity beans are persistent, transactional, server-side components. They are used to model persistent business-domain objects such as bank accounts, orders, and products. Each of these has behavior that is typically stored in a database.

There are two types of entity bean, distinguished by how their persistence is managed: *bean-managed persistence (BMP)* and *container-managed persistence (CMP)*. A BMP entity bean is responsible for managing its own relationships and persistence state in the database. A developer defining a BMP bean writes the database-access logic directly into the bean class. A CMP entity bean, by contrast, leaves management of its persistent state and relationships to an EJB container. Database-access code is generated automatically at deployment time.

Developers might use *message-driven beans* to integrate an EJB system with a legacy system, or to enable business-to-business interactions. While a message-driven bean consists of a bean class and an XML deployment descriptor, it does not have a remote or home interface (EJBObject or EJBHome references). All message-driven beans respond only to asynchronous messages delivered from JMS and, therefore, are not distributed components. They are stateless, server-side components used to receive and process messages that Java clients send to them via JMS. They are used to model processes and routers that operate on inbound enterprise messages.

Passivation and Activation

EJB has built-in passivation and activation support. Passivation is the process of temporarily storing the state of the shopping cart to persistent storage if a customer has not completed the cycle of shopping or checkout. Activation occurs when the customer returns to complete his checkout.

These capabilities are not provided by CORBA or RMI. The CORBA Portable Object Adapter (POA) did provide this capability, but it was somewhat of a latecomer within the CORBA world, not well supported, and rather difficult to use.

CORBA Component Model

The CORBA Component Model is similar to EJB. Before it made its appearance on the market, not every CORBA ORB supported transactions, security, and persistence services. The persistence service was hardly implemeneted or used at all. These services were not tightly integrated into the server architecture as they are in EJB where the container automates the calling of these services.

Exhibit 8.   AlphaBean Examples

AlphaBean	Functions
CryptoBeans	Perform various cryptographic transformations with CryptoBeans Bean Suite (symmetric encryption, password-based encryption, and hash calculation)
Directory EJB	DirectoryEJB extends functionality of the Directory Bean Suite on the client/server technology.
Common Application Functions	Get access to printer, fax, and mail systems in Java applications and servlets with Common Application Functions Bean Suite
FolderSychronizer	Keep folders up-to-date
Authentication	Authenticate users with new Authentication Bean Suite

In CORBA, application code is needed to call these services. This resulted in more lines of code to develop and maintain. Although EJB minimizes the amount of coding, it adds more work to the task of configuration and deployment.

AlphaBean Examples

To try out a bean or two, one can download the alphaBeans listed in Exhibit 8 and use them to work with JDK 1.2. Other beans (at www.alphabeans.com) may require a different JDK level.

OpenEJB and CVS

OpenEJB is an open-source EJB 1.1/2.0 container system, is JDK 1.2 compliant, and provides for Java Authentication and Authorization Support (JAAS). JAAS extends the security architecture of the Java 2 Platform with additional support to authenticate and enforce access controls upon users. It builds on the javax.security package in the core SDK, the Java Secure Socket Extension (JSSE), the Java Cryptography Extension (JCE), and the Java Security Tools.

As a container system, OpenEJB works like a big plug-in for middleware servers such as Web servers, CORBA servers, and application servers. By plugging OpenEJB into these servers, one can obtain instant EJB 1.1/2.0 compliance for hosting Enterprise JavaBeans.

OpenEJB provides a clear separation of responsibilities between the EJB container and the EJB server. The application server and OpenEJB container system interact through an open programming interface, which forms the container/server contact. This contract is defined by the Container Provider Interface (CPI), which is a small and simple set of classes and interfaces.

Through the server/container interface (SCI), an application server vendor can use the OpenEJB container system to create an instant and customizable EJB 2.0 platform. Through the service/provider interface (SPI), primary services can be interchanged to match any target environment's specific requirements. For details, go to http://www.openejb.org/specification.html.

OpenEJB is the first EJB container system that allows EJB platform developers to assemble it from existing products rather than construct it from scratch. These developers can create applications or modify existing ones in an open, distributed environment. One problem is that some developers have no way of knowing who has developed what objects or applications. There is always a possibility of overwriting someone else's work by mistake.

One way of getting around this problem is to use the Concurrent Versions Systems (CVS), allowing developers to control source codes over the network. CVS has four basic functions:

1. Maintain a history of all changes made to each directory tree it manages.
2. Provide hooks to support process control and change control.
3. Provide reliable access to its directory trees from remote hosts using Internet protocols.
4. Support parallel development, allowing more than one developer to work on the same sources at the same time.

To download source code and other files from a CVS server, one needs a CVS client. Go to http://www.cvshome.org/downloads.html and select the appropriate code for a platform of one's choice — BeOS, Linus, Machintosh, OS/2, UNIX, VMS, or Windows 95/NT/2000.

There is no "Install Shield" for CVS. One must put the CVS executable in any directory and then include that directory in the PATH system variable. One can then execute CVS commands from anywhere in the command shell.

Java 2 Enterprise Edition

In January 2001, Sun announced Java 2 Enterprise Edition (J2EE) v1.3, offering simplified connectivity and faster time to market. It is the primary development platform for server-side enterprise application development. It includes EJB, Java Server Pages (JSP) servlets, Java Database Connectivity (JDBC), JNDI, as well as specification for interoperability and connections in Legacy and ERP systems (see Exhibit 9).

New in J2EE 1.3 are JMF 2.1, EJB 2.0, and enhanced XML support, including Java API for XML Parsing (JAXP), Java API for XML Messaging (JAXM), and Java API for Data Binding (JAXB). These are open sourced through Apache's Jakarta project. These along with the JXTA networking application API make up JAX (Java, Apache, and XML).

Exhibit 9 shows most features in J2EE. For example, if the second column is not blank (e.g., SQL, SQLJ), it means those items are a natural flow from the corresponding item (e.g., JDBC) in the first column. The first seven items are part of the EJB framework.

Integration with Legacy, ERP, CRM, and SCM Applications

Enterprise JavaBeans in the J2EE framework provide the ability to create and package integration points in the EAI space. By leveraging J2EE technologies

Exhibit 9. Java API Flows in J2EE

JDBC	SQL, SQLJ
EJB	
JMS	
JMX	
JTA/JTS	
JMF[a]	
JAXP[a]	
JAXM[a]	
JAXB[a]	
JXTA[a]	
JAX[a]	Java, Apache, XML
J2EE Interoperability	COM, CORBA, CCM, XML
XML/JAX/JDOM	CORBA
Servets, JSP, JSP Taglibs	
JDNI	
J2EE Connection API	Legacy/ERP
Java OSS	OSS Trouble Ticket API
	OSS Quality of Service API
	OSS Service Activation API
Security	JCE, JSSE, JAAS

[a] New features in J2EE v1.3.

Should be included: CORBA's dependence on RMI/IIOP and Java IDL to run the applications.

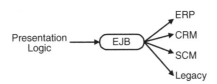

Exhibit 10.   Back-End Applications: ERP, CRM, SCM, and Legacy

such as JMS in combination with Enterprise Information System (EIS) integration brokers and business-to-business integration brokers, components can be created that allow standard access to enterprise computing assets. The backbone of the modern enterprise is spread across a diverse set of technology and applications, including legacy, ERP, CRM, and SCM applications (see Exhibit 10).

To accomplish E-business integration, an integration platform must be created that combines the presentation capabilities and technologies required of Internet-based applications with the multitude of technologies that can be utilized to integrate application systems. There are several approaches to creating such an integration architecture, including:

- Point-to-point integration that leverages APIs to create reusable components
- EAI integration brokers that provide single-point access to a variety of back-end systems using a uniform API
- B2B integration brokers that provide access to external data in the form of XML messages
- Composite platforms that utilize a combination of the above to achieve maximum "connectivity"

At the heart of the J2EE platform are EJB components and containers. The EJB component model defines the interfaces between the bean and container that provide enterprise-computing capabilities, including security and transaction support. The behavior of these capabilities is dictated by instructions specified in the bean's deployment descriptor, allowing control outside of program code.

With bean-managed components, the developer is responsible for writing code to persist specific attributes of the bean. This has the added advantage of allowing bean attributes to be stored in technologies other than a relational database. This is important because a significant portion of legacy, ERP, and CRM information is provided via non-database access.

Key enabling technologies can be utilized to create integration points. JDBC is used to re-face database queries and tables as EJB objects. Transactional CICS[6] systems can be accessed using IBM's External Call Interface (ECI), which allows communication. JMS can be used to provide the underlying messaging interface.

The integration broker provides a single interface for accessing legacy, CRM, or ERP assets, leveraging XML as a standard message format. The point integration solutions — such as JDBC, ECI, JMS, and MQSeries — are replaced by a single API set — the J2EE Connector architecture.

J2EE 1.3 adds support for the connector architecture that defines a standard architecture for connecting J2EE components to heterogeneous EISs, including ERP, mainframe systems, database systems, and legacy applications not written in Java. This J2EE Connector achitecture is an open standard alternative to time-consuming customizations on proprietary products in providing connectivity between the EIS systems and application servers (e.g., databases, client applications, and Web components).

This architecture provides containers for an assortment of components, including EJB and JSP. This allows enterprises to encapsulate parts of existing applications with them. It also provides a standard set of services to permit integration of new applications with virtually any back-end enterprise information system. These services are supplied as plug-in connectors — resource adapters that will be supplied by EIS and Java software application server vendors.

An EIS vendor provides a pluggable resource adapter for an application server environment to establish connectivity between an EIS, the application server, and the enterprise application. This means an application server or client can use the resource adapter to make the connection. For multiple EISs, one needs a resource adapter for each EIS type. It is possible to plug in multiple resource adapters in an application server. All adapters provide support for connection, transaction, and security management in a manner similar to EJB containers.

In addition, the J2EE Connector architecture defines a Common Client Interface (CCI) for EIS access. It acts as an integration enabler of application components and EAI frameworks across heterogeneous EISs. This capability of using multiple adapters and the CCI enables EJB and other J2EE components in the application server to access the underlying multiple EISs.

Several ERP vendors are getting a jump on the new architecture by releasing connectors that are compatible with popular application servers. Two examples are PeopleSoft and SAP. By using PeopleSoft's Component Interfaces, third-party systems can synchronously invoke PeopleSoft business logic via EJB. SAP validates third-party products for SAP's Business Technology that supports development of business logic in Java and data transfer using XML.

As industry pressure to implement E-business initiatives increases and other trends such as mergers and acquisitions accelerate, the need to integrate legacy systems with the new "E-conomy" will only increase. The need for architected composite integration platforms will also increase as the industry continues to mature and product vendors rush to keep pace and vie for IT dollars in a very competitive marketplace.

Oracle9i AS Containers for J2EE

Oracle9i Application Server Containers for J2EE (OC4J) is available on all standard operating system and hardware platforms, including Solaris, HP-UX, AIX, Tru64, Windows NT, and Linux. With Oracle9i AS v1.0.2.2 release, it is certified to run on the JDK 1.3 Java Virtual Machine (JVM).

OC4J provides a complete J2EE container that includes a JSP Translator, a Java servlet engine, and an EJB. It also supports the JMS and several other Java specifications. Oracle9i AS v1.0.2.2 provides full support for all of the J2EE APIs, including:

- EJB 1.1 and several parts of the EJB 2.0 specification, including EJB 2.0 style enterprise beans and message-driven beans
- Servlet 2.2 (and Servlet 2.3 including facilities such as Servlet Chaining and Filters)
- JSP 1.1
- JTA 1.0.1
- JNDI 1.2
- JMS 1.0.1
- JDBC 2.0
- JavaMail 1.1.2

Internet applications are designed and implemented as multi-tier applications. A middle-tier application server provides a runtime environment for the application and access to existing business functions, legacy systems, and data. The J2EE reduces the cost and complexity of developing these multi-tier

Exhibit 11.   JDBC Drivers and Associated Databases

Oracle	Oracle9*i* AS
Non-Oracle	IBM DB/2
	Microsoft SQL Server
	Informix
	Sybase

applications by defining a standard application model and a standard set of programming interfaces for developing multi-tier Internet applications. Application servers that support J2EE provide a standard "container" environment for executing J2EE applications, allowing application developers to write once and target server environments provided by a number of vendors.

Oracle offers JDeveloper as a Java development tool (Java IDE) and two different database access interfaces (JDBC and embedded SQL in Java (SQLJ)). Oracle JDeveloper integrates an object-relational mapping — Business Components for Java — that supports one-to-one and one-to-many mappings between Java classes and database schemas and allows the use of SQL to query the database.

Java applications built with any development tool can be deployed against OC4J. This container supports standard J2EE deployment packages[7] of J2EE Archive (EAR), Web Component (WAR), EJB Java Archive (JAR), or Application Client JAR files. Applications deployed with OC4J can be debugged using standard java profiling and debugging capabilities. OC4J provides four logging services: Web access, server and application activities, RMI activities, and JMS activities

Oracle also recommends the use of Merant's JDBC drivers to access non-Oracle databases, including IBM DB/2, Microsoft SQL Server, Informix, and Sybase from Java (see Exhibit 11). (Merant is an Oracle Partner.) Oracle also provides a standard way to embed SQL statements in Java programs. It offers a much simpler and higher productive programming API than JDBC. One can use SQLJ to develop both client-side and middle-tier applications that access databases from Java and to define stored procedures, triggers, methods, etc. within the database server in Java in a portable manner.

Oracle recognizes that users partition their Internet Application code into three layers: Web presentation logic, business logic, and data manipulation logic. In J2EE applications, the Web presentation logic is developed using JSPs or servlets; the business logic is developed as EJBs. To support J2EE Applications, Oracle9*i* AS provides a standards-compliant J2EE container that executes on any JDK JVM (provided on each operating system and hardware platform).

Configuring and Assembling J2EE Applications

This section looks at the configuration and assembly of a J2EE application. The typical configuration is an application component deployed in a container

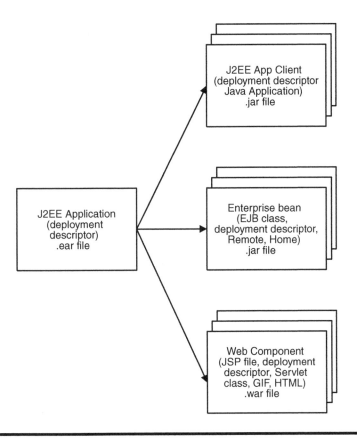

Exhibit 12.   Contents of J2EE Application

provided by an application server. The application component needs transactional access to multiple resource managers and uses a transaction manager that is responsibile for managing transactions across multiple resource managers.

A resource manager can support two types of transactions:

- *JTA/XA Transaction.* Java Transaction API specifies standard Java interfaces between a transaction manager and the parties involved in a distributed transaction system: the resource manager, the application server, and the transactional applications. Also known as the transaction manager, it is external to the resource manager.
- *RM/Local Transaction.* The transaction manager that controls and coordinates the transaction is internal to the resource manager. The coordination of such transactions involves no external transaction managers. This means the Transaction Manager component is part of the Resource Manager.

To assemble a J2EE application, one needs three kinds of modules: enterprise beans, Web components, and J2EE application clients (see Exhibit 12). These modules are reusable; one can build new applications from existing enterprise beans and components. And because the modules are portable, the application they comprise will run on any J2EE server that conforms to the specifications.

An enterprise bean is composed of three class files: the EJB class, the remote interface, and the home interface. The Web component may contain files of the following types: servlet class, JSP, HTML, and GIF. A J2EE application client is a Java application that runs in an environment (container) that allows it to access J2EE services.

Each J2EE application, Web component, enterprise bean, and J2EE application client has a deployment descriptor. A deployment descriptor is an .xml file that describes the component. An EJB deployment descriptor, for example, declares transaction attributes and security authorizations for an enterprise bean. Because this information is declarative, it can be changed without requiring modifications to the bean's source code. At runtime, the J2EE server reads this information and acts upon the bean accordingly.

One bundles each module into a file with a particular format: a J2EE application into an .ear file, an enterprise bean into an EJB .jar file, a Web component into a .war file, and a J2EE application client into a .jar file. An .ear file, for example, contains an .xml file for its deployment descriptor, and one or more EJB .jar and .war files. An EJB .jar contains its deployment descriptor and the .class files for the enterprise bean.

As one can see, JAR is a platform-independent file format that aggregates many files into one. Multiple Java applets and their requisite components (.class files, images, and sounds) can be bundled in a JAR file and subsequently downloaded to a browser in a single HTTP transaction, greatly improving the download speed. The JAR format also supports compression, which reduces the file size, further improving the download time. In addition, the applet author can digitally sign individual entries in a JAR file to authenticate their origin. It is fully backward-compatible with existing applet code and is fully extensible.

Enterprise Servlets with J2EE

To learn how servlets can be distributed, look at EJB technology, a server-side component model for implementing distributed business objects. EJB is designed from the ground up as distributable objects. An EJB implements business logic and lets the *container* (essentially the server) in which it runs manage services such as transactions, persistence, concurrency, and security. An EJB can be distributed across a number of back-end machines and can be moved between machines at the container's discretion. To enable this distribution model, EJB must follow a strict specification-defined ruleset for what they can and cannot do.

Servlet distribution (often called clustering) is an optional feature of a servlet container, and servlet containers that do support clustering are free to do so in several different ways. As shown in Exhibit 13, there are four standard architectures, listed here from the simplest to the msot advanced. As is obvious, one cannot have session migration without clustering. Likewise, one must

Exhibit 13. Clustering

Level	Clustering	Session Migration	Session Failover
NA	NA	NA	NA
Simple	X	NA	NA
Intermediate	X	X	NA
Advanced	X	X	X

have clustering and session migration in place to take advantage of session failover capabilities.

J2EE 1.2 and higher collect together several server-side APIs, including Servlet API 2.2, JSP 1.1, EJB, JavaMail, JMS, JTA, CORBA, JDBC, JAXP, and JNDI. J2EE defines how these technologies can interoperate and make use of one another, and provides certification that certain application servers are J2EE compliant, meaning they provide all the required services as well as the extra connection glue.

J2EE Security Model for OC4J

The J2EE security model lets one configure a Web or enterprise bean component so system resources are accessed only by authorized users. For example, a Web component can be configured to prompt for a user name and password. An enterprise bean component can be configured so only persons in specific groups can invoke certain kinds of its methods. Alternatively, a servlet component might be configured to have some of its methods accessible to everyone and a few methods accessible to only certain privileged persons in an organization. The same servlet component can be configured for another environment to have all methods available to everyone, or all methods to only a select few.

OC4J has an Access Control List (ACL) mechanism that allows for fine-grained control of the usage of components running on the server. One can define what can or cannot be executed by which user or group of users, right down to the Java method level.

Security realms allow the administrator to import information from existing authorization or authentication systems into the ACL. One can thus import information from the NT/2000 security system, from an LDAP system, from the UNIX password file, or from the database. Oracle9i AS v1.0.2.2 is fairly complete with respect to security. It includes all of the classes for Secure Sockets Layer (SSL) v3, RSA Encryption, and Support for X.509 certificates.

Another related security topic is the functionality of *firewall tunneling*. Oracle9i AS v1.0.2.2 provides the ability to go through firewalls and proxies via HTTP and HTTPS tunneling. With Oracle9i AS release 2.0, the J2EE security facilities will support the Oracle Login Server for single-sign-on and single station administration of security.

Exhibit 14.   Tiers and Deployment Types

Tiers	Deployment Types
Web server	HTTP listeners
Web presentation	JSPs and servlets
EJB	Business logic

RMI and Tunneling Services

When J2EE Applications are deployed, they are typically divided into two or three tiers: the Web server tier where the HTTP listeners are deployed; the Web presentation tier where the JSPs and servlets are deployed; and the EJB tier where the business logic defined as EJBs is deployed (see Exhibit 14). Smaller Web sites combine these different tiers into one physical mid-tier; larger Web sites divide these different tiers into two or three separate physical tiers for security, scalability, and load-balancing purposes.

Oracle9*i* AS takes these architectural issues into consideration and is designed to meet these needs, as shown in Exhibit 15.

Java Messaging Service

One should know about JMS before discussing message-driven beans. JMS makes available common sets of interfaces for sending and receiving messages reliably and asynchronously. Asynchronous messaging is an obvious choice for use with disconnected clients such as cell phones and PDAs. In addition, JMS is a means of integrating enterprise systems in a loosely coupled (if not completely decoupled) manner with the primary objective of creating applications that are seemingly portable across messaging vendors.

There are lots of messaging systems, each with their own API. Messaging systems provide a way to exchange events and data asynchronously. Let us quickly go through some of the basics of the JMS APIs.

Messaging Domains

Message systems have several models of operation. The JMS API provides separate domains that correspond to the different models. A JMS provider can implement one or more of the domains. The two most common domains are Point-to-Point and Publish/Subscribe. Both domains have the following concepts.

- *Destination:* the object that a client uses to specify the target of messages it sends/receives
- *Producer:* a client that sends a message to a destination
- *Consumer:* a client that receives messages from a destination

Exhibit 15. Architectural Issues

Web Server to JSP/ Servlet Engine Connectivity	The Web server can either use the Apache JServ Protocol (AJP) or HTTP to direct requests to the JSP/servlet engine. As a result, the Web server can even be placed outside a firewall and can direct request to the servlet engine that is placed behind the firewall.
JSP/Servlet-to-EJB and EJB-to-EJB Connectivity	Communication from the presentation logic tier to business logic tier and between EJBs is done using standard RMI, which gives any client or Web tier program accessing an EJB direct access to the services in the EJB tier. These services include JNDI for looking up and referencing EJBs, JMS for sending and receiving asynchronous messages, and JDBC for relational database access.
HTTP and HTTP-S Tunneling	Oracle9*i* AS also supports the ability to tunnel RMI over HTTP and HTTP-S. RMI over HTTP/HTTP-S tunneling can be used for Java-based clients when they need to communicate with Oracle9*i* AS and the only option is to use HTTP. Typically, HTTP tunneling provides a way to simulate a stateful socket connection between a Java client and Oracle9*i* AS and to "tunnel" this socket connection through an HTTP port in a security firewall. HTTP is a stateless protocol, but Oracle9*i* AS provides tunneling functionality to make the connection appear to be a regular stateful RMI connection. Under HTTP, a client can only make a request, and then accept a reply from a server. The server cannot voluntarily communicate with the client, and the protocol is stateless, meaning that a continuous two-way connection is not possible. Oracle9*i* AS's HTTP tunneling simulates an RMI connection via HTTP, thus, overcoming these limitations.

Point-to-Point

One form of JMS is a point-to-point (P2P) model designed for use in a one-to-one delivery of messages. An application developer should use P2P messaging when every message must be successfully processed. Unlike the Publish/Subscribe model, P2P messages are always delivered. It has the following characteristics:

- A P2P producer is a sender.
- A P2P consumer is a receiver.
- A P2P destination is a queue.
- A message can only be consumed by one receiver.

In addition, messages are sent to specific queues, and clients will extract messages from specific queues established to hold their messages. Queues retain all messages sent until such time as the messages are consumed or expire. Each message has only one consumer although multiple receivers may connect to the queue. Messages are removed from the start of the queue. Receivers acknowledge the successful receipt of a message. For example, a call center application may use a P2P domain. A phone call enters the queue and an operator takes care of that call. The phone call does not go to all of the operators.

Publish/Subscribe

Another form of JMS is a Publish/Subscribe (pub/sub) application model designed for one-to-many broadcasts of messages. An application developer may wish to use pub/sub messaging when it is acceptable for some level of unreliability to exist. It is possible that all consumers will not receive all messages or no consumer will receive any message. The model has the following characteristics:

- A pub/sub producer is a publisher.
- A pub/sub consumer is a subscriber.
- A pub/sub destination is a topic.
- A message may have multiple subscribers.

In addition, publishers and subscribers are usually anonymous. The system takes care of distributing the messages arriving from a topic's publishers to its subscribers. Producers and messages via topics and consumers receive those messages by subscribing to a topic. Messages are retained only as long as it takes to distribute them to the registered subscribers. Each message may have multiple subscribers. There are time dependencies that exist between publishers and subscribers. Subscribers to a topic can only consume messages published after a subscription is created. Subscribers must maintain their subscription to a topic to continue receiving messages.

An e-mail newsletter application, for example, may use a pub/sub model. Everyone who is interested in the newsletter becomes a subscriber; and when a new message is published (say the head of Human Resources sends out new information), that message is sent to all subscribers.

EJB 2.0: Message-Driven Beans

Having discussed the fundamentals of JMS, we can now move on to the message-driven bean, a new component type that is in the EJB 2.0 specification. Suppose a sender puts messages on the queue, and a receiver reads the messages and uses that information to send out e-mail. This receiver could be a program that starts up, subscribes to the "EmailQueue," and deals with the messages that come in. Instead of doing this every time one needs a receiver, it makes more sense to have a component architecture that allows for the concurrent processing of a stream of messages, is transactionally aware, and takes care of the infrastructure code, thus allowing one to work on the business logic.

This is where message-driven beans enter the picture. A message-driven bean is simply a JMS message consumer. A client cannot access a message-driven bean directly (as one does with session and entity beans). The only interface to the message-driven bean is by sending a JMS message to the destination to which the message-driven bean is listening. To allow reuse, as with the other EJBs, a lot of information is provided in the EJB deployment descriptor.

OpenJMS

OpenJMS is an open-source implementation of Sun Microsystems' Java Message Service API 1.0.2 Specification. The architecture and design were completed in late February 2000, implementation began in early March 2000, and a functional prototype was released in mid-May 2000.

OpenJMS allows developers to assemble message services from existing products rather than construct an application from scratch. These developers can create applications or modify existing ones in an open, distributed environment. One problem is that some developers have no way of knowing which person has developed what objects or applications. There is always a possibility of overwriting someone else's work by mistake.

One way of getting around this problem is to use the CVS, allowing developers to control source codes over the network. CVS has four basic functions:

1. Maintaining a history of all changes made to each directory tree it manages
2. Providing hooks to support process control and change control
3. Providing reliable access to its directory trees from remote hosts using Internet protocols
4. Supporting parallel development, thus allowing more than one developer to work on the same sources at the same time

To download source code and other files from a CVS server, one needs a CVS client. Go to http://www.cvshome.org/downloads.html and select the appropriate code for a platform of choice — BeOS, Linux, Machintosh, OS/2, UNIX, VMS, or Windows 95/NT/2000.

There is no "Install Shield" for CVS. Just put the CVS executable in any directory and then include that directory in the PATH system variable. Then execute CVS commands from anywhere within the command shell.

One can download the latest stable OpenJMS release with source code, test harness, and example code. One can also look at a number of examples (http://openjms.exolab.org/examples.html).

Java Naming and Directory Interface

The Java Naming and Directory Interface (JNDI) is an API specified in Java that provides access to different naming and directory services. Application developers can use the JNDI API to access files, devices, objects, and many other types of data available in different kinds of naming and directory services.

Software vendors such as Novell, Sun, HP, and IBM create Java packages that plug into JNDI and provide access to a specific naming or directory service.

These JNDI implementations can be created for naming services such as the Internet DNS and those employed by distributed object systems (CORBA, RMI, etc.), or directory services such as Novell's NetWare, Sun Solaris' NIS+, LDAP, and many others. JNDI is very similar to other JavaSoft APIs, like JDBC and JavaMail, where vendor-specific implementations of a particular technology can be used interchangeably through a common API.

Naming Systems and Services

A naming system provides a natural, understandable way of identifying and associating names with data. Computing systems use naming systems to provide a natural way of organizing and acting on data and objects. Examples of Naming Services include DNS, CORBA, RMI, and directory services such as X.500 and LDAP.

DNS

The Internet's Domain Name System (DNS) is perhaps the largest and best-known naming service. It allows Internet users to refer to host computers through easily recognizable names. The DNS is a global distributed naming service. The bindings that link names with actual host computers are distributed across many Name Servers.

CORBA and RMI

CORBA and RMI are examples of distributed object systems that employ naming services. In these types of systems, the naming service associates names with live objects, thus allowing an application on one computer to access live objects from a different computer.

Directory Services

The directory service is a natural extension of the naming service. Directory services are typically organized as hierarchical naming services, organizing data and objects within the context of directories and subdirectories.

Enterprise-level directory services allow all kinds of resources to be arranged and managed, including files, printing services, computing devices, user accounts, security, and business objects — practically any device or functionality found on a network. The real power of a full-featured directory service is its capacity to represent, manage, and provide access to a diverse set of resources. Directory services can be central to a local area network or global, providing access to widely distributed resources. The following paragraphs provide brief descriptions of both local and global enterprise-level directory services. Exhibit 16 gives JNDI directory service examples.

Exhibit 16. JNDI Directory Services

X.500	Defined by ISO, X.500 can be used for many types of data. X.500 is a very robust data model and set of operations that has been adopted in part by several other directory service implementations.
LDAP	The University of Michigan introduced the Lightweight Directory Access Protocol (LDAP) directory service as a lightweight version of X.500 that could run on the TCP/IP protocol stack.
NDS	NetWare Directory Service (NDS) is Novell's proprietary directory service. NDS organizes objects in a distributed database, independent of their physical location, and can be used for acting on both physical and logical entities within a NetWare network.
NIS+	Network Information Service Plus (NIS+) is Sun Microsystems' proprietary directory service for Sun Solaris 2.0. NIS+ is an enterprise network administration tool and repository for information about network entities such as users, servers, and printers. NIS+ improves on an older directory service called NIS.

Naming and directory services vary in their exact implementation from one service to the next. NDS, NIS+, LDAP, and X.500 are all directory services, but they use different servers, bindings, protocols, and clients. The same is true of the DNS and naming systems such as those utilized by CORBA and Java RMI. The differences in naming and directory services, however, are encapsulated in their implementations and APIs: the basic architecture of these systems are the same.

Directory and naming services usually employ two layers: a client layer and a server layer. The server is responsible for maintaining and resolving the actual name-object bindings, controlling access, and managing operations performed on the structure of the directory service. The client acts as an interface that applications use to communicate with the directory service.

JNDI is a client API that provides naming and directory functionality specifically for Java applications. JNDI is specified in Java and is designed to provide an abstraction that represents those elements most common to naming and directory service clients. JNDI is not intended as an alternative to established naming and directory services; rather, it is designed to provide a common interface for accessing existing services such as DNS, NDS, LDAP, CORBA, and RMI.

JNDI Architecture

The JNDI architecture is separated into two main interfaces: the API and SPI. The JNDI API provides a set of classes and interfaces that application developers use for navigating across multiple naming systems. The JNDI API shields application developers from the nuts and bolts of how different naming and directory services function. Vendors who are developing service providers for JNDI can use the JDNI SPI. This interface provides the classes and interfaces that a directory service must implement to be available to a JNDI client.

The JNDI API is divided into two packages: the javax.naming and javax.naming.directory packages. This is a natural and logical packaging system for representing naming and directory services. As previously discussed, a directory service is a type of naming service; thus, it is natural and logical that the directory package would be largely derived from the naming package.

The Naming Package

The javax.naming.Context interface is the most important type in the JNDI API. It provides access to name-object bindings, the heart of any naming system. A Context object provides methods for resolving named objects, binding and unbinding names to objects, and creating and destroying subcontexts. In JNDI, a type of Context called InitialContext — the root of a client's naming system — is used as a starting point for navigating a namespace.

The javax.naming.Reference class is the heart of JNDI's federated naming facilities. It enables different service providers to cooperate, producing seamless transitions from one directory or naming service to the next. A reference can be thought of as a pointer from one namespace to another. It is named and placed in a binding just like any other context or named object. When an object of type Reference is resolved, however, JNDI automatically detects that it is a Reference and uses the information it contains to transition the client to the service provider, namespace, and appropriate object described by the Reference.

A Reference object is really just a collection of strings that JNDI uses to load and initialize a service provider. It describes the type of service, the name of the server, the object name, and a URL for dynamically loading the appropriate service provider.

This gives JNDI the ability to dynamically load service providers as needed and to store links to other namespaces. Everyone involved in developing and using JNDI, from the vendor that creates service providers to the application developer to the user, is insulated from the mechanics of JNDI's federated naming facilities. To allow a JNDI client to cross from one namespace to another, a simple Reference can be created and stored in the server — JNDI takes care of the rest.

The Directory Package

DirContext interface is as important to the directory package as Context is to the naming package. In fact, DirContext extends javax.naming.Context by adding methods for examining and searching attributes associated with a directory object. The defining difference between a directory service and a naming service is that a directory service is organized as a hierarchical naming system that includes functionality for evaluating and modifying attributes attached to contexts and the ability to search a context using attributes as a filter. The concept of a directory service with a hierarchical structure is very easy to model with JNDI.

Exhibit 17.   New JNDI 1.2 Features

Event Notification	The `javax.naming.event` package contains classes and interfaces for supporting event notification in naming and directory services.
LDAP v3 Extensions and Controls	The `javax.naming.ldap` is for applications and service providers that deal with LDAP v3 extended operations and controls.
Using Resources for Configurations	A mechanism using resources is defined for service providers and applications to provide configuration information to JNDI.
Service Provider Support	*Storing Objects* defines a mechanism for service providers to transform the state of an object into a form that can be stored into naming/directory services. *Federation* specifies the policy for how a service provider should support dynamic location of the next naming system. *Environment Properties* specifies how a convention is defined for the naming of environment properties to prevent namespace collisions.
Modification to JNDI 1.1 Packages	Several modifications are made to the `javax.naming`, `javax.naming.directory,` and `javax.naming.spi` packages.

Every DirContext object contains zero or more objects of class Attribute. Every Attribute object has a String identifier — a name — and a set of values. Because a directory has attributes and also extends the Context class, it can be both described and used as a naming context. A person's e-mail address, phone number, and other personal information, for example, could all be available through the Attributes of a DirContext associated with a specific person. In addition, resources specific to that person, such as their printer, fax machine, and scheduler, could be obtained through a lookup.

JNDI 1.2

JNDI 1.2 is a major new upgrade release that adds new functionality to the basic naming and directory support offered in the 1.1.x releases. New features include event notification, and LDAP v3 extensions and controls. This release contains valuable contributions from the following companies: Netscape, Novell, Tarantella, Sun, and BEA.

JNDI 1.2 is a Java Standard Extension, running on all compatible platforms. Exhibit 17 shows what new features have been added since JNDI 1.1.

Java Media Framework

Java Media Framework (JMF) 2.1 provides a unified architecture for the capture, playback, streaming, and transcoding of media content — such as audio and video — across most major operating systems. It enables developers to incor-

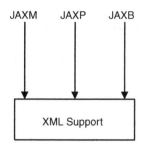

Exhibit 18.   XML Support

porate time-based media content into Java applications and applets. JMF 2.1.1 extends the Java platform by offering advanced media processing capabilities, including media capture, compression, streaming, playback, and support for important media types and codecs such as M-JPEG, H.263, MP3, Real-Time Transport Protocol and Real-time Streaming Protocol (RTP/RTSP), Macromedia's Flash, IBM's HotMedia, and Beatnik's Rich Media Format (RMF). JMF 2.1.1 also supports popular media types such as Quicktime, Microsoft's Audio-Video Interleaved (AVI) format, and Motion Picture Experts Group-1 (MPEG-1). In addition, JMF 2.1.1 includes an open media architecture, allowing developers to access and manipulate individual components of the media playback and capture process, such as effects, tracks, and renders, or to utilize their own custom plug-in components.

JMF 2.1.1 technology ships in four different versions tailored to meet specialized developer needs, starting with the most portable version, written entirely in the Java programming language, and designed to work with any Java-compatible system. JMF source code will be released under Sun Community Source Licensing (SCSL).

Java APIs: XML Messaging, XML Parsing, and Data Binding

JAXM, JAXP, and JAXB form the core of XML support in the J2EE platform. These Java technologies for XML give developers an API toolset for developing and deploying Java technology-based applications that harness the synergies of the Java platform's portable code and XML's portable data (see Exhibit 18). All three technologies are being developed through the Java Community Program (JCP) program, the open, community-based organization that stewards the evolution of the Java platform.

The Java API for XML Messaging

JAXM enables the packaging, routing, and transport of both XML and non-XML business messages across a number of key communications infrastructures, such as those based on HTTP, SMTP, and FTP protocols. By supporting industry-standard packaging and an asynchronous messaging model, Java technology programmers can build and secure B2B E-commerce applications with JAXM.

JAXM supports a variety of XML messaging methods, such as the evolving XML messaging standard being defined in the ebXML framework. ebXML is intended to provide a global standard for simple, robust, low-cost trade facilitation and is a joint development effort between the Organization for the Advancement of Structured Information Standards (OASIS) and the United Nations Centre for Trade Facilitation and Electronic Business (UN/CEFACT). Sun is involved in defining ebXML and is contributing to multiple working groups, such as the Transport/Routing & Packaging group, and leading the Proof-of-Concept working group.

The Java API for XML Parsing

JAXP enables the reading, manipulating, and generating of XML documents through Java APIs by providing a standard way to seamlessly integrate any XML-compliant parser with a Java technology-based application. JAXP v.1.1 supports the latest XML standards, including the Document Object Model (DOM) level 2, a W3C recommendation that was recently released; Simple API for XML (SAX) level 2, the industry standard for XML parsing; and XSL Transformations (XSLT), an integrated XML transformation standard defined by the W3C.

With JAXP, developers can swap XML parsers, depending on the needs of the application, without actually changing any code. One XML parser that could be used is "Crimson," which was developed at Sun and donated to the Apache Software Foundation. Crimson is used as the default XML parser with JAXP v.1.1; however, the technology's pluggable architecture allows any XML-conformant parser to be used, including the existing xml.apache.org XML parser, code named Xerces.

The Java API for Data Binding

JAXB, formerly Project Adelard, enables Java technology developers to deliver and maintain high-performance, XML-enabled applications with a minimum of development effort. JAXB provides two-way mapping between XML documents and Java technology-based objects along with a schema compiler tool. The compiler automatically generates Java technology classes from XML schemas without requiring developers to write any complex parsing code. In addition, the compiler contains automatic error and validity checking of XML messages, helping to ensure that only valid, error-free messages are accepted and processed by a system.

JXTA Project

The goal of Project JXTA is to leverage distributed computing by providing direct access or communication to resources from one node (device) on the network to another, without any centralized server control. As wireless mobile devices such as personal data assistants (PDAs), cell phones, pagers, and laptops increasingly become connected to the Internet, and become nodes on a peer-to-peer[8] network, it will be possible for a PDA to directly access information from a laptop, without requiring a centralized server.

JXTA's four key concepts are:

1. *Peer groups*: the ability to create groups of groups in a dynamic, fluid, flexible environment; the ability to allow different ways for people to become aware of each other, trust one another, and aggregate content logically and cohesively
2. *Peer pipes*: the ability to connect one peer to another across the network in a distributed fashion
3. *Peer monitoring*: the ability to know what is going on and to establish control policies among peers
4. *Security*: a mechanism available to ensure privacy, confidentiality, identity, and controlled access to services

JavaSpaces and Jini Technologies

The JavaSpaces technology allows dynamic communication, coordination, and sharing of objects between Java technology-based network resources such as clients and servers. In a distributed application, this technology acts as a virtual space between providers and requestors of network resources or objects. Participants can use Java objects to exchange tasks, requests, and information.

The JavaSpaces technology is a Jini technology — an architecture for the construction of systems from objects and networks. The Jini architecture lets programs use services in a network without knowing about the wire technology the service uses. One implementation of a service might be XML based, another RMI based, and a third CORBA based. A service is defined by its programming API, making itself known by publishing an object that implements the service API.

To find the service, the client looks for an object that supports the API. When the object is found, it will download any code in order to talk to the service. The programmer who implements the service chooses how to translate an API request into bits using RMI, CORBA, or a private protocol.

Notes

1. For more information about ERP, CRM, and SCM, go to the section on "Java 2 Enterprise Edition."
2. See "Configuring and Assembling J2EE Applications" in this chapter.
3. The container defines the part of the EJB server that hosts instances of enterprise beans.
4. JNDI is a vendor-neutral Java API that can be used with any kind of naming or directory service, such as CORBA naming or LDAP. For more information, go to the section on JNDI in this chapter.

5. See the "Java Messaging Service" section in this chapter.

6. CICS applications written in Java indicate that the enterprises are moving into the world of objects from CICS, using a native IIOP interface for a CORBA-compliant client. CICS support for Java enables delvelopers to exploit the JavaBeans component model. CICS is being transformed into an Enterprise Java Server to extend support for Enterprise APIs and e-Business Connectors for enterprise systems.

7. For more information on .ear, .jar, and .war files, go to the section on "Java Applications."

8. The term "peer-to-peer" currently has no single definition. Taken literally, a peer-to-peer transaction involves servers talking to one another; but in practice, peer-to-peer expands beyond servers and decentralizes transactions on the Internet.

Chapter 5

Web Services: Hot Stuff

This chapter discusses Web services and related technologies (front-end, back-end) and standards. It covers how various vendors and organizations define Web services and present Web services architecture traffic. The chapter also looks at Universal Description, Discovery and Integration (UDDI) technology, Web service brokerage, and some third-party tools; provides workflow process examples; and briefly discusses versioning of Web services.

Introduction

Web services are designed for incorporation into software for human intervention. Operating at a code level, Web services call and are called by other Web services and other components to exchange information.

Web services technology can be thought of as an evolution of Common Object Request Broker Architecture (CORBA). Its major advantage over CORBA is that Web services do not require integration of an ORB. The underlying transport protocol behind Web services is based on eXtensible Markup Language (XML) over the Hypertext Transport Protocol (HTTP). Another advantage is that Web services are stateless[1] and connectionless,[2] while CORBA is stateful.

As of August 30, 2001, Jupiter Media Matrix, a leading company in Internet and new technology measurement analysis, reports that the U.S. Web services revolution will not reach full scale for another 18 to 24 months. It expects "that enterprise application vendors will begin to remake pieces of their applications around the Web services architecture by late 2002."

Most of the companies employing Web services use them for internal application, such as retrieving customer information from a customer relationship management (CRM) system or passing a transaction from a front-office system to a back-office system. Some will deploy Web services technology for interaction with existing suppliers and partners for purposes such as authorizing credit-card transactions or conducting credit checks.

Wily Technologies offers Version 2.6 of its monitoring and measuring software for Enterprise JavaBeans (EJBs). It has been extended to Web services.

Web Services

Before discussing what a Web services stack is, we need to define what Web services are. The problem here is that there are so many definitions for them. There is no standard definition for Web services. Where a definition could not be provided or found, it is replaced with a short description.

Defining or Describing Web Services

As one will notice below, the definitions or descriptions range from very easy to understand to very abstract that only a few people will know exactly what they really mean. Some are very short while others are very wordy.

> Web services are encapsulated, loosely coupled [and] contracted functions offered through standard protocols.
>
> — WebServices.org

> Web services allows the customer to rent components from various sources on the Internet, and mix and match them to create new applications [over the Internet].
>
> — Scott Leibs,
> "Web Services: The Great Buildup,"
> *CFO*, May 2001

> Web services are defined as loosely coupled applications that can be exposed as services and easily consumed by other publication using Internet standard technologies (XML, SOAP, WSDL, UDDI). Web services are URL addressable resources that exchange information and execute processes automatically without human interventions.
>
> — The Grand Central (Third-Party)
> Scott Durchslag, Craif Donato, and John Hagel, III
> Web Services: Enabling the Collaborative Enterprise

> The Stencil defines Web services as loosely coupled, reusable software components that semantically encapsulate discrete functionality and are distributed and programmatically accessible over standard Internet protocols.
>
> — The Stencil Group (Market Services)

A Web service is an interface that ... [is] network accessible through ... XML messaging, ... transport protocols. The interface hides the implementation details ... Web services ... applications ... [are] loosely coupled ... [It] can be used alone or with other Web services to carry out a complex aggregation or a business transaction.

> — Heather Kreger,
> WebServices Conceptual Architecture (WSCA 1.0)
> IBM Software Group, May 2001

A Web service is defined from existing applications, Web sources, databases, or other sources of content or functionality using XML. Developers and administrators create services by defining ... the syntax of the service request and response. The resulting *service package* is ... a local directory that contains a ... descriptor file in XML.

> — Developing, Deploying,
> Managing Web Services with Oracle9*i*
> June 2001

Web services are functional software components that can be accessed over the Internet. They combine the best aspects of component-based development and the Web, delivering true distributed "peer-to-peer" computing. Based on open Internet standards, Web services enable the construction of Web-based applications using any platform, object model, or programming language.

> — Cape Clear (Third-Party)

... a *Web service* is a programmable application component that is accessible through standard Web protocols. There are four categories of Web services that will be delivered to the Internet:

1. Public .NET Web Services
2. Commercial .NET Building Block Web Services
3. Ready-to-use, out-of-the-box Web Services
4. Custom-developed Web Services

> — Michael Herman,
> Developing Collaborative Microsoft .NET Solutions
> EC3 Enterprise Consulting Competency Centers, Microsoft
> Microsoft .NET Framework

A Web service is an application that accepts requests from other *systems* across the Internet or an intranet, mediated by lightweight, vendor-neutral communications technologies.

> — SunOne Architecture
> James Kao,
> Building XML-based Web Services with the Java 2 Platform
> Enterprise Edition (J2EE), June 2001

Web services can be described as the protocols, conventions, and network facilities that expose business functions to authorized parties over the Internet from any Web-connected device.

— BEA Systems WebLogic

Web services are modular and reusable software components that are created by wrapping a business application inside a Web service interface.

— Hewlett Packard NetAction

Web services can for example comprise financial, logistic or auctioning services.

— SAP

Web services are software components that can be housed in an application on a local network or the Internet, and are accessible by applications....

— Romin Irani,
"Part II — ebXML and Web Services:
The Way to Do Business"
Web Services Architect, July 25, 2001

Web services can ... connect applications using standard XML formats over ... Internet protocols to virtually any client, including desktop applications, Web browsers, mobile devices, and PDAs. ... [They] interconnect applications from ... different hardware platforms, such as mainframes, application servers, and Web servers ... [via] Windows, Java, and UNIX.

— Borland Web Services

Comparing Definitions or Descriptions

Note that the first example as given by WebServices.org, a standards organization, is quite abstract, while the second example from the *CFO* magazine is very easy to understand. Both mean almost the same thing.

Like CORBA, Web services are components that one can reuse in building applications. The tasks that Web services perform when customers reuse and put together the components are not seen from the outside. This is known as the encapsulation. Encapsulated tasks are transparent. Reusable components can be encapsulated.

When a customer mixes and matches components, it means that the Web services are reconfigurable or, in a more formal sense, loosely coupled. Although tasks are reconfigurable, a change in the implementation of one function does not require a change to the invoking function. "Loosely coupled" does not refer to communications between two applications, as Web services rely on a remote procedure call (RPC) in which queries and responses are exchanged in XML over HTTP.

Loosely coupled also means that Web services can send messages to a queue for later retrieval, as in a workflow process. It is not necessary for a receiver to be present when a sender transmits a message; the receiver can get it at a later time — from a queue. It is also not necessary for the sender to get a response immediately after sending a message.

Encapsulated and loose coupling require wire-level messaging protocols to perform the data transfer between functions, independent of the runtime environment. XML, being a self-description language, is used and the Simple Object Access Protocol (SOAP) acts as the "envelope" for the messages. These messages must be routed with reliability and have transactions support (such as the SQL Commit statement).

Web services require contracted functions, meaning that there are publicly available functions (in addition to private ones not available to public applications). They include interfaces for standard description languages, such as discovery, workflow, and standard taxonomies used to search and store information a private directory (e.g., stock service brokerage) or public directory (e.g., UDDI).

The contracted functions can be extended to aggregations of Web services, transactions, and workflow, all of which require quality of service (QoS), security for confidentiality, authorization, data integrity, message origin authentication (not a replay of old message), and non-repudiation, as well as management for process execution at all levels.

For our own purpose, contracted functions are grouped into the following:

- Web description languages
- Discovery, workflow, and standard taxonomies
- Negotiation-runtime agreement on the protocols for Web services aggregations
- Management, security, and quality of service (QoS)

All definitions or descriptions indicate implicitly or explicitly that Web services use standard protocols to distribute them over the Internet — in a format common to the customers. Standard protocols are widely published and freely available for anyone to implement. Standard organizations such as the World Wide Web Consortium (W3C) and the Organization for the Advancement of Structured Information Standards (OASIS) facilitate agreement and collaboration between companies on messaging standards. These protocols refer to the Open Standards component of the Web services stack.

Web Services Stack

As with the above definitions or descriptions, the architecture of the Web services stack varies from one vendor to another and from one standard

Exhibit 1.   WebServices.org Web Services Stack

Service Negotiation — Trading Partner Agreement	Management Quality of Service Security Open Standards
Workflow, discovery, registries (UDDI and ebXML registries), IBM WSFL, MS XLANG[a]	
Service Description Language — WSDL/WSCL	
Messaging — SOAP/XML Protocol	
Transport HTTP, FTP, SMTP	
Internet	

[a] An XML language to describe processes and spawn them.

organization to another. A Web services stack is either short and simple, or long and abstract. Where information on a stack architecture is unavailable, the organization presents a similar content in a narrative format (see the section entitled "Web Services Architecture (Narrative)").

In a stack, a Web service interface can be implemented using an Internet protocol, such as SOAP, SOAP Messages with Attachments (SwA), ebXML Message Service, e-Speak, XML-RPC, CORBA, Java Remote Method Invocation (RMI), or COM+. This makes it possible to achieve interoperability between Web services client operations and application server middleware, such as CORBA, Java 2 Enterprise Edition (J2EE), EJB applications, connected to UDDI Registry and Wireless Service Applications.

We first present the stacks from WebServices.org, IBM, The Stencil Group, W3C WebServices Workshop, Microsoft, Sun, Oracle, BEA systems, and Hewlett Packard (see Exhibits 1 through 10) and then compare some of them.

Exhibit 1 displays the Web services stack from WebServices.org. If one transforms this exhibit into a pyramid with the Service Negotiation layer at the top, one sees that business logic process goes from one layer to another in succession — from top to down. The stack starts with, for example, two trading partners who negotiate and agree on the protocols to aggregate Web services.

Then they move to the next lower layer to establish workflow processes using Web Services Flow Language (WSFL)[3] to specify how a Web service is interfaced with another, and how it can either function as an activity in one workflow or consist of a series of sequenced activities or workflows. Some Web services, however, are private; they cannot expose details of these services to public applications.

Web services that can be exposed may, for example, get the information on credit validation activities from a public directory or registry, such as UDDI. The ebXML, E-Services Village, BizTalk.org, and xml.org registries and a stock service brokerage are other directories that could be used with UDDI in conjunction with Web services for business-to-business (B2B) transactions in a complex Enterprise Application Integration (EAI) infrastructure.

Exhibit 2. The Stencil Group Web Services Technology Stack

Other Business Rules (not yet defined)	Emerging Layers
Web Services Flow Language (WSFL)	
Universal Description, Discovery and Integration (UDDI)	
Web Services Description Language (WSDL)	
Simple Object Access Protocol (SOAP)	Core Layers
eXtensible Markup Language (XML)	
Common Internet Protocols (TCP/IP, HTTP)	

The first release of UDDI was published in May 2001. Before year's end, additional revisions to this registry were planned before it was turned over to a standards organization. Microsoft has worked with IBM, Ariba, CommerceOne and some 200+ companies in developing and revising UDDI.

As one can see when moving down the stack, one needs an XML-based Web Services Description Language (WSDL) that one can use to connect to a Web service. This language describes in an abstract way the services' connections and various protocols and their uses, forming a key element to the directory.

One also needs Web Service Conversational Language (WSCL)[4] to help the developers better describe the XML schema, so they will know what a given Web service can do. WSCL can be used to specify a Web service interface and to describe service interactions.

WSDL help service requestors "find, bind, and publish" the results of getting the information on services from UDDI. Now we are getting to the Messaging layer where SOAP acts "as the envelope" for XML-based messages. Messages are sent back and forth regarding the status of various Web services as the work progresses (e.g., from customer order to shipping product).

After this, Web services have one more door to enter: the Transport layer that uses HTTP, File Transfer Protocol (FTP), and Standard Mail Transfer Protocol (SMTP). Then, Web services take a ride over the Internet to provide services to a service requestor or to give a status to a service provider or service broker.

The Stencil Group presents the stack shown in Exhibit 2. This stack is similar to that of WebServices.org except that ebXML and WSCL are not considered part of the emerging layers.

IBM looks at the stack in a slightly different way, as indicated in Exhibit 3. The IBM Web Services Stack does not show WSCL and ebXML, as shown in WebServices.org's stack. It refers, in the Network layer, to IBM MQSeries messaging systems and the Internet Inter-ORB Protocol (IIOP) — a protocol CORBA uses to transmit data, information, and messages between applications. The stack also applies QoS, management, and security to all six layers.

Exhibit 3. IBM Conceptual Web Services Stack

WSFL	Service Flow	
Static → UDDI	Service Directory	Quality of Service Management Security
Direct → UDDI	Service Publication	
WSDL	Service Description	
SOAP	XML-Based Messaging	
HTTP, FTP, e-mail , MQ, IIOP	Network	

Exhibit 4. W3C Web Services Wire Stack

Other "extensions"	
Attachments	Routing
Security	Reliability
SOAP/XML Protocol	
XML	

As of May 2001, IBM announced software and tools that enable businesses to create, publish, securely deploy, host, and manage Web services applications. They include WebSphere Application Server Version 4.0, WebSphere Studio Technology Preview for Web Services, WebSphere Business Integrator, DB2 Version 7.2, Tivoli Web Services Manager (to monitor performance of all aspects of the Web services environment), and Lotus software suite (to enable Web collaboration, knowledge management, and distance learning).

In addition, IBM's Web Services ToolKit (WSTK) provides a runtime environment as well as demo/examples to design and execute Web-service applications to find one another and collaborate in business transactions without programming requirements or human intervention. The WSTK demonstrates how some of the emerging technology standards such as UDDI and WSDL work together and provides simple-to-use examples of Web services.

The W3C Web Services Workshop, led by IBM and Microsoft, has agreed that the architecture stack consists of three parts: wire, description, and discovery. Exhibit 4 shows which layers constitute the Wire Stack. This Wire Stack has extensions to two layers: SOAP and XML. This means that whenever the SOAP is used as the envelope for the XML messages, they must be secure, reliable, and routed to the intended service requestor or provider.

The Description Stack consists of five layers as shown in Exhibit 5. As shown, the Service Description layer comprises two parts: Service Interface and Service Implementation, both of which require WSDL. As the name

Exhibit 5.   W3C Web Services Description Stack

Business Process Orchestration		
Message Sequencing		
Service Capabilities Configuration		
Service Description (WSDL)	Service Interface	WSDL
	Service Implementation	
XML Schema		

Exhibit 6.   W3C Web Services Discovery Stack

Discovery UDDI
Inspection

Exhibit 7.   W3C Services Architecture Stack

	Other "extensions"			
	Attachments	Routing		
Wire Stack	Security	Reliability		
	SOAP/XML			
	XML			
	Business Process Orchestration			
	Message Sequencing			
Description Stack	Service Capabilities Configuration			
	Service Description (WSDL)		Service Interface	WSDL
			Service Implementation	
	XML Schema			
Discovery Stack	Directory (UDDI)			
	Inspection			

implies, the Discovery Stack (see Exhibit 6) involves the use of the UDDI, allowing businesses and trading partners to find and discover one another over the Internet.

All three stacks form the Architecture Stack (see Exhibit 7).

Web Services Architecture (Narrative)

This section covers Web services architecture as presented by Microsoft, Sun, Oracle, BEA Systems, Hewlett-Packard, and Borland. Each has a different perspective.

Microsoft .NET Web Services

Microsoft is offering .NET as "a platform for Web services." Loosely coupled .NET Framework allows a Web service consumer to send and receive using XML, including a description of the Web services it and other consumers offer. The SOAP is used to invoke Web services and is supported by XML Schema Datatypes (XSD), Service Contract Language (SCL), and XML/HTTP protocols such as Web Distributed Authoring and Versioning (WebDAV).

The first commercial Web services that Microsoft will make available are currently known by the codename "HailStorm." In launching Web services at the beginning of 2002 (the .NET Platform is due out in November 2001), Microsoft offers user-centric Web services.

Included in the 14 services scheduled for the HailStorm release are:

1. myProfile (name, nickname, special dates, picture)
2. myContacts (electronic relationships/address book)
3. myNotifications (notification subscription, management and routing)
4. myCalendar (time and task management)
5. myDocuments (raw document storage)
6. myWallet (receipts, payment instruments, coupons and other transaction records)
7. myDevices (device settings, capabilities)

Sun's ONE Web Services

SunOne presents the ONE Web services developer model as a way of building Web services with XML and Java technologies (see Exhibit 8). The Java platform includes native support for XML.

The SunOne architecture recommends four types of XML messagaing systems: SOAP, SwA, ebXML Message Service, and XML Protocol (XMLP). ebXML Message Service is an XML messaging service designed to support the requirements of B2B E-commerce. It extends SwA by adding a QoS framework that ensures reliable and secure message delivery. An ebXML message can transport any number of XML documents and nonXML attachments. However, the ebXML Message Service does not support an RPC programming convention.

As of Summer 2001, XMLP specification was under development. Its stated goal was to be an extensible, general-purpose XML protocol. The XMLP Activity used the SOAP V1.1 specification as a starting point.

Exhibit 8. Java Technologies

Java API for XML Processing (JAXP)	Provide a native Java interface to DOM, SAX, and XSLT.
Java API for XML Data Binding (JAXB)	Bind XML data to Java code. A developer uses JAXB to compile XML schema information into Java objects. At runtime, JAXB automatically maps the XML document data to the Java object, and vice versa.
Java API for XML Messaging (JAXM)	Provide native Java interface to XML messaging systems, such as the ebXML Message Service, XMLP, and SOAP.
Java API for XML Registries (JAXR)	Provide an interface to XML registries and repositories, such as the ebXML Registry and Repository, and the UDDI Business Registry.
Java APIs for XML-based RPC (JAX/RPC)	Provide direct support for an RPC programming convention for XML messaging systems, such as SOAP and XMLP.

Exhibit 9. Oracle Web Services Architecture (Partial)

Web Services Broker		
Input/Output transformers	Execution modules	Protocol adapters
Registry cache		
Service Registry	Application Profile Registry	
Oracle Internet Directory (OID) Server		

Oracle Web Services

The core of the Oracle9*i* Web Services Framework is the Web Service Broker, a J2EE execution engine deployed in Oracle9*i* Application Server (see Exhibit 9). Application developers can access the engine using the Oracle Web Services Java client APIs, which provide a level of abstraction over the communication protocol used by the client library to connect to the execution engine (direct Java method calls, PL/SQL calls, HTTP, HTTPS, or JMS messages).

Oracle9*i* AS contains the Web Services Broker and registry cache and protocol adapters within it. The Web Services Broker is a policy and service management engine that executes services. It retrieves the service descriptor, sets up the execution environment, issues execution requests to the resource providers, receives responses from the resource provider, and transforms them for the client.

Registry cache caches service definitions from the Web Services Registry, which stores service definitions containing information. This registry enables the Web Services Broker to set up and execute services, and access distributed sources. Different registry options can be used without affecting the client. Developers will be able to access the registry, which is based on the Oracle Internet Directory (OID) through Lightweight Directory Access Protocol (LDAP) or the UDDI interface layer.

Protocol adapters transform the standard service requests to the input needed by the service following the underlying protocol. They include Web service, database service, and other service providers.

BEA Web Services

BEA Systems develops Web services on the J2EE platform using the SOAP protocol. Future J2EE products will eventually support and possibly standardize how Web services will work as part of complex business processes participating in business transactions.

J2EE applications expose EJBs and JMS destinations as Web services. Exposed services use WSDL as the service description language and provide access to components. Private registries (possibly based on UDDI) are used to integrate with partners by some applications. Typical enterprise application integration is based on the J2EE Connector Architecture (J2EE CA).

BEA uses the Business Transaction Protocol (BTP) — an XML dialect for orchestrating inter-enterprise business transactions that address the unique business-to-business (B2B) requirements. This protocol is stack agnostic, so it can be easily implemented in conjunction with other standards, such as ebXML or SOAP. For example, a header can be added to the ebXML message envelope to carry the transaction context defined by BTP.

Hewlett-Packard Web Services

The Hewlett-Packard Web Services Platform supports both Web service interactions and Web service implementation bindings via an architecture that addresses three key infrastructure service areas:

- Messaging
- Interaction control
- Application processing

In addition to the these key infrastructure services, supporting functions that handle transactional semantics, security, availability and scalability, and monitoring and management are provided by the underlying HP Total-e-Server platform (see Exhibit 10).

Exhibit 10. HP Web Services Architectural Overview

	Security
Application Processing (Workflow, Servlet EJB, JSP, Cocoon)	Transactions
	Availability
Interaction Control (Envelope Processing, Dispatch to Application Components)	Scalability
	Monitoring
Messaging (Transports, Listeners, Content Format Handlers)	Management
	Tools

Borland Web Services

Delphi 6 Borland provides three new key features needed to build and deploy Web services. They are:

- *BizSnap*: simplifies E-business integration by creating and using XML/SOAP-based Web services.
- *WebSnap*: a component-based Web application development framework that supports leading Web application servers, including Apache, Netscape, and Microsoft Internet Information Services (IIS).
- *DataSnap*: a Web service-enabled database middleware that enables any client application or service to easily connect with any major database over the Internet. It supports all major database servers such as Oracle, MS-SQL Server, Informix, IBM DB2, Sybase, and InterBase. Client applications connect to DataSnap servers through industry-standard SOAP/XML HTTP connections over the Internet without bulky database client drivers and complex configuration requirements. DCOM, CORBA, and TCP/IP connections are also supported.

Each feature forms the basis for the Web services architecture. DataSnap is apparently the core of this architecture, as it is the middleware for Web services. See Chapter 6 for more information on DataSnap.

Emerging Stack Layers

This section cites the following as possible emerging stack layers:

- Web Services User Interface (WSUI)
- Security Assertion Markup Language (SAML)
- eXtensible Access Control Markup Language (XACML)
- XML Key Management Specification (XKMS)

To use Web services for application integration, several extensions must be added to the collection of Web services specifications, including security and user interfaces. Web services currently lack a mechanism to encapsulate a user interface. This encapsulation allows packaging of an application and embedding it into another application.

As a partial solution, the WSUI Initiative, drawn up in June 2001, defines the concept of what views the developers should use to display a Web service on a screen. It specifies that views employ eXtensible Stylesheet Language Transformation (XSLT) to transform into a HyperText Markup Language (HTML) or Wireless Markup Language (WML) script.

Web services, in addition, lack security facilities. The application of Web services for business-to-business integration (B2Bi) will be limited if services for authentication, encryption, access control, and data integrity are not available. Web services cannot certify the identity of the publisher or consumer of a Web service. There are no facilities to restrict access to a Web service to a group of authorized users. As a partial solution, the XML-Based Security Services Technical Committee from the OASIS is working on a specification for SAML. OASIS is also working on XACML that would allow organizations to limit access to services to authenticated, authorized users.

Among other system standards being developed regarding the implementation of low-level security services is the XKMS proposed by Microsoft, VeriSign, and webMethods. This specification aims at reducing the complexity of creating products that support public key infrastructure (PKI).

UDDI Registration

Today, organizations find it difficult to locate a business offering services that best fit their needs. UDDI[5] makes it possible for organizations to quickly discover the right business out of the millions that are currently online via known identifiers (e.g., DUNS, Thomas Registry), standard taxonomies (e.g., NAICS, UN/SPSC), or business services.

Once an organization finds a potential business partner, there is no standard mechanism to figure out how to conduct electronic business with this partner. UDDI makes it possible for organizations to programmatically describe their services and specify how they prefer to conduct business, so that partners can quickly and easily begin trading.

UDDI can give a business visibility on a global scale by providing the means for an organization to advertise its business and services in a global registry. It can help a business develop new E-business partnerships by enabling businesses to quickly and dynamically discover and interact with each other on the Internet. The ultimate goal is to offer the basic infrastructure for dynamic, automated integration of all E-commerce transactions and Web services.

The information provided in the UDDI Business Registry consists of three components: "white pages" of company contact information, "yellow pages" that categorize businesses by standard taxonomies, and "green pages" that document the technical information about services that are exposed. The registry does not list an organization's catalog of products and available services. Exhibit 11 provides examples of what information the companies need to register about their business and Web-based services.

Exhibit 11. UDDI Business Registry

White pages	Business name
	Contact information
	Human-readable description
	Identifiers (DUNS, NAICS, UNSPSC, ISO 3166, SIC, tax ID, etc.)
Yellow pages	Services and products index
	Industry codes
	Geographic index
Green pages	E-business rules
	Service descriptions
	Application invocation
	Data binding

Alternatively, a business can have a registrar perform UDDI registration services on its behalf. The registrar can help the business compose its registry information, including its list of services and the models that describe those services.

The UDDI Business Registry is the implementation of the specification developed by uddi.org. It is a core element of the infrastructure that supports Web services, and provides a place for a company to register its business and the services it offers. People or businesses that need a service can use this registry to find a business that provides the service.

This registry is operated as a distributed service. Currently, IBM and Microsoft operate registry nodes. Additional operators will bring more nodes online in the future. Hewlett-Packard has signed an agreement to operate another registry node. An Operator's Council sets policy and quality of service guidelines for the operators.

Exhibit 12 shows how the information is organized in the registry.

The UDDI specification does not dictate registry implementation details. It defines an XML-based data model and a set of SOAP APIs to access and manipulate that data model. A UDDI implementation could be built on an LDAP directory as long as it conforms to the specified behavior. Thus far, all UDDI implementations have been built on relational databases.

Businesses that offer ebXML or e-Speak business services will want to register their businesses and their services in the UDDI Business Registry. The UDDI business services, service types, and specification pointers could point to the ebXML Registry and Repository or E-Services Village for business and technical descriptions of the services.

Businesses that register their schemas and style sheets in BizTalk.org or xml.org will want to register these business formats as service types in the UDDI Business Registry. The UDDI tModel specification pointers could point to these schemas and style sheets in BizTalk.org or xml.org.

Exhibit 12. Organization of UDDI Information

Business Entity	A business entity represents information about a business. Each business entity contains a unique identifier, the business name, a short description of the business, some basic contact information, a list of categories and identifiers that describe the business, and a URL pointing to more information about the business.
Business Service	Associated with the business entity is a list of business services offered by the business entity. Each business service entry contains a business description of the service, a list of categories that describe the service, and a list of pointers to references and information related to the service.
Specification Pointers	Associated with each business service entry is a list of binding templates that point to specifications and other technical information about the service. For example, a binding template might point to a URL that supplies information on how to invoke the service. The specification pointers also associate the service with a service type.
Service Types	Multiple businesses can offer the same type of service, such as the name of the organization that published the tModel, a list of categories that describe the service type, and pointers to technical specifications for the service type such as interface definitions, message formats, message protocols, and security protocols.

The UDDI Business Registry will help businesses in different marketplaces determine which potential trading partners use the same technology they do, and it will encourage the creation of new Web services to translate from one technology to another. This will help unify businesses and marketplaces through the use of a common set of specifications for description and integration.

RosettaNet defines standard set of protocols and message formats for supply chain integration, called Partner Interface Processes (PIPs). The RosettaNet PIPs have been registered as service types in UDDI, and businesses can associate their services with these RosettaNet service types. Users can search the UDDI registry for businesses that support these PIPs. Other industry organizations can also register their service types in UDDI.

One can start registering at www.uddi.org where it provides links that take one to the registration forms at the various distributed UDDI Business Registry nodes. One should register at only one of the operator nodes (IBM or Microsoft currently, or Hewlett Packard at a future date). One's data will be automatically replicated to the other nodes. Once one registers with an operator, that operator node will be the custodian of the registration. One must use this same operator node to make changes to a registration.

If the marketplace provides a way of accepting electronic orders and other business documents, then one will need to work with that marketplace provider to correctly describe one's services. The specific marketplace with which one currently participates may programmatically register one's organization with UDDI.

UDDI Registrars and Services

Peregrine Systems has integrated UDDI into its Get2Connect.net Web site and serves as a UDDI registrar, enabling its users to register and update their businesses and services in the UDDI Registry. Peregrine also allows its users to search UDDI directly from its Web site. RealNames will act as a registrar, providing single-click UDDI registration when customers are establishing a RealNames Keyword.

The ResolveNet Global Business Registry (GBR) has integrated its business registry with UDDI. This gives those registering for the GBR the option of simultaneously publishing their profiles to UDDI. Riskebiz Internet Services Inc. has established an E-marketplace UDDI for the insurance industry. As a registrar, Riskebiz will provide an environment for finding insurance-related Web services.

RealNames and Microsoft have enabled UDDI search directly from the address bar of the Internet Explorer browser utilizing RealNames Keywords, making Internet Explorer the first major discovery and distribution channel for UDDI data available from every desktop. RealNames will also register their Keywords customers into the UDDI Business Registry with a single click, making RealNames a registrar for UDDI.

Web Services Brokerage

Salcentral.com and Xmethods are among the two leading Web services brokerage firms providing their own centralized Web services network. Salcentral.com sees its network as a benefit to UDDI and will be able (as of August 2001) to search the UDDI project for Web services. Such a centralized brokerage aims to help customers find Web services and assist Web service providers in advertising their functionality.

Salcentral.com provides five benefits to Web service users: find Web services, buy access to Web services, watch Web services, get Web service support, and use the specialized searching facility. The Web service providers would benefit from promoting, selling, testing, and supporting Web services and using the searching facility.

Salcentral.com currently gives a short tutorial on how to create a Web service with Visual Basic (Version 5 and 6). At a future date, it will provide tutorials on using other languages to create Web services. Another service that this brokerage offers includes various utilities that convert schemas to the WDSL format.

The RDF Site Summary (RSS) format news feed standard is used to publicize a Web services list that changes on a daily basis. RSS is a file format that uses XML and is defined as a lightweight multi-purpose extensible metadata description and syndication format. One can create it by hand or with any Web content management system.

To better understand how RSS works, take a look at its background. In March 1999, Netscape introduced the RDF Site Summary (RSS) 0.9 format as a way of syndicating Netcenter channels. Since then, many Web sites have adopted the format for everything from syndicating news feeds to threaded messages. Along the way, RSS 0.91 moved away from RDF in favor of a Data Type Definition (DTD) that is used to describe the format of an XML document. Netscape called it the Rich Site Summary.

In time, RSS evolved to meet the demands of users who wanted Weblogs, message boards, catalogs, event feeds, and data exchange. Users began to extend RSS by adding their own tags in the RSS files and some editors began inserting non-RSS elements and tags such as HTML. This caused problems when exchanging these files with the public.

The RSS 1.0 proposal reintroduced the use of RDF (visit http://purl.org/rss/1.0/for full specification). It was developed to meet the growing requirements for flexible extensibility that maintain its ability to be shared with third parties.

Now, let us continue the discussion of the Web services brokerage. Here is a business architecture of support and sales services that SalCentral recommends. The architecture shows that there are 11 parts of the development process of a Web service grouped under four categories: Creation, Publication, Promotion, and Selling. Obviously, the Creation category involves four key players — the designer, the developer, the distributor, and a third-party company to test the service's interoperability. Good technical documentation about a Web service is required of these four categories.

To publish the Web service, the developer's source codes and scripts need to be kept in a secure storage area and version control must be in place to track changes to the codes. An organization must be specified to host the compiled Web service and to set up a data warehouse for the data used by the Web service.

Promotion in the business architecture is another way of saying Web service discovery. It provides a means to locate (or discover) a Web service by browsing or using a specialized Web service directory. Promotion also provides value-added services for customers and accreditation to be given to Web services hosting and development organizations.

The Selling category focuses on Web service auditor and accounts. The auditor part refers to the:

- Organizations that review and check the Web services their customers are using
- Customers who check that the Web service complies with the service level agreement (SLA)

Xmethods currently offers a directory of publicly available web services, hosting and deployment facilities for service developers, SOAP interoperability Testbed, and forums for discussing Web services. Some examples of Web services in its registry include text-to speech (TTS), e-mail, EDGAR search, currency exchange rate, and a mechanism that allows a customer system to check real-time inventory levels. Xmethods offers a built-in UDDI interface using GLUE and provides links to IBM UDDI, MS UDDI, Sun UDDI, and Java-based (jUDDI).

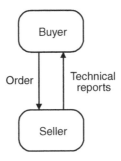

Exhibit 13.   Simple Workflow

Bowstreet developed jUDDI as one of the industry's first implementations of UDDI. The implementation came less than four weeks after Ariba, IBM, and Microsoft unveiled a draft specification of the standard. Bowstreet introduced jUDDI as free, open-source Java-based software that has been architected to allow it to act as the UDDI front end on top of existing directories and databases. jUDDI-enabled applications can look up services in the UDDI registry and then proceed to "call" those Web services directly.

Bowstreet incorporates jUDDI technology into its products, including the Bowstreet Business Web Factory. Customers can point-and-click to search, select, and acquire Web services from the UDDI registry with the jUDDI-enabled Bowstreet Business Web Factory. They can then combine these Web services, incorporate them with Web services within companies and in other directories across the Web, and customize and proliferate the results.

Workflow Processes

A Web service that serves as an activity in one workflow can consist of a series of sequenced activities or a workflow. One can compose a Web service from a workflow.

Start with a simple Web service workflow: a publisher service and an author service (see Exhibit 13), the seller service whose interface is defined using WSDL. The buyer service is invoking the technical report order on the seller service using SOAP and WSDL. It knows what the SOAP reply message looks like as defined in the WSDL language.

As shown in Exhibit 14, the seller service is a workflow encapsulated as a single Web service. The seller service consists of a credit validation activity, document listing activity, and buyer accounting service. The system uses WSDL to interface the seller service with the buyer interface. The seller service does not expose the details of these services to public applications and services that seek to use the seller service.

Now one can expand the workflow to include several activity steps for the Document Listing Web Service (see Exhibit 15). The Credit Validation Service hidden from public view uses a Pubic Credit Service over the Internet from a UDDI registry.

Now assume that the Buyer Accounting Service is an encapsulated EJB and replace the activities in the Document Listing Service as EJBs (see

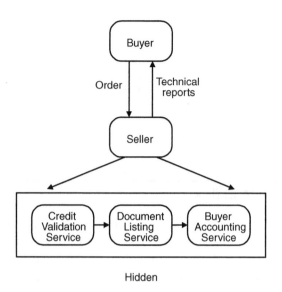

Hidden

Exhibit 14.   Complex Workflow (Hidden)

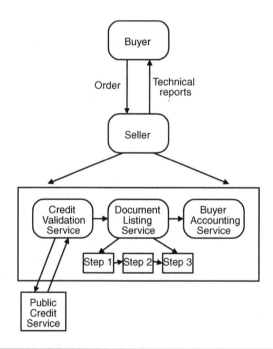

Exhibit 15.   Complex Workflow (Public Credit Service)

Exhibit 16). Also add an encapsulated EJB to serve as a Web service client application between the Credit Validation Service and the Public Credit Service. This workflow also calls out middleware products that currently support or will support WSFL. After the WSFL has been standardized, it is more likely that it will be used more widely as Web services reach full scale by the end of 2002.

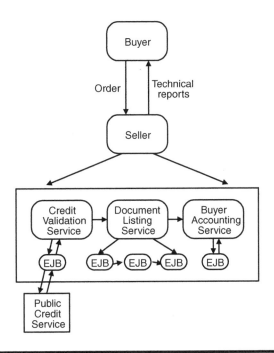

Exhibit 16. EJB-Based Workflows

Versioning of Web Services

As the Web services market matures, large organizations (as well as medium-sized businesses and small shops) will be faced with the enormous task of maintaining different versions of Web services for different customers. Suppose an organization decides to Web service-enable system modules of an enterprise planning resource (ERP) system (sales, human resources, finance, accounting, inventory, customer) as a group of integrated Web services, and defines WSDL interfaces to hook up to the modules of this distributed version. The organization publishes these interfaces in a Web services brokerage firm's[6] private registry or the publicly accessible UDDI registry.

When the organization releases a new version of its product and upgrades it to the current ones, it does not mean all customers will use the latest versions. One or two may wish to stay with the older version. Some may require customizations to the product to suit their special requirements. The organization will find it more difficult to maintain older versions while improving on the latest version of its products and customizing for a few customers.

If the WSDL changes drastically, the organization will need service broker to scan incoming requests and inform the older interface invocations of incompatibility. It can also make use of services provided by Web services brokerages, such as salcentral.com, that provide services of scanning WSDL schemas for changes in their structures. After finding a change, the service e-mails, stating that a change has occurred. Maintaining different versions of Web services at a central place, however, can be a problem when the organization customizes Web services on a global scale.

Third-Party Tools

This section takes a look at the Grand Central, Cape Clear, Silverstream, and IONA Technologies and what tools each offers.

The Grand Central

As the major vendors keep pushing their Web services strategies, third parties continue to emerge and offer complementary technologies. Grand Central, for instance, has launched its Web services Network to enable companies to partner for online business transactions by providing many-to-many and one-to-many use cases.

The Grand Central Network uses a SOAP native interface. Applications that speak native SOAP typically require little or no changes to work with the Grand Central Network. For existing applications that are not SOAP based, Grand Central provides lightweight, standards-based SDKs for Java, Perl, and COM that allow applications to post and receive SOAP messages via the Network. Using emerging standards such as XML, SOAP, UDDI, and WSDL, the Grand Central Network enables companies to connect, integrate, and manage their business processes with those of their partners and customers.

Grand Central's service consists of four layers, as indicated in Exhibit 17. The Grand Central Network leverages Web services standards to provide the foundation that businesses require to enable inter-enterprise collaboration. Web services are a simple, lightweight, and standards-based way to connect applications to one another. They have entered into the third wave of the Internet, allowing companies to connect their systems and business processes with those of their partners and customers. As such, the third wave has evolved from the second wave, whereby the Web sites are connected to people, and, in turn, from the first wave, in which e-mail is used to connect with people.

As a service, the Grand Central Network integrates Web services — far cheaper than the more expensive EAI solutions that require highly skilled support staff. Pricing for the service is subscription based, and developers can take advantage of the company's two-month, no-risk, free trial.

The Grand Central's Web Services Network complements the Web services strategies outlined by IBM, BEA, and Sun with a suite of services that provide the capabilities necessary for inter-enterprise collaboration — reliable messaging between Web services, the ability to manage and provision Web services interfaces, and the tools to organize logical chains of Web services into business processes. Other partners include Verisign, Salesforce.com, Tarrific, and Blue Matrix.

Cape Clear

Cape Clear Software offers CapeConnect with the iPlanet Application Server, among others. In addition, CapeConnect now includes fine-tuned support for the recently announced CapeStudio, which is a rapid application development

Exhibit 17. Grand Central Service Layers

Secure, reliable messaging	This feature includes guaranteed delivery, even if the receiving is temporarily down or unavailable, allowing both senders and receivers of messages to specify their delivery preference. The Grand Central Network acts as a third party in any application-to-application communication, providing non-repudiation and tracking capabilities that allow the delivery status of any message to be confirmed or diagnosed.
Service management	The Grand Central Network allows companies to effectively manage and provision Web services interfaces that are exposed for consumption by partners and customers. Companies can configure levels of service, allowing them to determine which partner or customer can access Web services at certain levels.
Business process orchestration	Enterprises can use the Network to logically chain Web services into inter-enterprise business processes. Grand Central offers "message routers" that allow companies to program the Network with their specific business processes. It provides networking capabilities that allow enterprises to view the status of any business process.
Discovery services	The Central Network offers a directory of Web services and metering service to allow companies to track how their services are used. It provides companies with a gateway to connect with others, including those who run both proprietary and nonproprietary services.

tool for Web services, updated interoperability with other leading SOAP-enabled products, and an enhanced SOAP client builder.

CapeConnect is a complete Web services platform that allows one to automatically expose existing Java, EJB, and CORBA components as Web services without writing code. CapeConnect Web services provide full support for SOAP, WSDL, and UDDI.

Web services created with CapeConnect use SOAP to communicate, are described in WSDL, and can be published to the UDDI repositories. CapeConnect is compatible with leading J2EE application servers, such as WebLogic, WebSphere, and iPlanet. Supported CORBA platforms include Orbix, Visibroker, and WebLogic Enterprise. CapeConnect is also compatible with Microsoft .NET technology.

CapeConnect comes in two versions: CapeConnect One for CORBA and CapeConnet Two for J2EE. Its architecture contains three core components as shown in Exhibit 18.

Silverstream

SilverStream Software offers SilverStream Application Server 3.7.3 with full Web services capabilities, including support for XML, SOAP, WSDL, and UDDI.

Exhibit 18.   CapeConnect Architecture

CapeConnect gateway	A servlet that runs on the servlet engine of the Web server. It acts as a communication bridge between remote clients and the CapeConnect XML engine.
CapeConnect XML engine	Converts SOAP messages from the gateway to EJB calls on back-end components. It then converts the results of these EJB calls to XML documents and returns these documents to the gateway.
CapeConnect J2EE (EJB container)	Represents a single standard for implementing and deploying Web-enabled applications that include enterprise beans, servlets, and JavaServer Pages (JSP). Using J2EE, these technologies can work together to provide a complete solution. The CapeConnect J2EE engine employs these technologies to enable developers to quickly create and deploy multi-tier solutions. It is possible to use other third-party J2EE products, such as BEA WebLogic, IBM WebSphere, and Sun Microsystems iPlanet.

In addition to providing a J2EE-certified platform for building and deploying enterprise-class Web applications, the SilverStream Application Server features the SilverStream eXtend Workbench to streamline J2EE and Web services-based application development.

The Silverstream eXtend Workbench includes jBroker Web, a Web services engine that assists developers in building and deploying Web services using Java. Like other SilverStream products, it supports J2EE application servers beyond the company's own server, including IBM WebSphere, BEA WebLogic, and Oracle9*i* AS.

IONA Technologies

IONA XMLBus is an enabling technology for the IONA e-Business Platform for Total Business Integration. Used in conjunction with IONA's EAI and business-to-business integration (B2Bi) technologies, IONA XMLBus contributes to IONA's support for end-to-end E-business integration. For example, coupled with IONA Enterprise Integrator, IONA XMLBus provides a platform for building service-oriented architectures. When coupled with IONA B2B Integrator, IONA XMLBus provides a platform for business process collaboration among trading partners.

Using IONA XMLBus technology, Web services created in .NET can be utilized in J2EE environments. This allows developers to build Web services from J2EE applications running on the IONA iPortal, BEA WebLogic, or IBM WebSphere application servers. Sun's Java Management Extensions (JMX) instrumentation ensures that customers can administer and manage Web services in the same way that they manage their existing systems.

The XMLBus technology provides support for SwA, allowing the development of Web services based on document passing style. Multi-part MIME attachments within a SOAP message can transmit XML documents, images, arbitrary binary data, and encrypted messages across the wire. This implementation demonstrates IONA's commitment to ebXML.

XMLBus provides tools and a runtime environment to turn existing Java and J2EE applications into Web services without having to write code. Java classes and EJBs can be exposed as standard Web services. IONA XMLBus generates Java code for the appropriate Web server container, and enlists the Web service to the specified UDDI registry.

This technology provides a portable Web services container that can be installed on top of an existing J2EE environment or run as a stand-alone application. Web services are deployed into the container with automatic connection to back-end resources, via dispatchers. The container is available on most application server platforms or as an XMLBus stand-alone.

Dispatchers are provided for Java classes and Enterprise JavaBeans (EJBs). No programming is required to bind new Web services to preexisting application functionality supported by these dispatchers. Future dispatchers will include support for IONA Enterprise Integrator, IONA B2B Integrator, CORBA 2.3, JMS, and MQSeries.

Web services include gateways into back-end systems. They can be used in banking, insurance, brokerage, telecommunications services, retailing, manufacturing and supply chain management, and many other industries to expose existing systems via either the public Internet or private intranets and extranets within service-oriented architectures.

The following are Web service examples to demonstrate various features of XMLBus and Web services.

1. Interoperability Test Web Service
2. 1999 WSDL Interoperability Test Web Service
3. Length Conversion Web Service
4. Broker and Supplier Web Service
5. SOAP with Attachments Web Service
6. Postage Rate Calculator Web Service
7. Knowledge Base Web Service
8. Finance Web Service
9. Electricity Web Service

The WSDL examples shown here include Interoperability Test Web Service, Broker and Supplier Web Service, Postage Rate Calculator Web Service, Finance Web Service, and Electricity Web Service. All XML documents have a .wsdl file extension.

Interoperability Test Web Service Description

To concretely measure the ability of a SOAP implementation to work with other SOAP implementations, a set of tests has been devised by the SOAP developers' community to validate the interoperability of each SOAP platform. These tests are encapsulated by the Interoperability Test Web Service. Clients generated from this Web service can be used to test the interoperability of other SOAP implementations. Likewise, clients based on other toolkits can be used to test the interoperability of IONA's XMLBus.

Appendix A includes a client built with Microsoft's SOAP toolkit and a client built with Microsoft's .NET platform. These clients can be used to talk to Interoperability Test Web Service.

To test this service using other vendor's SOAP implementations, or to test the XMLBus interoperability client against other servers, visit http://www.xmethods.com/ilab.

Broker and Supplier Web Service Description

There are two primary supplier Web services representing online bookstores called "Anaconda" (see Appendix B) and "FarmsAndRegal" (see Appendix C). The "Broker" Web service (Appendix D) acts as a middleman. End customers send purchase orders to the broker, the broker forwards them to each of the suppliers, and then the broker returns a composite quote with the best prices from each supplier. In addition to the Java clients, Appendices B through D include a Microsoft .NET client to demonstrate the interoperability of XMLBus with .NET.

Postal Rate Calculator Web Service Description

Appendix E consists of a domestic postage rate calculator. This service takes in a query string as an argument and returns a quote for that query. The user enters all the necessary information about a package to be sent via the United States Postal Service (USPS). This information is sent to the USPS server as a query and the results are returned to the user and displayed.

Finance Web Service Description

Appendix F provides financial computations related to interest, APR, future value, tax rates, and mortgages. One can also use this service to compare the compound interest accumulated with a rule-of-72 estimate to that of the exact compound interest calculated.

Electricity Web Service Description

Appendix G computes Watt, volt, and ampere relationships. Using this service, one can also calculate the correct cable size for household appliances.

Notes

1. *Stateless* means there is no record of previous interactions and each interaction request has to be handled based entirely on the information that comes with it. *Stateful* means an entity, such as CORBA, keeps track of the state of interaction. Stateful and stateless are derived from the usage of *state* as a set of conditions at a moment in time.

2. For connectionless communications, the calling program does not enter into a connection with the target process. The receiving application acts on the request and responds if required. In contrast, connection-oriented communications involve the two parties who first connect, exchange messages, and then disconnect.

3. MQ Series Workflow, a middleware product from IBM, supports the WSFL. It defines workflows composed of Web services.

4. WSCL has been recently submitted to W3C (Summer 2001).

5. Among the first technology leaders to endorse and collaborate on the UDDI Project, a cross-industry initiative designed to accelerate and broaden business-to-business integration and commerce on the Internet, are American Express Co., Andersen Consulting, Ariba Inc., Bowstreet, Cargill Inc., Clarus Corp., Commerce One Inc., CommerceQuest Inc., Compaq Computer Corp., CrossWorlds Software Inc., Dell Computer Corp., Descartes, Extricity Software Inc., Fujitsu Ltd., Great Plains, i2, IBM Corp., Internet Capital Group, Loudcloud Inc., match21, Merrill Lynch & Co. Inc., Microsoft Corp., NEON, Nortel Networks Corp., NTT Communications Corp., Rational Software Corp., RealNames Corp., Sabre Holdings Corp., SAP AG, Sun Microsystems Inc., TIBCO Software Inc., Ventro Corp., Versata Inc., VeriSign, VerticalNet Inc., and webMethods Inc.

6. Examples include www.salcentral.com and www.xmethods.net.

Appendix A: Interoperability Test WDSL Example

```
<?xml version="1.0" encoding="UTF-8" ?>
- <definitions name="InteropTestService"
    targetNamespace="http://soapinterop.org/"
    xmlns="http://schemas.xmlsoap.org/wsdl/"
    xmlns:SOAP-ENC="http://schemas.xmlsoap.org/soap/encoding/"
    xmlns:soap="http://schemas.xmlsoap.org/wsdl/soap/"
    xmlns:tns="http://soapinterop.org/"
    xmlns:xsd="http://www.w3.org/2001/XMLSchema"
    xmlns:xsd1="http://soapinterop.org/xsd"
    xmlns:xsi="http://www.w3.org/2001/XMLSchema-instance">
  - <types>
    - <schema targetNamespace="http://soapinterop.org/xsd"
        xmlns="http://www.w3.org/2001/XMLSchema"
        xmlns:wsdl="http://schemas.xmlsoap.org/wsdl/">
      - <complexType name="SOAPStruct">
        - <all>
            <element name="varFloat" type="xsd:float" />
            <element name="varInt" type="xsd:int" />
            <element name="varString" type="xsd:string" />
          </all>
        </complexType>
      - <complexType name="ArrayOffloat">
        - <complexContent>
          - <restriction base="SOAP-ENC:Array">
              <attribute ref="SOAP-ENC:arrayType" wsdl:arrayType="xsd:float[]" />
            </restriction>
          </complexContent>
        </complexType>
      - <complexType name="ArrayOfstring">
        - <complexContent>
          - <restriction base="SOAP-ENC:Array">
              <attribute ref="SOAP-ENC:arrayType" wsdl:arrayType="xsd:string[]" />
            </restriction>
          </complexContent>
        </complexType>
      - <complexType name="ArrayOfint">
        - <complexContent>
          - <restriction base="SOAP-ENC:Array">
              <attribute ref="SOAP-ENC:arrayType" wsdl:arrayType="xsd:int[]" />
            </restriction>
          </complexContent>
        </complexType>
      - <complexType name="ArrayOfSOAPStruct">
        - <complexContent>
          - <restriction base="SOAP-ENC:Array">
              <attribute ref="SOAP-ENC:arrayType"
              wsdl:arrayType="xsd1:SOAPStruct[]" />
            </restriction>
          </complexContent>
        </complexType>
      </schema>
    </types>
  - <message name="echoStructRequest">
      <part name="inputStruct" type="xsd1:SOAPStruct" />
    </message>
  - <message name="echoStructResult">
      <part name="return" type="xsd1:SOAPStruct" />
    </message>
  - <message name="echoBooleanRequest">
      <part name="inputBoolean" type="xsd:boolean" />
    </message>
  - <message name="echoBooleanResult">
      <part name="return" type="xsd:boolean" />
    </message>
  - <message name="echoDateRequest">
      <part name="inputDate" type="xsd:dateTime" />
    </message>
  - <message name="echoDateResult">
      <part name="return" type="xsd:dateTime" />
    </message>
  - <message name="echoFloatArrayRequest">
      <part name="inputArray" type="xsd1:ArrayOffloat" />
```

```
    </message>
  - <message name="echoFloatArrayResult">
      <part name="return" type="xsd1:ArrayOffloat" />
    </message>
  - <message name="echoFloatRequest">
      <part name="inputFloat" type="xsd:float" />
    </message>
  - <message name="echoFloatResult">
      <part name="return" type="xsd:float" />
    </message>
  - <message name="echoStringArrayRequest">
      <part name="inputArray" type="xsd1:ArrayOfstring" />
    </message>
  - <message name="echoStringArrayResult">
      <part name="return" type="xsd1:ArrayOfstring" />
    </message>
  - <message name="echoIntegerArrayRequest">
      <part name="inputArray" type="xsd1:ArrayOfint" />
    </message>
  - <message name="echoIntegerArrayResult">
      <part name="return" type="xsd1:ArrayOfint" />
    </message>
  - <message name="echoStructArrayRequest">
      <part name="inputArray" type="xsd1:ArrayOfSOAPStruct" />
    </message>
  - <message name="echoStructArrayResult">
      <part name="return" type="xsd1:ArrayOfSOAPStruct" />
    </message>
  - <message name="echoDecimalRequest">
      <part name="inputDecimal" type="xsd:decimal" />
    </message>
  - <message name="echoDecimalResult">
      <part name="return" type="xsd:decimal" />
    </message>
    <message name="echoVoidRequest" />
    <message name="echoVoidResult" />
  - <message name="echoStringRequest">
    <part name="inputString" type="xsd:string" />
    </message>
  - <message name="echoStringResult">
      <part name="return" type="xsd:string" />
    </message>
  - <message name="echoIntegerRequest">
      <part name="inputInteger" type="xsd:int" />
    </message>
  - <message name="echoIntegerResult">
      <part name="return" type="xsd:int" />
    </message>
  - <message name="echoBase64Request">
      <part name="inputData" type="xsd:base64Binary" />
    </message>
  - <message name="echoBase64Result">
      <part name="return" type="xsd:base64Binary" />
    </message>
  - <portType name="InteropTestPortType">
    - <operation name="echoStruct">
        <input message="tns:echoStructRequest" name="echoStruct" />
        <output message="tns:echoStructResult" name="echoStructResult" />
      </operation>
    - <operation name="echoBoolean">
        <input message="tns:echoBooleanRequest" name="echoBoolean" />
        <output message="tns:echoBooleanResult" name="echoBooleanResult" />
      </operation>
    - <operation name="echoDate">
        <input message="tns:echoDateRequest" name="echoDate" />
        <output message="tns:echoDateResult" name="echoDateResult" />
      </operation>
    - <operation name="echoFloatArray">
        <input message="tns:echoFloatArrayRequest" name="echoFloatArray" />
        <output message="tns:echoFloatArrayResult" name="echoFloatArrayResult" />
      </operation>
    - <operation name="echoFloat">
        <input message="tns:echoFloatRequest" name="echoFloat" />
        <output message="tns:echoFloatResult" name="echoFloatResult" />
      </operation>
```

```
-   <operation name="echoStringArray">
      <input message="tns:echoStringArrayRequest" name="echoStringArray" />
      <output message="tns:echoStringArrayResult" name="echoStringArrayResult" />
    </operation>
-   <operation name="echoIntegerArray">
      <input message="tns:echoIntegerArrayRequest" name="echoIntegerArray" />
      <output message="tns:echoIntegerArrayResult" name="echoIntegerArrayResult" />
    </operation>
-   <operation name="echoStructArray">
      <input message="tns:echoStructArrayRequest" name="echoStructArray" />
      <output message="tns:echoStructArrayResult" name="echoStructArrayResult" />
    </operation>
-   <operation name="echoDecimal">
      <input message="tns:echoDecimalRequest" name="echoDecimal" />
      <output message="tns:echoDecimalResult" name="echoDecimalResult" />
    </operation>
-   <operation name="echoVoid">
      <input message="tns:echoVoidRequest" name="echoVoid" />
      <output message="tns:echoVoidResult" name="echoVoidResult" />
    </operation>
-   <operation name="echoString">
      <input message="tns:echoStringRequest" name="echoString" />
      <output message="tns:echoStringResult" name="echoStringResult" />
    </operation>
-   <operation name="echoInteger">
      <input message="tns:echoIntegerRequest" name="echoInteger" />
      <output message="tns:echoIntegerResult" name="echoIntegerResult" />
    </operation>
-   <operation name="echoBase64">
      <input message="tns:echoBase64Request" name="echoBase64" />
      <output message="tns:echoBase64Result" name="echoBase64Result" />
    </operation>
  </portType>
- <binding name="InteropTestBinding" type="tns:InteropTestPortType">
    <soap:binding style="rpc" transport="http://schemas.xmlsoap.org/soap/http" />
-   <operation name="echoStruct">
      <soap:operation soapAction="urn:soapinterop" style="rpc" />
    - <input name="echoStruct">
        <soap:body encodingStyle="http://schemas.xmlsoap.org/soap/encoding/"
          namespace="http://soapinterop.org/" use="encoded" />
      </input>
    - <output name="echoStructResult">
        <soap:body encodingStyle="http://schemas.xmlsoap.org/soap/encoding/"
          namespace="http://soapinterop.org/" use="encoded" />
      </output>
    </operation>
-   <operation name="echoBoolean">
      <soap:operation soapAction="urn:soapinterop" style="rpc" />
    - <input name="echoBoolean">
        <soap:body encodingStyle="http://schemas.xmlsoap.org/soap/encoding/"
          namespace="http://soapinterop.org/" use="encoded" />
      </input>
    - <output name="echoBooleanResult">
        <soap:body encodingStyle="http://schemas.xmlsoap.org/soap/encoding/"
          namespace="http://soapinterop.org/" use="encoded" />
      </output>
    </operation>
-   <operation name="echoDate">
      <soap:operation soapAction="urn:soapinterop" style="rpc" />
    - <input name="echoDate">
        <soap:body encodingStyle="http://schemas.xmlsoap.org/soap/encoding/"
          namespace="http://soapinterop.org/" use="encoded" />
      </input>
    - <output name="echoDateResult">
        <soap:body encodingStyle="http://schemas.xmlsoap.org/soap/encoding/"
          namespace="http://soapinterop.org/" use="encoded" />
      </output>
    </operation>
-   <operation name="echoFloatArray">
      <soap:operation soapAction="urn:soapinterop" style="rpc" />
    - <input name="echoFloatArray">
        <soap:body encodingStyle="http://schemas.xmlsoap.org/soap/encoding/"
          namespace="http://soapinterop.org/" use="encoded" />
      </input>
    - <output name="echoFloatArrayResult">
```

```
          <soap:body encodingStyle="http://schemas.xmlsoap.org/soap/encoding/"
            namespace="http://soapinterop.org/" use="encoded" />
        </output>
      </operation>
  -   <operation name="echoFloat">
        <soap:operation soapAction="urn:soapinterop" style="rpc" />
    -   <input name="echoFloat">
          <soap:body encodingStyle="http://schemas.xmlsoap.org/soap/encoding/"
            namespace="http://soapinterop.org/" use="encoded" />
        </input>
    -   <output name="echoFloatResult">
          <soap:body encodingStyle="http://schemas.xmlsoap.org/soap/encoding/"
            namespace="http://soapinterop.org/" use="encoded" />
        </output>
      </operation>
  -   <operation name="echoStringArray">
        <soap:operation soapAction="urn:soapinterop" style="rpc" />
    -   <input name="echoStringArray">
          <soap:body encodingStyle="http://schemas.xmlsoap.org/soap/encoding/"
            namespace="http://soapinterop.org/" use="encoded" />
        </input>
    -   <output name="echoStringArrayResult">
          <soap:body encodingStyle="http://schemas.xmlsoap.org/soap/encoding/"
            namespace="http://soapinterop.org/" use="encoded" />
        </output>
      </operation>
  -   <operation name="echoIntegerArray">
        <soap:operation soapAction="urn:soapinterop" style="rpc" />
    -   <input name="echoIntegerArray">
          <soap:body encodingStyle="http://schemas.xmlsoap.org/soap/encoding/"
            namespace="http://soapinterop.org/" use="encoded" />
        </input>
    -   <output name="echoIntegerArrayResult">
          <soap:body encodingStyle="http://schemas.xmlsoap.org/soap/encoding/"
            namespace="http://soapinterop.org/" use="encoded" />
        </output>
      </operation>
  -   <operation name="echoStructArray">
        <soap:operation soapAction="urn:soapinterop" style="rpc" />
    -   <input name="echoStructArray">
          <soap:body encodingStyle="http://schemas.xmlsoap.org/soap/encoding/"
            namespace="http://soapinterop.org/" use="encoded" />
        </input>
    -   <output name="echoStructArrayResult">
          <soap:body encodingStyle="http://schemas.xmlsoap.org/soap/encoding/"
            namespace="http://soapinterop.org/" use="encoded" />
        </output>
      </operation>
  -   <operation name="echoDecimal">
        <soap:operation soapAction="urn:soapinterop" style="rpc" />
    -   <input name="echoDecimal">
          <soap:body encodingStyle="http://schemas.xmlsoap.org/soap/encoding/"
            namespace="http://soapinterop.org/" use="encoded" />
        </input>
    -   <output name="echoDecimalResult">
          <soap:body encodingStyle="http://schemas.xmlsoap.org/soap/encoding/"
            namespace="http://soapinterop.org/" use="encoded" />
        </output>
      </operation>
  -   <operation name="echoVoid">
        <soap:operation soapAction="urn:soapinterop" style="rpc" />
    -   <input name="echoVoid">
          <soap:body encodingStyle="http://schemas.xmlsoap.org/soap/encoding/"
            namespace="http://soapinterop.org/" use="encoded" />
        </input>
    -   <output name="echoVoidResult">
          <soap:body encodingStyle="http://schemas.xmlsoap.org/soap/encoding/"
            namespace="http://soapinterop.org/" use="encoded" />
        </output>
      </operation>
  -   <operation name="echoString">
        <soap:operation soapAction="urn:soapinterop" style="rpc" />
    -   <input name="echoString">
          <soap:body encodingStyle="http://schemas.xmlsoap.org/soap/encoding/"
            namespace="http://soapinterop.org/" use="encoded" />
```

```
      </input>
    - <output name="echoStringResult">
        <soap:body encodingStyle="http://schemas.xmlsoap.org/soap/encoding/"
          namespace="http://soapinterop.org/" use="encoded" />
      </output>
    </operation>
  - <operation name="echoInteger">
      <soap:operation soapAction="urn:soapinterop" style="rpc" />
    - <input name="echoInteger">
        <soap:body encodingStyle="http://schemas.xmlsoap.org/soap/encoding/"
          namespace="http://soapinterop.org/" use="encoded" />
      </input>
    - <output name="echoIntegerResult">
        <soap:body encodingStyle="http://schemas.xmlsoap.org/soap/encoding/"
          namespace="http://soapinterop.org/" use="encoded" />
      </output>
    </operation>
  - <operation name="echoBase64">
      <soap:operation soapAction="urn:soapinterop" style="rpc" />
    - <input name="echoBase64">
        <soap:body encodingStyle="http://schemas.xmlsoap.org/soap/encoding/"
          namespace="http://soapinterop.org/" use="encoded" />
      </input>
    - <output name="echoBase64Result">
        <soap:body encodingStyle="http://schemas.xmlsoap.org/soap/encoding/"
          namespace="http://soapinterop.org/" use="encoded" />
      </output>
    </operation>
  </binding>
- <service name="InteropTestService">
  - <port binding="tns:InteropTestBinding" name="InteropTestPort">
      <soap:address location="http://www.xmlbus.com:9010/xmlbus/container/
        InteropTest/InteropTestService/InteropTestPort/" />
    </port>
  </service>
</definitions>
```

Appendix B: Broker and Supplier Web Service: Anaconda WSDL Example

```
<?xml version="1.0" encoding="UTF-8" ?>
- <definitions name="AnacondaService"
    targetNamespace="urn:target-anaconda-service"
    xmlns="http://schemas.xmlsoap.org/wsdl/"
    xmlns:SOAP-ENC="http://schemas.xmlsoap.org/soap/encoding/"
    xmlns:soap="http://schemas.xmlsoap.org/wsdl/soap/"
    xmlns:tns="urn:target-anaconda-service"
    xmlns:xsd="http://www.w3.org/2001/XMLSchema"
    xmlns:xsd1="uri:Anacondadata-namespace"
    xmlns:xsi="http://www.w3.org/2001/XMLSchema-instance">
  - <types>
    - <schema targetNamespace="uri:Anacondadata-namespace"
        xmlns="http://www.w3.org/2001/XMLSchema"
        xmlns:wsdl="http://schemas.xmlsoap.org/wsdl/">
      - <complexType name="com_iona_xmlbus_examples_brokerDemo_brokerIntf_
          PurchaseOrder">
        - <all>
            <element name="CustomerName" type="xsd:string" />
            <element name="TotalPrice" type="xsd:float" />
            <element name="LineItems"type="xsd1:ArrayOfcom_iona_xmlbus_examples_
              brokerDemo_brokerIntf_LineItem" />
          </all>
        </complexType>
      - <complexType name="com_iona_xmlbus_examples_brokerDemo_brokerIntf_LineItem">
        - <all>
            <element name="SupplierName" type="xsd:string" />
            <element name="UnitPrice" type="xsd:float" />
            <element name="TotalPrice" type="xsd:float" />
            <element name="Quantity" type="xsd:float" />
            <element name="ProductName" type="xsd:string" />
```

```
      </all>
    </complexType>
  - <complexType name="ArrayOfcom_iona_xmlbus_examples_brokerDemo_brokerIntf_
    LineItem">
    - <complexContent>
      - <restriction base="SOAP-ENC:Array">
          <attribute ref="SOAP-ENC:arrayType" wsdl:arrayType="xsd1:com_iona_
            xmlbus_examples_brokerDemo_brokerIntf_LineItem[]" />
        </restriction>
      </complexContent>
    </complexType>
  - <complexType name="ArrayOfstring">
    - <complexContent>
      - <restriction base="SOAP-ENC:Array">
          <attribute ref="SOAP-ENC:arrayType" wsdl:arrayType="xsd:string[]" />
        </restriction>
      </complexContent>
    </complexType>
  </schema>
</types>
- <message name="requestQuoteRequest">
    <part name="requestForQuote"
      type="xsd1:com_iona_xmlbus_examples_brokerDemo_brokerIntf_PurchaseOrder" />
  </message>
- <message name="requestQuoteResult">
    <part name="return"
      type="xsd1:com_iona_xmlbus_examples_brokerDemo_brokerIntf_PurchaseOrder" />
  </message>
  <message name="getCatalogRequest" />
- <message name="getCatalogResult">
    <part name="return" type="xsd1:ArrayOfstring" />
  </message>
  <message name="getSupplierNameRequest" />
- <message name="getSupplierNameResult">
    <part name="return" type="xsd:string" />
  </message>
- <portType name="AnacondaPortType">
  - <operation name="requestQuote">
      <input message="tns:requestQuoteRequest" name="requestQuote" />
      <output message="tns:requestQuoteResult" name="requestQuoteResult" />
    </operation>
  - <operation name="getCatalog">
      <input message="tns:getCatalogRequest" name="getCatalog" />
      <output message="tns:getCatalogResult" name="getCatalogResult" />
    </operation>
  - <operation name="getSupplierName">
      <input message="tns:getSupplierNameRequest" name="getSupplierName" />
      <output message="tns:getSupplierNameResult" name="getSupplierNameResult" />
    </operation>
  </portType>
- <binding name="AnacondaBinding" type="tns:AnacondaPortType">
    <soap:binding style="rpc" transport="http://schemas.xmlsoap.org/soap/http" />
  - <operation name="requestQuote">
      <soap:operation soapAction="urn:target-anaconda-service/requestQuote"
        style="rpc" />
    - <input name="requestQuote">
        <soap:body encodingStyle="http://schemas.xmlsoap.org/soap/encoding/"
          namespace="urn:target-anaconda-service" use="encoded" />
      </input>
    - <output name="requestQuoteResult">
        <soap:body encodingStyle="http://schemas.xmlsoap.org/soap/encoding/"
          namespace="urn:target-anaconda-service" use="encoded" />
      </output>
    </operation>
  - <operation name="getCatalog">
      <soap:operation soapAction="urn:target-anaconda-service/getCatalog"
        style="rpc"
        />
    - <input name="getCatalog">
        <soap:body encodingStyle="http://schemas.xmlsoap.org/soap/encoding/"
          namespace="urn:target-anaconda-service" use="encoded" />
      </input>
    - <output name="getCatalogResult">
        <soap:body encodingStyle="http://schemas.xmlsoap.org/soap/encoding/"
```

```
          namespace="urn:target-anaconda-service" use="encoded" />
      </output>
    </operation>
  - <operation name="getSupplierName">
      <soap:operation soapAction="urn:target-anaconda-service/getSupplierName"
        style="rpc" />
    - <input name="getSupplierName">
        <soap:body encodingStyle="http://schemas.xmlsoap.org/soap/encoding/"
          namespace="urn:target-anaconda-service" use="encoded" />
      </input>
    - <output name="getSupplierNameResult">
        <soap:body encodingStyle="http://schemas.xmlsoap.org/soap/encoding/"
          namespace="urn:target-anaconda-service" use="encoded" />
      </output>
    </operation>
  </binding>
- <service name="AnacondaService">
  - <port binding="tns:AnacondaBinding" name="AnacondaPort">
      <soap:address location="http://www.xmlbus.com:9010/xmlbus/container/Anaconda/
        AnacondaService/AnacondaPort/" />
    </port>
  </service>
</definitions>
```

Appendix C: Broker and Supplier Web Service: FarmsandRegal WSDL Example

```
<?xml version="1.0" encoding="UTF-8" ?>
- <definitions name="FarmsAndRegalService"
    targetNamespace="urn:target-farmsandregal-service"
    xmlns="http://schemas.xmlsoap.org/wsdl/"
    xmlns:SOAP-ENC="http://schemas.xmlsoap.org/soap/encoding/"
    xmlns:soap="http://schemas.xmlsoap.org/wsdl/soap/"
    xmlns:tns="urn:target-farmsandregal-service"
    xmlns:xsd="http://www.w3.org/2001/XMLSchema"
    xmlns:xsd1="uri:FarmsAndRegaldata-namespace"
    xmlns:xsi="http://www.w3.org/2001/XMLSchema-instance">
  - <types>
    - <schema targetNamespace="uri:FarmsAndRegaldata-namespace"
        xmlns="http://www.w3.org/2001/XMLSchema"
        xmlns:wsdl="http://schemas.xmlsoap.org/wsdl/">
      - <complexType name="com_iona_xmlbus_examples_brokerDemo_brokerIntf_
          PurchaseOrder">
        - <all>
            <element name="CustomerName" type="xsd:string" />
            <element name="TotalPrice" type="xsd:float" />
            <element name="LineItems"
              type="xsd1:ArrayOfcom_iona_xmlbus_examples_brokerDemo_brokerIntf_
              LineItem" />
          </all>
        </complexType>
      - <complexType name="com_iona_xmlbus_examples_brokerDemo_brokerIntf_LineItem">
        - <all>
            <element name="SupplierName" type="xsd:string" />
            <element name="UnitPrice" type="xsd:float" />
            <element name="TotalPrice" type="xsd:float" />
            <element name="Quantity" type="xsd:float" />
            <element name="ProductName" type="xsd:string" />
          </all>
        </complexType>
      - <complexType name="ArrayOfcom_iona_xmlbus_examples_brokerDemo_brokerIntf_
          LineItem">
        - <complexContent>
          - <restriction base="SOAP-ENC:Array">
              <attribute ref="SOAP-ENC:arrayType"
                wsdl:arrayType="xsd1:com_iona_xmlbus_examples_brokerDemo_brokerIntf_
                LineItem[]" />
            </restriction>
          </complexContent>
        </complexType>
```

```
    - <complexType name="ArrayOfstring">
      - <complexContent>
        - <restriction base="SOAP-ENC:Array">
            <attribute ref="SOAP-ENC:arrayType" wsdl:arrayType="xsd:string[]" />
          </restriction>
        </complexContent>
      </complexType>
    </schema>
  </types>
- <message name="requestQuoteRequest">
    <part name="requestForQuote" type="xsd1:com_iona_xmlbus_examples_brokerDemo_
    brokerIntf_PurchaseOrder" />
  </message>
- <message name="requestQuoteResult">
    <part name="return" type="xsd1:com_iona_xmlbus_examples_brokerDemo_brokerIntf_
    PurchaseOrder" />
  </message>
  <message name="getCatalogRequest" />
- <message name="getCatalogResult">
    <part name="return" type="xsd1:ArrayOfstring" />
  </message>
  <message name="getSupplierNameRequest" />
- <message name="getSupplierNameResult">
    <part name="return" type="xsd:string" />
  </message>
- <portType name="FarmsAndRegalPortType">
  - <operation name="requestQuote">
      <input message="tns:requestQuoteRequest" name="requestQuote" />
      <output message="tns:requestQuoteResult" name="requestQuoteResult" />
    </operation>
  - <operation name="getCatalog">
      <input message="tns:getCatalogRequest" name="getCatalog" />
      <output message="tns:getCatalogResult" name="getCatalogResult" />
    </operation>
  - <operation name="getSupplierName">
      <input message="tns:getSupplierNameRequest" name="getSupplierName" />
      <output message="tns:getSupplierNameResult" name="getSupplierNameResult" />
    </operation>
  </portType>
- <binding name="FarmsAndRegalBinding" type="tns:FarmsAndRegalPortType">
    <soap:binding style="rpc" transport="http://schemas.xmlsoap.org/soap/http" />
  - <operation name="requestQuote">
      <soap:operation soapAction="urn:target-farmsandregal-service/requestQuote"
      style="rpc" />
    - <input name="requestQuote">
        <soap:body encodingStyle="http://schemas.xmlsoap.org/soap/encoding/"
        namespace="urn:target-farmsandregal-service" use="encoded" />
      </input>
    - <output name="requestQuoteResult">
        <soap:body encodingStyle="http://schemas.xmlsoap.org/soap/encoding/"
        namespace="urn:target-farmsandregal-service" use="encoded" />
      </output>
    </operation>
  - <operation name="getCatalog">
      <soap:operation soapAction="urn:target-farmsandregal-service/getCatalog"
      style="rpc" />
    - <input name="getCatalog">
        <soap:body encodingStyle="http://schemas.xmlsoap.org/soap/encoding/"
        namespace="urn:target-farmsandregal-service" use="encoded" />
      </input>
    - <output name="getCatalogResult">
        <soap:body encodingStyle="http://schemas.xmlsoap.org/soap/encoding/"
        namespace="urn:target-farmsandregal-service" use="encoded" />
      </output>
    </operation>
  - <operation name="getSupplierName">
      <soap:operation soapAction="urn:target-farmsandregal-service/getSupplierName"
      style="rpc" />
    - <input name="getSupplierName">
        <soap:body encodingStyle="http://schemas.xmlsoap.org/soap/encoding/"
        namespace="urn:target-farmsandregal-service" use="encoded" />
      </input>
    - <output name="getSupplierNameResult">
        <soap:body encodingStyle="http://schemas.xmlsoap.org/soap/encoding/"
```

```
            namespace="urn:target-farmsandregal-service" use="encoded" />
        </output>
      </operation>
    </binding>
  - <service name="FarmsAndRegalService">
    - <port binding="tns:FarmsAndRegalBinding" name="FarmsAndRegalPort">
        <soap:address location="http://www.xmlbus.com:9010/xmlbus/container/
        FarmsAndRegal/FarmsAndRegalService/FarmsAndRegalPort/" />
      </port>
    </service>
  </definitions>
```

Appendix D: Broker and Supplier Web Services: Broker WSDL Example

```
<?xml version="1.0" encoding="UTF-8" ?>
- <definitions name="AnacondaService"
  targetNamespace="urn:target-anaconda-service"
  xmlns="http://schemas.xmlsoap.org/wsdl/"
  xmlns:SOAP-ENC="http://schemas.xmlsoap.org/soap/encoding/"
  xmlns:soap="http://schemas.xmlsoap.org/wsdl/soap/"
  xmlns:tns="urn:target-anaconda-service"
  xmlns:xsd="http://www.w3.org/2001/XMLSchema"
  xmlns:xsd1="uri:Anacondadata-namespace"
  xmlns:xsi="http://www.w3.org/2001/XMLSchema-instance">
  - <types>
    - <schema targetNamespace="uri:Anacondadata-namespace"
      xmlns="http://www.w3.org/2001/XMLSchema"
      xmlns:wsdl="http://schemas.xmlsoap.org/wsdl/">
      - <complexType name="com_iona_xmlbus_examples_brokerDemo_brokerIntf_
        PurchaseOrder">
        - <all>
          <element name="CustomerName" type="xsd:string" />
          <element name="TotalPrice" type="xsd:float" />
          <element name="LineItems" type="xsd1:ArrayOfcom_iona_xmlbus_examples_
          brokerDemo_brokerIntf_LineItem" />
        </all>
      </complexType>
      - <complexType name="com_iona_xmlbus_examples_brokerDemo_brokerIntf_LineItem">
        - <all>
          <element name="SupplierName" type="xsd:string" />
          <element name="UnitPrice" type="xsd:float" />
          <element name="TotalPrice" type="xsd:float" />
          <element name="Quantity" type="xsd:float" />
          <element name="ProductName" type="xsd:string" />
        </all>
      </complexType>
      - <complexType name="ArrayOfcom_iona_xmlbus_examples_brokerDemo_brokerIntf_
        LineItem">
        - <complexContent>
          - <restriction base="SOAP-ENC:Array">
            <attribute ref="SOAP-ENC:arrayType"
            wsdl:arrayType="xsd1:com_iona_xmlbus_examples_brokerDemo_brokerIntf_
            LineItem[]" />
          </restriction>
        </complexContent>
      </complexType>
      - <complexType name="ArrayOfstring">
        - <complexContent>
          - <restriction base="SOAP-ENC:Array">
            <attribute ref="SOAP-ENC:arrayType" wsdl:arrayType="xsd:string[]" />
          </restriction>
        </complexContent>
      </complexType>
    </schema>
  </types>
  - <message name="requestQuoteRequest">
    <part name="requestForQuote"
    type="xsd1:com_iona_xmlbus_examples_brokerDemo_brokerIntf_PurchaseOrder" />
  </message>
```

```
   -  <message name="requestQuoteResult">
      <part name="return"
        type="xsd1:com_iona_xmlbus_examples_brokerDemo_brokerIntf_PurchaseOrder" />
     </message>
     <message name="getCatalogRequest" />
   -  <message name="getCatalogResult">
       <part name="return" type="xsd1:ArrayOfstring" />
     </message>
     <message name="getSupplierNameRequest" />
   -  <message name="getSupplierNameResult">
       <part name="return" type="xsd:string" />
     </message>
   -  <portType name="AnacondaPortType">
     -  <operation name="requestQuote">
         <input message="tns:requestQuoteRequest" name="requestQuote" />
         <output message="tns:requestQuoteResult" name="requestQuoteResult" />
       </operation>
     -  <operation name="getCatalog">
         <input message="tns:getCatalogRequest" name="getCatalog" />
         <output message="tns:getCatalogResult" name="getCatalogResult" />
       </operation>
     -  <operation name="getSupplierName">
         <input message="tns:getSupplierNameRequest" name="getSupplierName" />
         <output message="tns:getSupplierNameResult" name="getSupplierNameResult" />
       </operation>
     </portType>
   -  <binding name="AnacondaBinding" type="tns:AnacondaPortType">
       <soap:binding style="rpc" transport="http://schemas.xmlsoap.org/soap/http" />
     -  <operation name="requestQuote">
         <soap:operation soapAction="urn:target-anaconda-service/requestQuote"
           style="rpc" />
       -  <input name="requestQuote">
         <soap:body encodingStyle="http://schemas.xmlsoap.org/soap/encoding/"
           namespace="urn:target-anaconda-service" use="encoded" />
         </input>
       -  <output name="requestQuoteResult">
         <soap:body encodingStyle="http://schemas.xmlsoap.org/soap/encoding/"
           namespace="urn:target-anaconda-service" use="encoded" />
         </output>
       </operation>
     -  <operation name="getCatalog">
         <soap:operation soapAction="urn:target-anaconda-service/getCatalog"
           style="rpc" />
       -  <input name="getCatalog">
         <soap:body encodingStyle="http://schemas.xmlsoap.org/soap/encoding/"
           namespace="urn:target-anaconda-service" use="encoded" />
         </input>
       -  <output name="getCatalogResult">
         <soap:body encodingStyle="http://schemas.xmlsoap.org/soap/encoding/"
           namespace="urn:target-anaconda-service" use="encoded" />
         </output>
       </operation>
     -  <operation name="getSupplierName">
         <soap:operation soapAction="urn:target-anaconda-service/getSupplierName"
           style="rpc" />
       -  <input name="getSupplierName">
         <soap:body encodingStyle="http://schemas.xmlsoap.org/soap/encoding/"
           namespace="urn:target-anaconda-service" use="encoded" />
         </input>
       -  <output name="getSupplierNameResult">
         <soap:body encodingStyle="http://schemas.xmlsoap.org/soap/encoding/"
           namespace="urn:target-anaconda-service" use="encoded" />
         </output>
       </operation>
     </binding>
   -  <service name="AnacondaService">
     -  <port binding="tns:AnacondaBinding" name="AnacondaPort">
         <soap:address location="http://www.xmlbus.com:9010/xmlbus/container/Anaconda/
           AnacondaService/AnacondaPort/" />
       </port>
     </service>
   </definitions>
```

Appendix E: Postal Rate Calculator Web Service WSDL Example

```xml
<?xml version="1.0" encoding="UTF-8" ?>
- <definitions name="DomesticCalculatorService"
    targetNamespace="urn:target-domesticcalculator-service"
    xmlns="http://schemas.xmlsoap.org/wsdl/"
    xmlns:SOAP-ENC="http://schemas.xmlsoap.org/soap/encoding/"
    xmlns:soap="http://schemas.xmlsoap.org/wsdl/soap/"
    xmlns:tns="urn:target-domesticcalculator-service"
    xmlns:xsd="http://www.w3.org/2001/XMLSchema"
    xmlns:xsd1="uri:DomesticCalculatordata-namespace"
    xmlns:xsi="http://www.w3.org/2001/XMLSchema-instance">
  - <types>
    - <schema targetNamespace="uri:DomesticCalculatordata-namespace"
        xmlns="http://www.w3.org/2001/XMLSchema"
        xmlns:wsdl="http://schemas.xmlsoap.org/wsdl/">
      - <complexType name="ArrayOfstring">
        - <complexContent>
          - <restriction base="SOAP-ENC:Array">
              <attribute ref="SOAP-ENC:arrayType" wsdl:arrayType="xsd:string[]" />
            </restriction>
          </complexContent>
        </complexType>
      </schema>
    </types>
  - <message name="java_net_MalformedURLException">
      <part name="java_net_MalformedURLException" type="xsd:string" />
    </message>
  - <message name="java_io_IOException">
      <part name="java_io_IOException" type="xsd:string" />
    </message>
  - <message name="org_xml_sax_SAXException">
      <part name="org_xml_sax_SAXException" type="xsd:string" />
    </message>
  - <message name="java_lang_Exception">
      <part name="java_lang_Exception" type="xsd:string" />
    </message>
  - <message name="getDomesticRateRequest">
      <part name="query" type="xsd:string" />
    </message>
  - <message name="getDomesticRateResult">
      <part name="return" type="xsd1:ArrayOfstring" />
    </message>
  - <portType name="DomesticCalculatorPortType">
    - <operation name="getDomesticRate">
        <input message="tns:getDomesticRateRequest" name="getDomesticRate" />
        <output message="tns:getDomesticRateResult" name="getDomesticRateResult" />
        <fault message="tns:java_io_IOException" name="java_io_IOException" />
        <fault message="tns:java_lang_Exception" name="java_lang_Exception" />
        <fault message="tns:org_xml_sax_SAXException"
          name="org_xml_sax_SAXException"/>
        <fault message="tns:java_net_MalformedURLException"
          name="java_net_MalformedURLException" />
      </operation>
    </portType>
  - <binding name="DomesticCalculatorBinding" type="tns:DomesticCalculatorPortType">
      <soap:binding style="rpc" transport="http://schemas.xmlsoap.org/soap/http" />
    - <operation name="getDomesticRate">
        <soap:operation soapAction="urn:target-domesticcalculator-service/
          getDomesticRate" style="rpc" />
      - <input name="getDomesticRate">
          <soap:body encodingStyle="http://schemas.xmlsoap.org/soap/encoding/"
            namespace="urn:target-domesticcalculator-service" use="encoded" />
        </input>
      - <output name="getDomesticRateResult">
          <soap:body encodingStyle="http://schemas.xmlsoap.org/soap/encoding/"
            namespace="urn:target-domesticcalculator-service" use="encoded" />
        </output>
      - <fault name="java_io_IOException">
          <soap:fault encodingStyle="http://schemas.xmlsoap.org/soap/encoding/"
            name="java_io_IOException" namespace="urn:target-domesticcalculator-
```

```
            service" use="encoded" />
        </fault>
    - <fault name="java_lang_Exception">
        <soap:fault encodingStyle="http://schemas.xmlsoap.org/soap/encoding/"
          name="java_lang_Exception" namespace="urn:target-domesticcalculator-
          service" use="encoded" />
      </fault>
    - <fault name="org_xml_sax_SAXException">
        <soap:fault encodingStyle="http://schemas.xmlsoap.org/soap/encoding/"
          name="org_xml_sax_SAXException" namespace="urn:target-domesticcalculator-
          service" use="encoded" />
      </fault>
    - <fault name="java_net_MalformedURLException">
        <soap:fault encodingStyle="http://schemas.xmlsoap.org/soap/encoding/"
          name="java_net_MalformedURLException" namespace="urn:target-
          domesticcalculator-service" use="encoded" />
      </fault>
    </operation>
  </binding>
- <service name="DomesticCalculatorService">
  - <port binding="tns:DomesticCalculatorBinding" name="DomesticCalculatorPort">
      <soap:address location="http://www.xmlbus.com:9010/xmlbus/container/
        DomesticCalculator/DomesticCalculatorService/DomesticCalculatorPort/" />
    </port>
  </service>
</definitions>
```

Appendix F: Finance Web Service WSDL Example

```
<?xml version="1.0" encoding="UTF-8" ?>
- <definitions name="FinanceService"
  targetNamespace="urn:target-finance-service"
  xmlns="http://schemas.xmlsoap.org/wsdl/"
  xmlns:SOAP-ENC="http://schemas.xmlsoap.org/soap/encoding/"
  xmlns:soap="http://schemas.xmlsoap.org/wsdl/soap/"
  xmlns:tns="urn:target-finance-service"
  xmlns:xsd="http://www.w3.org/2001/XMLSchema"
  xmlns:xsd1="uri:Financedata-namespace"
  xmlns:xsi="http://www.w3.org/2001/XMLSchema-instance">
  - <message name="calculateTimeToDoubleUsingRuleOf72Request">
      <part name="InterestRate" type="xsd:double" />
    </message>
  - <message name="calculateTimeToDoubleUsingRuleOf72Result">
      <part name="return" type="xsd:int" />
    </message>
  - <message name="calculateRateToDoubleUsingRuleOf72Request">
      <part name="year" type="xsd:int" />
    </message>
  - <message name="calculateRateToDoubleUsingRuleOf72Result">
      <part name="return" type="xsd:float" />
    </message>
  - <message name="calculateFutureValueRequest">
      <part name="initial_amount" type="xsd:double" />
      <part name="rate" type="xsd:double" />
      <part name="compound_period" type="xsd:int" />
      <part name="total_period" type="xsd:int" />
    </message>
  - <message name="calculateFutureValueResult">
      <part name="return" type="xsd:double" />
    </message>
  - <message name="paymentMortgageRequest">
      <part name="LoanAmount" type="xsd:double" />
      <part name="InterestRate" type="xsd:double" />
      <part name="Period" type="xsd:int" />
    </message>
  - <message name="paymentMortgageResult">
      <part name="return" type="xsd:double" />
    </message>
  - <message name="calculateTimeToDoubleRequest">
      <part name="InterestRate" type="xsd:double" />
    </message>
```

```
- <message name="calculateTimeToDoubleResult">
    <part name="return" type="xsd:double" />
  </message>
- <message name="calculateRateToDoubleRequest">
    <part name="year" type="xsd:double" />
  </message>
- <message name="calculateRateToDoubleResult">
    <part name="return" type="xsd:double" />
  </message>
- <message name="periodMortgageRequest">
    <part name="MonthlyPayment" type="xsd:double" />
    <part name="LoanAmount" type="xsd:double" />
    <part name="InterestRate" type="xsd:double" />
  </message>
- <message name="periodMortgageResult">
    <part name="return" type="xsd:int" />
  </message>
- <message name="showTaxRateRequest">
    <part name="TaxStatus" type="xsd:int" />
    <part name="Income" type="xsd:float" />
  </message>
- <message name="showTaxRateResult">
    <part name="return" type="xsd:float" />
  </message>
- <message name="calculateRateRequest">
    <part name="APR" type="xsd:double" />
    <part name="compound_period" type="xsd:int" />
  </message>
- <message name="calculateRateResult">
    <part name="return" type="xsd:double" />
  </message>
- <message name="calculateAPRRequest">
    <part name="InterestRate" type="xsd:double" />
    <part name="compound_period" type="xsd:int" />
  </message>
- <message name="calculateAPRResult">
    <part name="return" type="xsd:double" />
  </message>
- <portType name="FinancePortType">
  - <operation name="calculateTimeToDoubleUsingRuleOf72">
      <input message="tns:calculateTimeToDoubleUsingRuleOf72Request"
        name="calculateTimeToDoubleUsingRuleOf72" />
      <output message="tns:calculateTimeToDoubleUsingRuleOf72Result"
        name="calculateTimeToDoubleUsingRuleOf72Result" />
    </operation>
  - <operation name="calculateRateToDoubleUsingRuleOf72">
      <input message="tns:calculateRateToDoubleUsingRuleOf72Request"
        name="calculateRateToDoubleUsingRuleOf72" />
      <output message="tns:calculateRateToDoubleUsingRuleOf72Result"
        name="calculateRateToDoubleUsingRuleOf72Result" />
    </operation>
  - <operation name="calculateFutureValue">
      <input message="tns:calculateFutureValueRequest"
        name="calculateFutureValue" />
      <output message="tns:calculateFutureValueResult"
        name="calculateFutureValueResult" />
    </operation>
  - <operation name="paymentMortgage">
      <input message="tns:paymentMortgageRequest" name="paymentMortgage" />
      <output message="tns:paymentMortgageResult" name="paymentMortgageResult" />
    </operation>
  - <operation name="calculateTimeToDouble">
      <input message="tns:calculateTimeToDoubleRequest"
        name="calculateTimeToDouble" />
      <output message="tns:calculateTimeToDoubleResult"
        name="calculateTimeToDoubleResult" />
    </operation>
  - <operation name="calculateRateToDouble">
      <input message="tns:calculateRateToDoubleRequest"
        name="calculateRateToDouble" />
      <output message="tns:calculateRateToDoubleResult"
        name="calculateRateToDoubleResult" />
    </operation>
  - <operation name="periodMortgage">
```

```
        <input message="tns:periodMortgageRequest" name="periodMortgage" />
        <output message="tns:periodMortgageResult" name="periodMortgageResult" />
      </operation>
    - <operation name="showTaxRate">
        <input message="tns:showTaxRateRequest" name="showTaxRate" />
        <output message="tns:showTaxRateResult" name="showTaxRateResult" />
      </operation>
    - <operation name="calculateRate">
        <input message="tns:calculateRateRequest" name="calculateRate" />
        <output message="tns:calculateRateResult" name="calculateRateResult" />
      </operation>
    - <operation name="calculateAPR">
        <input message="tns:calculateAPRRequest" name="calculateAPR" />
        <output message="tns:calculateAPRResult" name="calculateAPRResult" />
      </operation>
    </portType>
  - <binding name="FinanceBinding" type="tns:FinancePortType">
      <soap:binding style="rpc" transport="http://schemas.xmlsoap.org/soap/http" />
    - <operation name="calculateTimeToDoubleUsingRuleOf72">
        <soap:operation soapAction="urn:target-finance-service/
          calculateTimeToDoubleUsingRuleOf72" style="rpc" />
      - <input name="calculateTimeToDoubleUsingRuleOf72">
          <soap:body encodingStyle="http://schemas.xmlsoap.org/soap/encoding/"
            namespace="urn:target-finance-service" use="encoded" />
        </input>
      - <output name="calculateTimeToDoubleUsingRuleOf72Result">
          <soap:body encodingStyle="http://schemas.xmlsoap.org/soap/encoding/"
            namespace="urn:target-finance-service" use="encoded" />
        </output>
      </operation>
    - <operation name="calculateRateToDoubleUsingRuleOf72">
        <soap:operation soapAction="urn:target-finance-
          service/calculateRateToDoubleUsingRuleOf72" style="rpc" />
      - <input name="calculateRateToDoubleUsingRuleOf72">
          <soap:body encodingStyle="http://schemas.xmlsoap.org/soap/encoding/"
            namespace="urn:target-finance-service" use="encoded" />
        </input>
      - <output name="calculateRateToDoubleUsingRuleOf72Result">
          <soap:body encodingStyle="http://schemas.xmlsoap.org/soap/encoding/"
            namespace="urn:target-finance-service" use="encoded" />
        </output>
      </operation>
    - <operation name="calculateFutureValue">
        <soap:operation soapAction="urn:target-finance-service/calculateFutureValue"
          style="rpc" />
      - <input name="calculateFutureValue">
          <soap:body encodingStyle="http://schemas.xmlsoap.org/soap/encoding/"
            namespace="urn:target-finance-service" use="encoded" />
        </input>
      - <output name="calculateFutureValueResult">
          <soap:body encodingStyle="http://schemas.xmlsoap.org/soap/encoding/"
            namespace="urn:target-finance-service" use="encoded" />
        </output>
      </operation>
    - <operation name="paymentMortgage">
        <soap:operation soapAction="urn:target-finance-service/paymentMortgage"
          style="rpc" />
      - <input name="paymentMortgage">
          <soap:body encodingStyle="http://schemas.xmlsoap.org/soap/encoding/"
            namespace="urn:target-finance-service" use="encoded" />
        </input>
      - <output name="paymentMortgageResult">
          <soap:body encodingStyle="http://schemas.xmlsoap.org/soap/encoding/"
            namespace="urn:target-finance-service" use="encoded" />
        </output>
      </operation>
    - <operation name="calculateTimeToDouble">
        <soap:operation soapAction="urn:target-finance-service/calculateTimeToDouble"
          style="rpc" />
      - <input name="calculateTimeToDouble">
          <soap:body encodingStyle="http://schemas.xmlsoap.org/soap/encoding/"
            namespace="urn:target-finance-service" use="encoded" />
        </input>
      - <output name="calculateTimeToDoubleResult">
```

```
            <soap:body encodingStyle="http://schemas.xmlsoap.org/soap/encoding/"
               namespace="urn:target-finance-service" use="encoded" />
          </output>
        </operation>
    - <operation name="calculateRateToDouble">
        <soap:operation soapAction="urn:target-finance-service/calculateRateToDouble"
           style="rpc" />
      - <input name="calculateRateToDouble">
            <soap:body encodingStyle="http://schemas.xmlsoap.org/soap/encoding/"
               namespace="urn:target-finance-service" use="encoded" />
          </input>
      - <output name="calculateRateToDoubleResult">
            <soap:body encodingStyle="http://schemas.xmlsoap.org/soap/encoding/"
               namespace="urn:target-finance-service" use="encoded" />
          </output>
        </operation>
    - <operation name="periodMortgage">
        <soap:operation soapAction="urn:target-finance-service/periodMortgage"
           style="rpc" />
      - <input name="periodMortgage">
            <soap:body encodingStyle="http://schemas.xmlsoap.org/soap/encoding/"
               namespace="urn:target-finance-service" use="encoded" />
          </input>
      - <output name="periodMortgageResult">
            <soap:body encodingStyle="http://schemas.xmlsoap.org/soap/encoding/"
               namespace="urn:target-finance-service" use="encoded" />
          </output>
        </operation>
    - <operation name="showTaxRate">
        <soap:operation soapAction="urn:target-finance-service/showTaxRate"
           style="rpc" />
      - <input name="showTaxRate">
            <soap:body encodingStyle="http://schemas.xmlsoap.org/soap/encoding/"
               namespace="urn:target-finance-service" use="encoded" />
          </input>
      - <output name="showTaxRateResult">
            <soap:body encodingStyle="http://schemas.xmlsoap.org/soap/encoding/"
               namespace="urn:target-finance-service" use="encoded" />
          </output>
        </operation>
    - <operation name="calculateRate">
        <soap:operation soapAction="urn:target-finance-service/calculateRate"
           style="rpc" />
      - <input name="calculateRate">
            <soap:body encodingStyle="http://schemas.xmlsoap.org/soap/encoding/"
               namespace="urn:target-finance-service" use="encoded" />
          </input>
      - <output name="calculateRateResult">
            <soap:body encodingStyle="http://schemas.xmlsoap.org/soap/encoding/"
               namespace="urn:target-finance-service" use="encoded" />
          </output>
        </operation>
    - <operation name="calculateAPR">
        <soap:operation soapAction="urn:target-finance-service/calculateAPR"
           style="rpc" />
      - <input name="calculateAPR">
            <soap:body encodingStyle="http://schemas.xmlsoap.org/soap/encoding/"
               namespace="urn:target-finance-service" use="encoded" />
          </input>
      - <output name="calculateAPRResult">
            <soap:body encodingStyle="http://schemas.xmlsoap.org/soap/encoding/"
               namespace="urn:target-finance-service" use="encoded" />
          </output>
        </operation>
      </binding>
    - <service name="FinanceService">
      - <port binding="tns:FinanceBinding" name="FinancePort">
          <soap:address location="http://www.xmlbus.com:9010/xmlbus/container/Finance/
             FinanceService/FinancePort/" />
        </port>
      </service>
    </definitions>
```

Appendix G: Electricity Web Service WSDL Example

```xml
<?xml version="1.0" encoding="UTF-8" ?>
- <definitions name="ElectricityService"
    targetNamespace="urn:target-electricity-service"
    xmlns="http://schemas.xmlsoap.org/wsdl/"
    xmlns:SOAP-ENC="http://schemas.xmlsoap.org/soap/encoding/"
    xmlns:soap="http://schemas.xmlsoap.org/wsdl/soap/"
    xmlns:tns="urn:target-electricity-service"
    xmlns:xsd="http://www.w3.org/2001/XMLSchema"
    xmlns:xsd1="uri:Electricitydata-namespace"
    xmlns:xsi="http://www.w3.org/2001/XMLSchema-instance">
  - <message name="computeVoltsRequest">
      <part name="Amps" type="xsd:int" />
      <part name="Watts" type="xsd:int" />
    </message>
  - <message name="computeVoltsResult">
      <part name="return" type="xsd:int" />
    </message>
  - <message name="computeWireSizeRequest">
      <part name="Amps" type="xsd:int" />
    </message>
  - <message name="computeWireSizeResult">
      <part name="return" type="xsd:string" />
    </message>
  - <message name="computeWattsRequest">
      <part name="Amps" type="xsd:int" />
      <part name="Volts" type="xsd:int" />
    </message>
  - <message name="computeWattsResult">
      <part name="return" type="xsd:int" />
    </message>
  - <message name="computeAmpsRequest">
      <part name="Volts" type="xsd:int" />
      <part name="Watts" type="xsd:int" />
    </message>
  - <message name="computeAmpsResult">
      <part name="return" type="xsd:int" />
    </message>
  - <message name="computeAmpacityRequest">
      <part name="wire" type="xsd:string" />
    </message>
  - <message name="computeAmpacityResult">
      <part name="return" type="xsd:int" />
    </message>
  - <portType name="ElectricityPortType">
    - <operation name="computeVolts">
        <input message="tns:computeVoltsRequest" name="computeVolts" />
        <output message="tns:computeVoltsResult" name="computeVoltsResult" />
      </operation>
    - <operation name="computeWireSize">
        <input message="tns:computeWireSizeRequest" name="computeWireSize" />
        <output message="tns:computeWireSizeResult" name="computeWireSizeResult" />
      </operation>
    - <operation name="computeWatts">
        <input message="tns:computeWattsRequest" name="computeWatts" />
        <output message="tns:computeWattsResult" name="computeWattsResult" />
      </operation>
    - <operation name="computeAmps">
        <input message="tns:computeAmpsRequest" name="computeAmps" />
        <output message="tns:computeAmpsResult" name="computeAmpsResult" />
      </operation>
    - <operation name="computeAmpacity">
        <input message="tns:computeAmpacityRequest" name="computeAmpacity" />
        <output message="tns:computeAmpacityResult" name="computeAmpacityResult" />
      </operation>
    </portType>
  - <binding name="ElectricityBinding" type="tns:ElectricityPortType">
      <soap:binding style="rpc" transport="http://schemas.xmlsoap.org/soap/http" />
    - <operation name="computeVolts">
        <soap:operation soapAction="urn:target-electricity-service/computeVolts"
          style="rpc" />
```

```
  - <input name="computeVolts">
     <soap:body encodingStyle="http://schemas.xmlsoap.org/soap/encoding/"
       namespace="urn:target-electricity-service" use="encoded" />
    </input>
  - <output name="computeVoltsResult">
     <soap:body encodingStyle="http://schemas.xmlsoap.org/soap/encoding/"
       namespace="urn:target-electricity-service" use="encoded" />
    </output>
   </operation>
 - <operation name="computeWireSize">
    <soap:operation soapAction="urn:target-electricity-service/computeWireSize"
      style="rpc" />
   - <input name="computeWireSize">
      <soap:body encodingStyle="http://schemas.xmlsoap.org/soap/encoding/"
        namespace="urn:target-electricity-service" use="encoded" />
     </input>
   - <output name="computeWireSizeResult">
      <soap:body encodingStyle="http://schemas.xmlsoap.org/soap/encoding/"
        namespace="urn:target-electricity-service" use="encoded" />
     </output>
    </operation>
 - <operation name="computeWatts">
    <soap:operation soapAction="urn:target-electricity-service/computeWatts"
      style="rpc" />
   - <input name="computeWatts">
      <soap:body encodingStyle="http://schemas.xmlsoap.org/soap/encoding/"
        namespace="urn:target-electricity-service" use="encoded" />
     </input>
   - <output name="computeWattsResult">
      <soap:body encodingStyle="http://schemas.xmlsoap.org/soap/encoding/"
        namespace="urn:target-electricity-service" use="encoded" />
     </output>
    </operation>
 - <operation name="computeAmps">
    <soap:operation soapAction="urn:target-electricity-service/computeAmps"
      style="rpc" />
   - <input name="computeAmps">
      <soap:body encodingStyle="http://schemas.xmlsoap.org/soap/encoding/"
        namespace="urn:target-electricity-service" use="encoded" />
     </input>
   - <output name="computeAmpsResult">
      <soap:body encodingStyle="http://schemas.xmlsoap.org/soap/encoding/"
        namespace="urn:target-electricity-service" use="encoded" />
     </output>
    </operation>
 - <operation name="computeAmpacity">
    <soap:operation soapAction="urn:target-electricity-service/computeAmpacity"
      style="rpc" />
   - <input name="computeAmpacity">
      <soap:body encodingStyle="http://schemas.xmlsoap.org/soap/encoding/"
        namespace="urn:target-electricity-service" use="encoded" />
     </input>
   - <output name="computeAmpacityResult">
      <soap:body encodingStyle="http://schemas.xmlsoap.org/soap/encoding/"
        namespace="urn:target-electricity-service" use="encoded" />
     </output>
    </operation>
  </binding>
 - <service name="ElectricityService">
  - <port binding="tns:ElectricityBinding" name="ElectricityPort">
     <soap:address location="http://www.xmlbus.com:9010/xmlbus/container/Electricity/
       ElectricityService/ElectricityPort/" />
    </port>
  </service>
</definitions>
```

Chapter 6

Database Middleware and Other Stuff

This chapter primarily focuses on relational databases — that is, data-level integration, SQL, XML, Java-based, XML-enabled, and Web-services enabled — as the middleware.

Introduction

Individuals use database applications to create, store, and manage raw data. People who need to see this data may be using different operating systems and applications than those who store the data. Middleware, in the form of relational database management systems and related products, bridges this gap.

Database middleware comes in various flavors: data-level integration, SQL, XML, and Java-based. Whatever the products an enterprise chooses, other middleware comes into play in collaboration efforts in integrating and transferring data. Among them are the Windows Telephony with TAPI, wireless APIs, and reliable messages.

Data-Level Integration

Information Builders' FOCUS is a family of enterprisewide data access and reporting tools, supporting the development of graphical client and server applications, as well as host-based, character-interface applications. FOCUS applications also support relational and non-relational data sources and can directly access many different data managers. Additional databases are supported through EDA/SQL middleware products.

Information Builders' EDA middleware provides data-level integration and built-in information access capabilities of WebFOCUS Business Intelligence Suite. This middleware product offers access to most database or application technologies on any computer platform. It works with all security systems and network architectures, allowing the widest universe of users — including Internet users — to interact with any information system in an enterprise. EDA also integrates with eXtensible Markup Language (XML), Enterprise JavaBeans (EJB), Distributed Component Object Model (DCOM), and other component-based technologies.

iWay Software, an Information Builders company specializing in middleware technology, adds enterprise application integration capabilities to EDA. iWay Software provides standard connections to over 120 back-office systems[1] and many front-end applications, enabling organizations to leverage technologies such as IBM MQSeries, XML, and Java. These connections provide the integration of E-business applications with the enterprise at all levels, including data, application, transition, and messaging.

WebFOCUS Business Intelligence Suite

WebFOCUS is designed to support today's most critical E-business and E-government initiatives — business-to-business (B2B), business-to-consumer (B2C), and business-to-enterprise (B2E). Whether one's needs are production reporting, complex analysis, supply chain management (SCM), customer relationship management (CRM), or self-service applications, WebFOCUS can help to quickly build and deploy Web reporting and transactional systems over intranets, extranets, and the Internet.

Features include:

1. Integration with Microsoft tools
2. Scalability
3. Multi-analytic viewpoints
4. Java-based report distribution
5. Wireless capabilities
6. ISO 9000 certification
7. Legacy–Web–ERP integration
8. Development tools
9. Components and services

Integration with Microsoft Tools

WebFOCUS features industry-leading integration with Microsoft Office 2000 and BackOffice 2000. For example, you can save complex WebFOCUS reports as Excel 2000 documents while preserving all formatting and drill-downs. From within WebFOCUS, you can even generate Excel Pivot Tables with a single click of a check box. WebFOCUS also integrates with Microsoft Online Analytical Processing (OLAP) Services, providing a single-vendor solution for high-performance reporting from cubes. In addition, Microsoft cube data can be combined with other sources for comprehensive enterprise reporting.

Scalability

WebFOCUS scales to the mainframe and runs on NT, UNIX, Linux, OS/400, OpenVMS, OS/390, MVS, and CMS. It provides a flexible architecture to fit into an infrastructure.

Multi-Analytic Viewpoints

Multi-dimensional analytic capabilities allow users to examine their data from many different points of view. Users can change sort fields, filter reports with varying selection criteria, or drill-down to view information in a whole new light. They can even look at multiple reports and graphs on a single page to easily compare data. Flexible styling allows each user to design reports that are most usable for his or her needs.

Java-Based Report Distribution

Both administrators and end users have the capability of scheduling and distributing reports. Reports can be delivered via e-mail, over intranet systems or the Internet, to network printers or to wireless devices.

Wireless Capabilities

WebFOCUS allows one to initiate queries from wireless devices such as Palm Pilots and retrieve reports that can be viewed on the devices' screens. Reports can even contain drill-down to detail data — exactly like the reports one would retrieve from one's office PC.

ISO 9000 Certification

WebFOCUS has been awarded the ISO 9002 certification. This certification is an internationally recognized standard for assessing the quality of business solutions.

Legacy–Web–ERP Integration

WebFOCUS leverages Information Builders' enterprise integration middleware to access over 85 data sources, including all major relational database structures, enterprise resource planning (ERP) packages (SAP and PeopleSoft), and legacy data (CICS and IMS transaction systems). This makes it easy to consolidate all data sources for the enterprise business intelligence.

Development Tools

From a single frontend, users can design Web pages that mix graphs, tabular reports, and spreadsheets. No prior knowledge of Hypertext Markup Language (HTML), Java, JavaScript, or other complex 3GL programming language is required to create applications. Users can use Microsoft FrontPage to integrate these Web pages into, for example, a multimedia Web site.

Components and Services

The components and services of the WebFOCUS solution are designed to meet the needs of a business enterprise. They include:

- Reporting, query, and analysis
- Report distribution
- Managed reporting
- Development and reporting tools
- Management and administration tools
- Report templates

iWay Software: EAI Solutions

iWay Software's products and reusable service channel architecture provide a complete E-business to Enterprise (E2e) infrastructure with everything needed for building end-to-end enterprise application integration (EAI) solutions. iWay works with all major integration brokers — the heart of EAI systems — so they can connect to virtually any transaction system, application, business package, or data source in an enterprise.

iWay's EAI solutions work with one's existing integration broker. These features include:

- iWay Enterprise Integrator[2] (see Exhibit 1)
- Connectors for one's existing current integration broker
- iWay Connector for IBM MQSeries Integrator, or the iWay IBM MQSeries Connector if one already uses MQSeries messaging and queuing
- iWay Network Adapters for virtually all enterprise network protocols
- Information for over 120 data sources from iWay's Enterprise Adapter Suite
- iWay Transaction Processing Adapters and the iWay Terminal Emulation Adapter to extend enterprise transaction systems and terminal applications for E-business

iWay Software: E-Business Integration

iWay Software's reusable service channel architecture provides E2e integration capabilities. With its simplified, universal view of all back-office information systems — no matter how complex — iWay's service channel architecture lets one create new composite applications and message flows (see Exhibit 2).

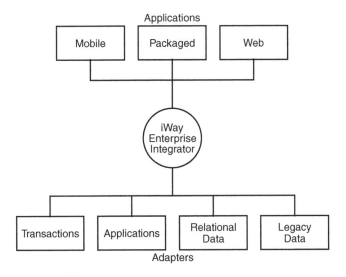

Exhibit 1.   iWay Enterprise Integrator

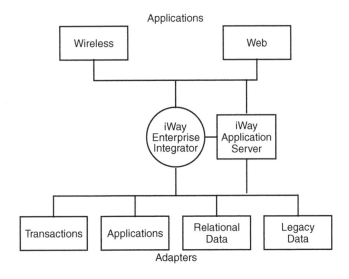

Exhibit 2.   E-Business Integration

Among the features are:

- iWay Application Server, including an embedded WebSphere Application Server Advanced Edition from IBM (One can optionally use one's own J2EE-compliant application server.)
- iWay Application Developer (One can optionally use one's own Java development environment.)
- iWay Enterprise Integrator, including an embedded MQSeries Integrator v 2.0 from IBM to provide integration broker-based EAI (One can optionally use one's existing integration broker. *Note:* If already using MQSeries Integrator, one may get the functionality of the iWay Enterprise Integrator via the iWay Connector for IBM MQSeries Integrator.)

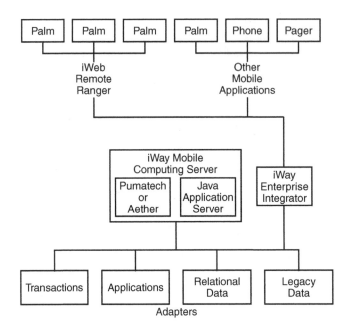

Exhibit 3. Mobile E-Business Integration

- iWay Network Adapters for virtually all enterprise network protocols
- Information adapters for over 120 data sources from iWay's Enterprise Adapter Suite
- iWay Transaction Processing Adapters and the iWay Terminal Emulation Adapter to extend enterprise transaction systems and terminal applications for E-business

iWay Software: Mobile E-Business Integration

E2e integration components aim at integrating mobile solutions with complex back-office environments. iWay mobile E-business solutions (see Exhibit 3) include its service channel architecture for connecting mobile applications to virtually any transaction system, application, business package, or relational or non-relational data source in an enterprise.

Features include:

- One or more applications from iWay Mobile Application Suite developed with NovaSync
- iWay Mobile Computering Server, a Java Application Server with available mobile technologies from Pumatech or Aether
- iWay Application Developer (One can optionally use Java development environment.)
- iWay Enterprise Integrator, including an embedded MQSeries Integrator v2.0 to provide integration broker-based EAI (One can optionally use one's existing integration broker. *Note:* If already using IBM's MQSeries Integrator,

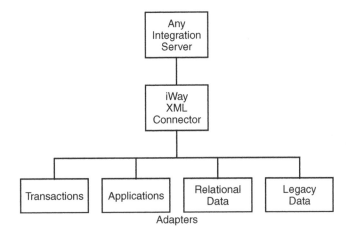

Exhibit 4.   B2B Integration

one may get the functionality of the iWay Enterprise Integrator using the iWay Connector for IBM MQSeries Integrator.)

- Information adapters for over 120 data sources from iWeb's Enterprise Adapter Suite
- iWay Network Adapters for virtually all enterprise network protocols

iWay Software: B2B Integration

iWay Software's B2B products work with most popular integration servers. Its reusable service channel architecture provides a simplified view of one's back office — even when one is using technologies such as XML, wireless, and IBM MQSeries. iWay's B2B integration solutions (see Exhibit 4) include:

- iWay Enterprise XML Connector
- iWay Connector for IBM MQSeries Integrator or the iWay IBM MQSeries Connector if already using MQSeries messaging and queuing
- iWay Network Adapters for virtually all enterprise network protocols
- Information adapters for over 120 data sources from iWay's Enterprise Adapter Suite

iWay Software: E-Commerce Integration

iWay Software's E-Commerce products and reusable service channel architecture provide a complete E2e infrastructure with everything needed for building end-to-end E-commerce solutions. That allows one to connect E-buying, E-selling, and other E-services to virtually any transaction system, application, or relational or non-relational data source in an enterprise.

The iWay e-Commerce Suite (see Exhibit 5) includes IBM's E-commerce technologies, together with value-added components that extend them to virtually all back-office environments.

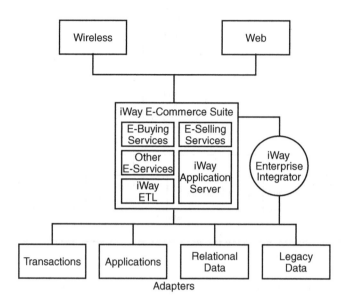

Exhibit 5.   E-Commerce Suite

E-commerce solutions include:

- iWay Commerce Suite, including an embedded WebSphere Application Server from IBM
- iWay ETL Manager for populating storefront databases from back-office systems
- For integration broker-based EAI, optional iWay Enterprise Integrator — or use existing integration broker
- iWay Application Developer (One can optionally use one's own Java development environment.)
- If already using IBM's MQSeries Integrator, one may get the functionality of the iWay Enterprise Integrator using the iWay Connector for IBM MQSeries Integrator
- iWay Network Adapters for virtually all enterprise network protocols
- Information adapters for over 120 data sources, from iWay's Enterprise Adapter Suite

DBMS/SQL Middleware

This section focuses on two types of DBMS middleware: Pervasive SQL and MERANT Java.

Pervasive.SQL Middleware

Pervasive Software's history began in 1982 when SoftCraft was founded to create the PC-based Btrieve database and market it to commercial developers building business-critical applications. In 1987, Novell acquired SoftCraft and merged Btrieve with the NetWare network operating system. As Btrieve's popularity grew, new products, such as the Scalable SQL relational database, were introduced to the market. In 1994, Novell sold its database business and Btrieve Technologies was born. Renamed Pervasive Software in 1996 to reflect a growing worldwide presence, Pervasive completed its initial public offering in September 1997.

Pervasive.SQL 2000/2000i is an evolution of the Btrieve database engine, provides a system analyzer, is platform independent, and has Object Database Connectivity (ODBC), Object Linking and Embedding Database data source (OLE DB), and Java Database Connectivity (JDBC) interfaces. Available on NT/2000, Netware, Solaris, and Linux (Red Hat, Caldera, SuSE), it plays well with Microsoft's Visual environment, as well as Delphi, Cobol, and Magic, and allows one to move between databases.

Samples on integration with Perl and PHP are provided. Pervasive.SQL 2000i has native support for all Btrieve applications and associated data, and provides samples on integration with Perl PHP.

MERANT Data Connectivity

MERANT[3] DataDirect offers two options for data connectivity for each standard API (JDBC, ODBC, and ADO): connect application components for a client- or server-based application, and SequeLink — end-to-end data middleware. With SequeLink, one can add on database servers or APIs to extend data access across the enterprise.

SequeLink Java Edition is a result of MERANT DataDirect's technological breakthrough that became the first JDBC driver to earn Sun's "100% Pure Java" certification. Recognizing Java's unique value to Internet applications, MERANT designed JDBC middleware with built-in features for online environments.

SequeLink Java, in particular, provides full multi-threaded Java-based connectivity to diverse data sources, including desktop, relational databases, enterprise resource planning (ERP), and mainframe and legacy data, across a wide variety of interfaces and operating systems. It offers multi-level security capabilities essential for secure business applications or online transactions. SequeLink Java includes the ability to spool or cache database requests.

XML Database Middleware

Database middleware is software used by data-centric applications to transfer data between XML documents and databases. It is written in various languages, but almost all use ODBC, JDBC, or OLE DB for relational databases. A Web server is required for most middleware products if one wants to take advantage of remote data access.

XML database middleware products are arbitrarily grouped into three parts: commercial, evaluation-only, and open-source products.

Commercial Products

The following products offer commercial license and allow data transfer in both directions: from XML to database and from database to XML, unless otherwise indicated.

1. ActiveX Data Object (ADO): Microsoft
2. Allora: HiT Sioftware
3. Attunity Connect
4. DB-X: Swift, Inc.
5. DB/XML Vision and xPower Transform: BDI Systems
6. Delphi: Borland
7. PerXML Smart Transformation System: PerCurrence
8. XML-DB Link: Rogue Wave Software
9. XML Junction and Data Junction Suite
10. XMLShark: infoShark
11. XML SQL Utility for Java (Oracle8i Application)
12. Net.Data: IBM

ActiveX Data Object (ADO): Microsoft

URL: http://www.microsoft.com/data/ado/
Data source: ADO/OLE DB, ODBC
Description: ADO can persist a Recordset object as an XML document and open the latter as a Recordset object. It provides a way to transfer data between XML and a database, using Recordsets as intermediate objects. The XML document is split into two parts: (1) the first part maps the XML in the second part to the Recordset, and (2) the second part contains the actual data in XML format.

ADO's use of XML allows a tree of nested elements to be opened as the tree of nested Recordsets, and vice versa. If the Recordset contains pending updates, deletes, or inserts, these are specifically flagged in the XML document with ADO-specific tags. One feature of ADO is Remote Data Service (RDS), which allows developers to create data-centric applications within ActiveX-enabled browsers such as Internet Explorer.

Allora: HiT Software

URL: http://www.hitsw.com/dsheets/alloramidware.htm
Data *source*: ODBC, OLE DB, JDBC
Description: Allora is an XML platform that consists of design-time tools for mapping XML to relational data and a set of APIs (runtime

engine) for building applications that are integrated with relational databases. The product can call to retrieve data from a table, result set, or catalog query as a Document Object Model (DOM) tree or as Simple API for XML (SAX) events.

Allora is available in Java and Windows versions. The Java version shows how the DOM tree is constructed, and how the changes to the tree are tracked. The Windows version comes with a graphical database viewer and a tool for tracing API calls.

ASP2XML: Stonebroom

URL: http://www.stonebroom.com/asp2xml.htm
Data source: ODBC, OLE DB
Description: ASP2XML provides an interface between almost any ODBC- or OLE DB-compliant data source and any XML-enabled client. It is designed for use with Microsoft Active Server Pages (ASP) scripts, or as a stand-alone COM-compliant ActiveX Dynamic Link Library (DLL) component. ASP2XML offers a range of options, including provision for creating XML documents as disk files.

Attunity Connect

URL: http://www.attunity.com/content/products/
Data Source: Relational and non-relational such as IMS, ADABAS, Enscribe, DB2, Sybase, and Oracle
Description: Attunity Connect integrates applications and data sources through industry-standard interfaces. It can receive SQL statements in XML and return results in XML, enabling solutions to construct complex XML documents using standard SQL statements.

DB-X: Swift, Inc.

URL: http://www.swiftinc.co.jp/en/frame/products/XMLServerWare/DB-X/
Data Source: Relational via ADO
Description: DB-X is a Windows-based component that connects to RDMS (like Oracle, SQL Server, ODBC data sources) and transforms data to XML format via an XSLT-like language. It transfers data from one or more ADO record sets to an XML document and uses DB-X-specific elements to embed queries in a template.

DB/XML Vision and xPower Transform: BDI Systems, Inc. (acquired by DataMirror Corp.)

URL: http://www.bdisystems.com/
Data Source: JDBC
Description: DB/XML Vision automatically creates XML documents containing hierarchical data from any database for B2B applications, and integration with EDI and databases. Its Tree-Structured-Query tool allows query-in-and-structured-XML-out with no need to write any code to structure result sets. xPower Transform provides an engine for bi-directional data transformation between XML, database, and text formats.

Delphi: Borland

URL: http://www.borland.com/delphi/del6/featurematrix/
                  bizsnap.html
Data Source: Relational, such as Borland Database Engine, ADO, InterBase
Description: Delphi is an application development tool that supports the transfer of data between XML documents and databases through the use of client data sets. Data set updates can be reflected in both the database and the XML document. *Note:* DataSnap, a Web services-enabled database middleware, is now available.

PerXML Smart Transformation System: PerCurrence

URL: http://www.percurrence.com/products/index.html
Data Source: Relational
Description: The PerXML Smart Transformation System includes a runtime engine to reduce the time and cost of building and maintaining XML applications. The PerXML Client supports major editing environments such as XML Spy and XMetal Pro, while the PerXML Server supports dynamic content integration and delivery in XML, HTML, Wireless Markup Language (WML), and most other Web environments.

PerXML transforms non-XML data into XML (e.g., database to XML), and integrates native XML and legacy data into XML documents. PerXML can accept all kinds of content (text, images, animations) for transformation into a common XML view with which the user can use PerXML to recombine the content into new objects.

XML-DB Link: Rogue Wave Software

URL: http://www.roguewave.com/products/xml/xmldblink/
Data Source: Relational via (OpenSQL — a Rogue Wave database API)

Description: XML-DB Link is a Web server plug-in that accesses relational databases based on predefined, parameterized SQL statements called "services." When XLM-DB Link receives a request for a Web service, it locates the appropriate service, accesses the database to get information, and executes the service. Results are transformed into XML as a SOAP document, and then sent back to the client where they are displayed or used by the requesting application.

XML Junction and Data Junction Suite

URL: http://www.xmljunction.net/; http://www.datajunction.com/
Data Source: ODBC, OLE DB, Native Drivers
Description: XML Junction is used for rapidly building E-business and application integration solutions and is a component within Data Junction's Integration Suite, the basis for B2B, EAI, and business intelligence solutions. Data Junction contains a transformation engine to convert databases into non-database formats (including XML) and vice versa. XML Junction is a visual mapping and integration tool that handles all dialects of XML as well as data type definitions (DTDs), external data representations (XDRs), and XML schema. One can map and move any type of data (including electronic data interchange (EDI), SQL, ASCII, COBOL, Binary) to or from XML, in batch mode or transaction mode (using Java Message Service (JMS), MQSeries, or Microsoft Message Queuing (MSMQ)). XML Junction is a free trial product.

XMLShark: infoShark

URL: http://www.infoshark.com/products/index.shtml
Data Source: Oracle, IBM DB2, Microsoft SQL Server and JDBC driver
Description: XMLShark is a software product for accomplishing distributed data exchange, allowing organizations to share information captured within corporate databases with anyone in the world by utilizing established XML document definitions. Developed in Java, it allows customers to achieve interoperability among diverse internal and external systems. Through a GUI, the user controlling the source database specifies what data to transfer, what server to use, and when to transfer the data. Similarly, the user controlling the target database specifies when to read data from the XML document.

XML SQL Utility for Java (Oracle8i Application)

URL: http://technet.oracle.com/docs/products/oracle8i/content.html
Data Source: JDBC

Description: XML SQL Utility for Java is a set of Java classes for transferring data between a relational database and an XML document. These classes are found in either a provided front end or in a user-written application. One must perform three steps when generating XML: (1) create a connection, (2) create an Oracle XMLQuery instance by supplying a SQL string or a ResultSet object, and (3) get the result as either a DOM tree or an XML string.

Net.Data: IBM

URL: http://www-4.ibm.com/software/data/net.data/
Data Source: ODBC, JDBC, Native Drivers (database to XML)
Description: Net.Data is a scripting language that allows one to create Web applications and is a no-cost feature of most versions of DB2 Universal Database. One can access data from DB2, Oracle, Distributed Relational Database Architecture (DRDA)-enabled data sources, and ODBC data sources, as well as flat file and Web Registry data. One can also use ASP to connect to DB2 through ODBC and ADO. Net.Data Version 7.2 for OS/2, Windows NT, and UNIX provides XML output, XHTML compatibility, file upload capability, and SQL statement nesting. Version 7 Net.Data for OS/390 and z/OS includes FastCGI, a COBOL language environment, and enhanced tracing.

Evaluation-Only Products

The following products are downloadable, are subject to evaluation, and have not yet been licensed. They allow data transfer in both directions: from XML to database, and from database to XML.

- DatabaseDom: IBM
- DataCraft: IBM

DatabaseDom: IBM

URL: http://www.alphaworks.ibm.com/tech/databasedom
Data Source: JDBC
Description: DatabaseDom is a combination of Java JDBC, IBM Data Access Bean, and DOM programming. It includes an XML template file to define the database and XML structure. A JavaBean is used to read the template, to create XML from the results of a database query, and to update the database based on a new or modified XML structure.

When the tree structure gets deep, recursive methods of searching through and rebuilding XML trees become inefficient.

As a partial solution, the faster hashtable data structure is used to search and update JDBC databases. The data from XML DOM tree format can be updated into JDBC database tables while XML files can be stored back into a database format.

DataCraft: IBM

URL: http://www.alphaworks.ibm.com/tech/datacraft
Data Source: DB2, Microsoft Access (database to XML)
Description: DataCraft is a tool targeted for Resource Description Framework (RDF)/XML applications within the context of Web-commerce applications and is a facility capable of generating visual query skeletons for use with IBM DB2 or Microsoft Access. It employs RDF and XML to describe data collection structures and to exchange resource schema and query between the server and client. Written in Java, DataCraft can be accessed by Web browsers.

Java-Based Database Middleware

Not all database middleware products are fully Java-compliant. Some contain JavaBeans while others do not. Not all fully JDBC-compliant products are certified by Sun as "100% Pure Java."

The following are examples of these products. Additional sources of information can be obtained from http://www.infoworld.com, and http://www.informationweek.com.

1. Business Sight Framework: Objectmatter
2. CocoBase (Free, Lite, Enterprise): Thought Inc.
3. CocoBase Enterprise Object to Relational Mapping: Thought Inc.
4. DataDirect SequeLink: MERANT
5. DB2 Universal Database: IBM
6. IBM dbANYWHERE Server: Symantec
7. DbGen Professional Edition: 2Link Consulting, Inc.
8. Enterprise Component Broker: Information Builders, Inc.
9. ExpressLane: XDB Systems
10. FastForward: Connect Software
11. Fresco: Infoscape Inc.
12. HiT JDBC/400: HiT Software Inc.
13. HiT JDBC/DB2: HiT Software, Inc.
14. IDS Server: IDS Software
15. Jaguar CTS: Sybase Inc.
16. Javabase/400: Telasoft Data Corporation
17. jConnect for JDBC: Sybase Inc.
18. JDBC Developer: Recital Corporation
19. JDBC Lite: Software Synergy Listing

20. JdbCache: Caribou Lake Software Inc.
21. jdbcKona: BEA Systems, WebXpress Division
22. JDX: Software Tree
23. JRB–Java Relational Binding: Ardent Software, Inc.
24. JSQL: Caribou Lake Software Inc.
25. Jsvr: Caribou Lake Software Inc.
26. JYD Object Database: JYD Software Engineering Pty Ltd.
27. ObjectStore PSE for Java: Object Design Inc.
28. OpenLink Data Access Drivers For JDBC: OpenLink Software Inc.
29. Oracle Lite: Oracle Corporation
30. POET Object Server Suite: POET Software Corporation
31. PRO/Enable: Black & White Software Inc.
32. Relational Object Framework: Watershed Technologies
33. RmiJdbc: GIE Dyade
34. SCO SQL-Retriever: SCO
35. SOLID JDBC Driver: Solid Information Technology Ltd.
36. SOLID Server: Solid Information Technology Ltd.
37. Versant ODBMS: Versant Object Technology
38. VisiChannel (JDBC): Visigenic Software Inc.

Business Sight Framework: Objectmatter

Platforms: Intel: Windows 95/98/NT/2000
Cert. 100% Pure: No
Java Bean: No
Description: Business Sight Framework is an object-relational Java class library. It allows Java objects to be saved and retrieved from relational databases accessible by JDBC, Remote Data Object (RDO), or ADO with Microsoft's ODBC drivers. The Framework supports local objects in a single-user or client/server configuration, as well as distributed business objects in a n-tier architecture. A graphical user interface (GUI) mapping tool can be used to reverse-engineer existing Java classes and database tables, and generate Java source templates and Data Definition Language (DDL) scripts.

CocoBase (Free, Lite, Enterprise): Thought Inc.

Platforms: Intel PC, SPARC, RS/6000, HP/9000, Mac, SGI, Alpha, AS/400, Windows 95/98/NT/2000, Solaris, AIX, HP/UX, MacOS, JavaOS, Irix, OS/2, OS/400
Cert. 100% Pure: No
Java Bean: Yes
Description: An object-to-relational mapping tool, CocoBase sits on top of the JDBC drivers and employs Common Object Request Broker Architecture (CORBA) or Remote Method Invocation (RMI) to access and manipulate databases and data stores

as application objects without using the SQL. It glues together the GUI, ORB (or RMI), and JDBC driver of the developer's choice. The Enterprise version includes tools for mapping objects, and converting classes into objects, and tables to objects.

CocoBase Enterprise Object to Relational Mapping: Thought Inc.

Platforms: Windows, Solaris, Linux, HP, SGI, AIX
Cert. 100% Pure: Yes
Java Bean: Yes
Description: CocoBase maps database tables or Java classes, creates Container or Bean Managed Persistent Beans (CMP/BMP), and generates Java Server Pages (JSPs) for the popular EJB J2EE application servers, including Allaire, BEA Weblogic, Borland, Bluestone, Gemstone, IBM WebSphere, iPlanet, JBOSS, and Sybase.

DataDirect SequeLink: MERANT

Platforms: Windows, Solaris, AIX, OS/400, DEC UNIX
Cert. 100% Pure: Yes
Java Bean: Yes
Description: SequeLink Java Edition delivers data integration for all major platforms and data stores. By implementing the full JDBC specification, it ensures database support and complete compatibility across the latest browsers and Java servers. This product provides direct, native access to data, thus eliminating the need for gateways or DBMS vendor middleware.

DB2 Universal Database: IBM

Platforms: Intel, SPARC, RS/600, HP/9000, Windows 95/NT, Solaris, AIX, HP/UX, OS/2
Cert. 100% Pure: No
Java Bean: No
Description: DB2 Universal Database is a multimedia, Web-enabled database for decision support, data warehousing and data mining, and OLAP and online transaction processing (OLTP).

dbANYWHERE Server: Symantec

Platforms: Intel PC, Windows 95/98/NT/2000
Cert. 100% Pure: No
Java Bean: No

Description: dbANYWHERE Server is a middleware application server
                               that manages transactions and connectivity between Java
                               clients and many databases — Oracle, Sybase, MS SQL
                               Server, Sybase SQL-Anywhere, MS Access, and other ODBC
                               sources, including DB2. This product is 100 percent JDBC
                               compliant.

DbGen Professional Edition: 2Link Consulting, Inc.

Platforms: Intel, SPARC, Windows 95/98/NT/2000, Solaris, x.86 Solaris
Cert. 100% Pure: No
Java Bean: Yes
Description: DbGen is an object-relational mapping tool that generates
                               Java objects to do basic insert, update, and delete operations
                               on the tables of a relational database via a JDBC driver.

Enterprise Component Broker: Information Builders, Inc.

Platforms: Intel, SPARC, HP/9000, RS/6000, Windows 95/98/NT/2000,
                               Solaris, OS/2, AIX, HP/UX, Netware 4.11
Cert. 100% Pure: No
Java Bean: Yes
Description: Enterprise Component Broker is an Application Server and
                               Java development platform for client- and server-side appli-
                               cations using the JavaBean component model. It enables
                               connections to Java applications for integration with trans-
                               action systems such as CICS and IMS, other applications,
                               and many databases.

ExpressLane: XDB Systems

Platforms: Intel PCs, Windows 95/98/NT/2000
Cert. 100% Pure: No
Java Bean: No
Description: ExpressLane optimizes performance of Java-based applets
                               and business applications when accessing MVS/DB2, IMS,
                               and VSAM data sources. It includes an optional RDBMS, a
                               native JDBC driver, as well as a smart ODBC driver, Link
                               software, and GUI tools for developing and deploying appli-
                               cations.

FastForward: Connect Software

Platforms: Intel, SPARC, Windows NT/95, Solaris
Cert. 100% Pure: No
Java Bean: No

Description:	FastForward is a JDBC implementation for Sybase and Microsoft SQL Server.

Fresco: Infoscape Inc.

Platforms:	Intel, SPARC, Mac, Windows 95/98/NT/2000, Solaris, System 7
Cert. 100% Pure:	Yes
Java Bean:	No
Description:	The Fresco product family is a suite of tools and servers for creating and deploying enterprise-scale intranet database applications. It includes Fresco Designer, a Java rapid application development tool; Fresco Information Server, an intranet application server; and Fresco Adapters, providing seamless connections to corporate databases.

HiT JDBC/400: HiT Software, Inc.

Platforms:	Windows, Solaris, Linux, AS/400
Cert. 100% Pure:	Yes
Java Bean:	Yes
Description:	HiT JDBC/400 is fully Java-compliant middleware for DB2/400 SQL that can access databases from custom applications and third-party products. HiT JDBC/400 accepts standard JDBC function calls; translates these into native DB2/400 SQL; and communicates with the AS/400 server to retrieve, update, and insert DB2 data (type 4 driver). All communication with the DB2/400 servers can be encrypted and authenticated via SSL v3.0. HiT JDBC/400 works with any operating system running Java Virtual Machine (JVM) 1.02 or later, including Windows, UNIX, Linux, IBM OS/400, and IBM OS/390.

HiT JDBC/DB2: HiT Software, Inc.

Platforms:	Windows, Solaris, Linux, AS/400
Cert. 100% Pure:	Yes
Java Bean:	Yes
Description:	HiT JDBC/DB2 accepts standard JDBC function calls; translates these into native DB2 SQL; and communicates with the DB2 servers to retrieve, update, and insert DB2 data (type 4 driver). All communication with the DB2 server can be encrypted and authenticated via SSL v3.0. Leveraging the IBM Distributed Relational Database Architecture (DRDA) protocol, HiT JDBC/DB2 uses native IBM server programs and does not require any additional DB2 server software. The middleware supports DB2 Universal Database (UDB)

for OS/390 and works with any operating system running
JVM 1.02 or later, including Windows, UNIX, Linux, IBM
OS/400, and IBM OS/390.

IDS Server: IDS Software

Platforms:	Windows 95/98/NT/2000
Cert. 100% Pure:	No
Java Bean:	No
Description:	IDS JDBC Driver, which comes with the IDS Server, is a Type-3 JDBC driver. It supports JDK 1.02 and JDK 1.1 browsers, zero client installation, public key encryption (Secure JDBC), firewall access, ResultSet caching, and any other features not found in competing JDBC drivers.

Jaguar CTS: Sybase Inc.

Platforms:	Intel, SPARC, HP/9000, RS/6000, Windows NT/2000, Solaris, HP/UX, AIX
Cert. 100% Pure:	No
Java Bean:	Yes
Description:	Jaguar is a component transaction server designed to deliver scalable, transaction-based applications for the Internet. It supports multiple component models, including JavaBeans, ActiveX, and C/C++ while providing connection management, session management, monitoring, multi-database connectivity, and point-and-click administration. The production version supports EJBs and a set of APIs to allow JavaBeans to run in a transaction server.

Javabase/400: Telasoft Data Corporation

Platforms:	Intel, AS/400, Windows 95, x.86 Solaris, OS/400
Cert. 100% Pure:	No
Java Bean:	Yes
Description:	Javabase/400 is a client/server application that provides Java with secure record-level access to the AS/400 relational database DB2/400. You can access record and field level database files, call AS/400 programs or commands, and return parameters.

jConnect for JDBC: Sybase Inc.

Platforms:	Intel, SPARC, Alpha, HP/9000, SGI, RS/6000, Mac, Windows 95/98/NT/2000, Solaris, DEC UNIX, HP/UX, Irix, AIX, System 7
Cert. 100% Pure:	Yes

Java Bean:	Yes
Description:	jConnect for JDBC translates JDBC calls directly into Sybase's native protocol, Tabular Data Stream (TDS), and is well suited for "thin-client" business applications where no client software installation is desired. It directly supports Sybase's SQL Server; SQL Anywhere; and more than 25 other data sources, including Oracle, DB2, and Informix and through Sybase's middleware products OmniConnect and Direct-Connect.

JDBC Developer: Recital Corporation

Platforms:	Windows, Solaris, Linux, BSD, HP/UX, Irix, AIX, OpenVMS
Cert. 100% Pure:	No
Java Bean:	Yes
Description:	JDBC Developer combines a JavaType 3/Type 4 JDBC 1.0 driver with a server architecture, allowing access to Recital, Oracle, Ingres, Informix, DB2/6000, C-ISAM, Digital RMS, dBase, FoxPro, Clipper, and ODBC data sources.

JDBC Lite: Software Synergy

Platforms:	Intel, Windows NT/95
Cert. 100% Pure:	No
Java Bean:	No
Description:	JDBC Lite is a lightweight JDBC driver, providing access to ODBC databases. The driver requires only a tiny memory footprint, and uses minimal overhead because it is downloaded with the applet. JDBC Lite works well on platforms with limited memory.

JdbCache: Caribou Lake Software Inc.

Platforms:	Windows, Solaris, Linux, AIX, HP/UX
Cert. 100% Pure:	Yes
Java Bean:	No
Description:	JdbCache is a class library for "caching" multiple JDBC connections within a multi-threaded Java application. It pools, reuses, and serves JDBC connections, thus allowing a Java application to reuse a small number of database connections to service many requests. Usage statistics are also provided.

jdbcKona: BEA Systems, WebXpress Division

Platforms:	Windows, Solaris, SunOS, HP/UX, AIX, Irix, OS/2, OS/400

Cert. 100% Pure: No
Java Bean: Yes
Description: The product includes JDBC drivers for Oracle, Sybase, Infor-
                   mix, and Microsoft SQL Server. Native drivers are JBDC-
                   compatible.

JDX: Software Tree

Platforms: Intel, SPARC, RS/6000, Windows 95/98/NT/2000, x.86
                   Solaris, Solaris, AIX
Cert. 100% Pure: No
Java Bean: No
Description: JDX provides transactional persistence of Java objects in
                   relational databases by mapping relational data to Java
                   objects. With JDX, programmers are not required to write
                   SQL statements.

JRB–Java Relational Binding: Ardent Software, Inc.

Platforms: Intel PC, SPARC, HP/9000, SGI, RS/6000, Windows 95/98/
                   NT/2000, Solaris 2.4/2.5
Cert. 100% Pure: No
Java Bean: Yes
Description: JRB bridges the gap between applications and databases,
                   while providing persistence for Java developers. Program-
                   mers can read Java objects from and write Java objects to
                   the database. Objects are automatically mapped into data-
                   base format, offering transparent management of persistent
                   Java objects. This eliminates the need for developers to
                   know the location of either the underlying database engine
                   or stored objects.

JSQL: Caribou Lake Software Inc.

Platforms: Windows, Solaris, Linux, AIX, HP/UX
Cert. 100% Pure: No
Java Bean: No
Description: JSQL is a multi-tier software suite designed for secure, robust
                   mission-critical Java applications requiring JDBC. The prod-
                   uct is compliant with Sun's JDBC 2.0 specification.

Jsvr: Caribou Lake Software Inc.

Platforms: Windows, Solaris Intel, Solaris, DEC UNIX, HP/UX, Irix, AIX
Cert. 100% Pure: Yes
Java Bean: Yes

Description: Jsvr is a JDBC connection server configurable with client-specified timeouts, meta data, BLOB support, complete connection logging, and advanced security features.

JYD Object Database: JYD Software Engineering Pty Ltd.

Platforms: Windows, Solaris, Linux
Cert. 100% Pure: No
Java Bean: No
Description: This product is an object DBMS for use by Java applications. It is a multi-user system with client/server support and garbage collection on the database.

ObjectStore PSE for Java: Object Design Inc.

Platforms: Intel, SPARC, Alpha, HP/9000, SGI, RS/6000, Mac, Windows 95//98/NT/2000, x.86 Solaris, OS/2, Solaris, Irix, System 7
Cert. 100% Pure: Yes
Java Bean: Yes
Description: The product is a full-featured pure Java database with a 150-kilobyte footprint. An object architecture, it reduces database and application memory requirements by 25 percent or more because no mapping code is needed.

ObjectStore DBMS: Object Design Inc.

Platforms: Intel, SPARC, Alpha, HP/9000, RS/6000, SGI, Windows NT, Solaris, Solaris x.86, DEC UNIX, HP/UX, AIX, Irix
Cert. 100% Pure: No
Java Bean: No
Description: ObjectStore is an object database management system (ODBMS) for Java, C++, and ActiveX developers. It manages data as objects rather than as rows and columns. Among its features are native object storage, distributed data caching, seamless Java integration, navigational access, and extensibility.

OpenLink Data Access Drivers for JDBC: OpenLink Software Inc.

Platforms: Intel, SPARC, Alpha, HP/9000, Mac, Windows, x.86 Solaris, Linux, BSD, Solaris, SunOS, DEC UNIX, HP/UX, MacOS, InixWare, SCO
Cert. 100% Pure: No
Java Bean: Yes
Description: The product contains JDBC drivers providing access to remote database engines from JDBC-compliant Java Applications, Applets, Serverlets, and Bean Components. It gives bi-

directional scrollable cursor support to all database engines supported by OpenLink Software: Oracle, Informix, CA/OpenIngres, Sybase, Progress, MS SQL Server, Unify, DB2, Postgres95, Kubl, and Velocis.

Oracle Lite: Oracle Corporation

Platforms: Intel, SPARC, Mac, Windows 95/98/NT/2000, Solaris, System 7
Cert. 100% Pure: Yes
Java Bean: No
Description: Oracle Lite is a single-user object-relational DBMS with Java object persistence, standard Oracle interfaces, Java stored procedures and triggers, and native JDBC driver. It includes replication to servers with SQL*Net, FTP, API, HTTP, mime or file-based protocols.

POET Object Server Suite: POET Software Corporation

Platforms: Windows, Linux, Solaris, HP/9000
Cert. 100% Pure: No
Java Bean: Yes
Description: POET Object Server Suite (OSS) 6.0 is a database solution for creating packaged, complex data applications. It combines POET's FastObject Technology with multi-threading and transaction capabilities.

PRO/Enable: Black & White Software Inc.

Platforms: Intel, SPARC, HP/9000, Windows 95/98/NT/2000, Solaris, HP/UX
Cert. 100% Pure: No
Java Bean: No
Description: PRO/Enable (Persistent Relational-Object) provides persistent relational-object mapping and application development for three-tier applications on UNIX and Windows platforms.

Relational Object Framework: Watershed Technologies

Platforms: Intel, HP/9000, RS/6000, Windows, Linux, HP/UX, AIX
Cert. 100% Pure: No
Java Bean: Yes
Description: Relational Object Framework (ROF) is a relational DBMS (RDBMS) to Java Object middleware layer for enterprise application development and is complementary to EJB, JSP, CORBA, and servlet solutions. It provides a bridge by mapping Java Objects to database elements. With ROF, developers

are not required to know about SQL in order to connect business objects to a relational database.

RmiJdbc: GIE Dyade

Platforms:	RS/6000; AIX
Cert. 100% Pure:	No
Java Bean:	No
Description:	RmiJdbc is a client/server JDBC driver that relies on Java RMI. All JDBC classes, such as Connection and ResultSet, are distributed as RMI objects.

SCO SQL-Retriever: SCO

Platforms:	Intel, SPARC, Alpha, HP/9000, RS/6000, Windows 95/98/NT/2000, SCO, Solaris, HP/UX, AIX
Cert. 100% Pure:	No
Java Bean:	No
Description:	SCO SQL-Retriever is designed for rapid development of database access solutions. It uses JDBC/ODBC to deliver UNIX-based SQL database information to PCs without the cost or complexity associated with proprietary database vendor networking products.

SOLID JDBC Driver: Solid Information Technology Ltd.

Platforms:	Intel, SPARC, HP/9000, RS/6000, SGI, Windows 95/98/NT/2000, Linux, SCO, UNIXWare, OS/2, Solaris, HP/UX, Irix, AIX, VxWorks
Cert. 100% Pure:	No
Java Bean:	No
Description:	SOLID JDBC Driver is a full Java implementation of JDBC, providing native database access to SOLID Server. It can be downloaded on the fly, enabling the use of SOLID database in thin-client Java applications.

SOLID Server: Solid Information Technology Ltd.

Platforms:	Intel, SPARC, HP/9000, RS/6000, SGI, Windows, Linux, SCO, UNIXWare, OS/2, Solaris, HP/UX, Irix, AIX, VxWorks
Cert. 100% Pure:	No
Java Bean:	No
Description:	SOLID Server is a compact database engine for embedded use in Web applications and packaged software. It has a native ODBC driver and a fully Java-compliant native JDBC driver.

Versant ODBMS: Versant Object Technology

Platforms: Intel, SPARC, HP/9000, SGI, RS/6000, Win NT/2000, Solaris, HP/UP, Irix, RS/6000

Cert. 100% Pure: No

Java Bean: No

Description: Versant Object Database Management System is Java-enabled persistent storage for objects. It supports the ODMG 2.0 standard for transactional object data management, and provides native thread support, Javasoft collections, high concurrency, and fault tolerance.

VisiChannel (JDBC) Visigenic Software Inc.

Platforms: Intel, SPARC, Windows NT, Solaris

Cert. 100% Pure: No

Java Bean: Yes

Description: A JDBC driver is well suited for most popular DBMSs via ODBC drivers and works with firewalls. It is fully JDBC compliant and built on top of company's VisiBroker CORBA product.

XML-Enabled Databases

XML-enabled databases are databases (usually relational) that contain extensions (either model- or template-driven) for transferring data between XML documents and themselves. They are generally designed to store and retrieve data-centric documents. This is because data is transferred to and from user-defined tables rather than database tables specifically designed to model XML documents.

Because many databases can publish documents to the Web, the line between XML-enabled databases and XML servers is blurred, although the latter are designed primarily for building Web-based applications. More distinct is the line between XML-enabled databases, XML application servers (which cannot receive data as XML), and content management systems (which are generally used for storing document-centric documents and contain features such as editors and version control).

This section describes the following XML-enabled databases.

1. DB2 XML Extender: IBM
2. Informix: IBM
3. Microsoft SQL Server 2000
4. Microsoft Access 2002
5. Oracle8*i*/9*i* Application Servers

DB2 XML Extender and DB2 Text Extender: IBM

URL: http://www-4.ibm.com/software/data/db2/extenders/ xmlext.html, http://www-4.ibm.com/software/data/db2/extenders/text.htm

Data Source: Relational

Description: The DB2 XML Extender is used to transfer data between XML documents and DB2. XML DTDs are mapped to relational schema (and vice versa) with the XML-based Data Access Definition (DAD) language. The language comes in two flavors: SQL mapping and relational database (RDB) node mapping. SQL mapping is a template-based language and can only be used to transfer data from the database to an XML document. RDB node mapping is a model-based language and uses object-relational mapping. It can be used to transfer data both to and from the database. Applications use stored procedures to invoke the extender, which then stores or retrieves data based on the DAD document. The DB2 Text Extender contains a variety of search technologies, such as fuzzy searches and synonym searches among others.

Informix: IBM

URL: http://www.informix.com/idn-secure/webtools/ot/, http://www.informix.com/datablades/dbmodule/informix1.htm

Data Source: Relational

Description: Informix supports XML through its Object Translator and the Web DataBlade. The Object Translator generates object code, including the ability of objects to transfer their data to and from the database. It also supports functionality such as transactions and optimistic and pessimistic locking. A GUI tool allows users to create object-relational mappings from XML documents to the database and specify how to construct intermediate objects. Object Translator Version 2.0 and higher supports SOAP as well as the capability to generate XML DTDs from object and relational schema.

The Web DataBlade is an application that creates XML documents from templates containing embedded SQL statements and other scripting language commands. It is run from a Web server and supports most major Web server APIs.

Microsoft SQL Server 2000

URL: http://msdn.microsoft.com/library/periodic/period00/sql2000.htm (see "XML Support" section), http://msdn.microsoft.com/library/periodic/period00/thexmlfiles.htm

Data Source: Relational
Description: Microsoft SQL Server 2000 supports XML in four ways:

- *The FOR XML clause in SELECT statements.* This clause has three options specifying how the SELECT statement is mapped to XML: RAW, AUTO, and EXPLICIT.
- *Xpath queries using annotated XML-Data Reduced schemas.* These mapping schemas specify an object-relational mapping between the XML document and the database, and are used to query the database using a subset of Xpath.
- *The OpenXML function in stored procedures.* This function uses a table-based mapping to extract parts of an XML document as a table and use it in most places where a table name can be used, such as the FROM clause of a SELECT statement. This can be used, for example, in conjunction with an INSERT statement to transfer data from an XML document to the database.
- *ADO 2.6.* One can use ADO as a tool to process XML directly without having to make conversions between XML and another format. The version of ADO must be 2.6 or later.

Microsoft Access 2002

URL: http://www.microsoft.com/office/access/
Data Source: Relational
Description: Microsoft Access 2002 is the Windows XP Office Database solution. It uses XML to publish and view reports on a Web browser with HTML 4.0 or higher. These reports may contain the results of data analysis using Microsoft PivotTable and Microsoft ChartTable that allow one to view the information in different ways. Access 2002 also imports XML documents into Access (Jet) or an SQL Server database and exports XML from Access into other formats. It can both upload tables to corporate-level, back-end SQL Server and access information from it. Access 2002 permits one to interact with data on the Web browser via a Web-enabled database.

Oracle8i/9i Application Servers

URL: http://technet.oracle.com/tech/xml/info/htdocs/relational/
                index.htm#ID795,
                http://technet.oracle.com/docs/products/ifs/doc_index.htm
                (registration required),
                http://technet.oracle.com/products/intermedia/,
                http://otn.oracle.com/products/reports/htdocs/
                reports_faq.htm#XML1
Data Source: Relational

Description: Oracle9*i* AS includes Native XML Database Support (XDB), and navigational search for XML documents. Oracle9*i* supports XML as a data source (including XML-Schema and xsql result sets). Developers can describe an entire report definition in XML and save the definition to either an RDF or XML file.

Oracle8*i* can store XML documents in three different ways:

- In the Internet File System (IFS)
- Using the XML SQL Utility for Java
- As a BLOB that can be searched using the Oracle Intermedia XML Search.

The first two employ an object-relational mapping tool while only IFS supports content management features such as check-in/check-out and versioning. Oracle8*i* includes the XML Class Generator to generate Java classes from a DTD.

Web Services-Enabled Database Middleware

DataSnap Enterprise Edition (see Exhibit 6) permits developers and companies to enable their existing RDBMS infrastructure with industry-standard Web services without major upgrades. It leverages distributed computing standards such as SOAP/XML, Web Services Definition Language (WSDL), COM, TCP/IP, and CORBA to allow the integration of existing systems with E-commerce applications.

This product is fully client- and server-side compatible with Borland MIDAS technologies. DataSnap optimizes RDBMS server connections and bandwidth by centralizing data access and updates among all E-business processes. DataSnap supports multiple Delphi data-access connectivity solutions with access to Access, dBase, FoxPro, MySQL, MyBase, Paradox, Oracle, DB2, the MS SQL server, Informix, Sybase, and InterBase. It runs on Microsoft Windows 2000, Windows Me, Windows 98, or Windows NT 4.0 with Service Pack 5 or later.

Windows Telephony with TAPI

Windows Telephony Applications Programming Interface (TAPI) 2.1, a part of the Windows Open System Architecture, lets developers create telephony applications. TAPI is an open industry standard, defined with considerable and ongoing input from the worldwide telephony and computing community. TAPI-compatible applications can run on a wide variety of PC and telephony hardware and can support a variety of network services.

Microsoft TAPI is a convergence platform that enables applications to provide a consistent user experience even when the applications are running on various topologies such as the public switched telephone network (PSTN), ISDN, PBX systems, and IP networks. With other Microsoft products such as

Exhibit 6.   Dephi 6 DataSnap Feature Matrix

Feature	Enterprise Edition	Professional Edition	Personal Edition
DataSnap Web-Service Enabled Database Middleware			
New! Web Client, GUI Client, and Web service access to any supported RDBMS	Y		
New! SOAP/XML, COM, CORBA, Web, and TCP/IP access connections available for maximum network connectivity and flexibility	Y		
New! Easily build XML/SOAP Web service interfaces to any enterprise-class database — Oracle, MS SQL Server, DB2, InterBase, and more	Y		
Dataset-based architecture for rapid learning curve — use existing skillsets to scale applications	Y		
Support for dbGo, BDE, IBX, and NewdbExpress data access architectures	Y		
High availability with the object broker failover safety to guarantee your data is ready when you need it	Y		
Load-balancing to promote the highest performance even when under the heaviest loads	Y		
Distributed data with transaction processing extends the reach of applications while maintaining data integrity	Y		
Automatic database constraint propagation brings the business rules to the client applications for local processing, conserving server horsepower	Y		
Low-maintenance, thin, and easily configured client-side applications to reduce deployment costs	Y		
High-speed database connectivity yields higher performance in applications	Y		
Server object pooling maximizes the conservation of resources on servers, keeping materials costs down	Y		
Supply data to thin-client applications rapidly, efficiently, and securely	Y		
Remote data broker to easily partition applications	Y		

Exhibit 6. Dephi 6 DataSnap Feature Matrix (Continued)

Feature	Enterprise Edition	Professional Edition	Personal Edition
TransactionResolver for transaction conflict resolution	Y		
Exclusive. Advanced Master/Detail Provider and Resolver support	Y		
BDE Resource Dispenser for MTS	Y		
Stateless DataBroker for more control in mobile and low-bandwidth situations	Y		
Server object pooling for complete scalability	Y		
Provider options increase control over how and what information is transmitted	Y		
DataSnap Development License included	Y		
Simple DataSnap deployment licensing	Y		
CORBAsupport			
New! VisiBroker 4.0.x for Delphi 6, including CORBA client and server development	Y		
New! Wizards to simplify development of CORBA clients and servers	Y		
New! BorlandAppServer v4.5 SIDL support — and build new rich applications and Web services with Delphi's RAD environment that uses EJBs for AppServer	Y		
Visual Type Library Editor — CORBA IDL Emitter	Y		
DataSnap CORBA connection component	Y		
Support for simultaneous COM and CORBA objects	Y		
Server object persistence model for greater scalability	Y		
Remote CORBA debugging/event stepping (multi-platform — UNIX/NT/Java)	Y		

Microsoft SNA Server and Microsoft Exchange Server, this integration extends to mainframe applications, messaging, and scheduling, among other things. TAPI 2.1 addresses the client/server need for call control. A telephony client application can integrate with the phone system via a link between the server and phone system, or via a link between the desktop PC and telephone set.

HTTPR

As of August 2001, developers consider Reliable HTTP (HTTPR) an unpopular item. Yet, reliable message support is not a new technology. Messaging middleware products such as the IBM MQSeries, Oracle Message Broker (Oracle8i), and MSMQ have supported it for years and are widely deployed in enterprise computing environments. Reliable messaging is currently supported via product-specific protocols.

As a partial solution, IBM is making the HTTPR specification available to the public to stimulate public discussion on reliable message delivery on the Internet. HTTPR is a protocol for the reliable transport of messages from one application program to another over the Internet, even in the presence of failures either of the network or the agents on either end. It is layered on top of HTTP.

Messaging agents can use HTTPR together with persistent storage capability to provide reliable messaging for applications. The specification of HTTPR does not include the design of a messaging agent, nor does it say what storage mechanisms should be used by a messaging agent. It does specify the state information needs to be in to be stored safely and when to store it so that a messaging agent can provide reliable delivery using HTTPR.

SOAP messages transported over HTTPR will have the same format as SOAP messages over HTTP. The additional information needed to correlate request and response in the HTTPR asynchronous (or pseudo-synchronous) environment is put into the HTTPR message context header. The `SOAPAction` parameter is carried in the HTTPR message context header as the type *app-soap-action*. Extensions to SOAP such as in ebXML and SOAP-RP contain application-level correlation information that must also be carried in the HTTPR message context header for this protocol.

SOAP can operate over HTTPR to allow Web services to make use of these reliability features. A WSDL specification for HTTPR will be almost precisely the same as for HTTP. For example, the following binding:

```
<soap:binding style = "…"
transport = "http://JohnIbbotson/ToFillIn/httpr"/>
```

will reference this HTTPR binding.

Notes

1. Here is a partial list of data adapters available for the following databases, ERPs, transaction systems, and files.
    a. *Relational and legacy data*: ADABAS, ALLBASE/SQL, ALL-IN-1, C-ISAM, CA-Datacom/DB, CA-IDMS, CA-Ingres, Cloudbase, DB2, DB2/2, DB2/400, DB2/6000, DBMS, dBASE, DL/1, DMS, ENSCRIBE, Essbase, FOCUS, IDS-II, IMS/DB, INFOAccess, Infoman, Informix, ISAM, KSAM, MODEL 204, MS SQL Server, MS OLAP Services, Mumps, Net-ISAM, Rdb, Tandem NonStop, Omnidex, Oracle, PACE, Pick Systems, Proprietary Files, Progress, QSAM, Red Brick, RMS, ShareBase, SQL/DS, SUPRA, Sybase, System 2000, Teradata, Total, TurboIMAGE, UFAS, Ultrix/SQL, UNIFY, UX, VSAM, WIIS
    b. *ERP systems*: SAP R/3, J.D. Edwards, PeopleSoft, Oracle, Baan, Walker Interactive, Millenium, Hogan Financials, Integral
    c. *OLTP/messaging*: CICS, IMS/DC, IMS/TM, MQSeries
    d. *Operating Platforms*: OS/390 Open Edition, VM, MVS, AIX, AIX/6000, OS/400, VMS, OpenVMS, Digital UNIX, AT&T UNIX, Sun Solaris, SunOS, HP-UX, Linux, Bull GCOS, Siemens, Windows NT, Windows 2000, IBM OS/2
2. iWay Enterprise Integrator integrates mobile, packaged and custom Web applications, using four types of adapters: transactions, applications, relational data, and legacy data.
3. MERANT is a strategic partner with Sun in the development of Java2 Enterprise Edition (J2EE), and Java Transaction Service (JTS), an API used by resource managers and transaction managers to incorporate database transaction capabilities.

Chapter 7

Bridging the Gap

Introduction

This chapter discusses how middleware such as Enterprise JavaBeans (EJBs) and markup languages such as XML can be used to bridge the gaps in an enterprisewide system. It looks at how a COBOL system is connected to EJBs, how Java is called from COBOL, and how COBOL classes are used to call from Java. The chapter presents what the advantages of using XML Schemas are in connecting E-commerce applications and shows why these schemas are better than DTDs. It also considers the role XML has played in TCP/IP Presentation layer and gives an overview of how XML is used to connect to an Oracle database over the air.

Bridging COBOL to Enterprise Java Beans

In view of the fact that the demand for mixing COBOL and Java is ever increasing, this section explains in detail how MERANT Micro Focus Net Express can be used to bridge COBOL to EJBs. It particularly focuses on accessing legacy COBOL assets from Java and EJBs, accessing Java objects from COBOL applications, invoking Object COBOL methods from Java and EJBs, and wrapping COBOL assets as COBOL EJBs.

Because these legacy systems include an estimated 200 billion lines of COBOL code, the ability of such enterprises to rapidly and reliably deliver COBOL business logic to the Internet is very important to the success and survival of organizations. It is impractical to convert all COBOL code to Java counterpart, as Java does not have certain features that COBOL has.

While it is obvious that Java will never completely replace COBOL, users can establish their legacy applications upon a strategic platform for extension toward E-business. Doing so will allow users to connect these legacy systems with new code written in Java, and reuse rather than rewrite legacy business logic, delivering it with application servers such as IBM WebSphere, BEA WebLogic, and others as part of EJBs.

Application Mining

The first step in building an application interface is to extract the business logic from the application. One can do this with the technique known as application mining, and offered by MERANT AssetMiner. This technique analyzes and modularizes the application that can interface with Java and wrap the COBOL as an EJB for deployment on Windows and UNIX systems.

While in the past the interfaces and capabilities provided by Web application servers differed considerably, they primarily targeted Java and C++, making it difficult for COBOL applications to interoperate with Java. To establish interoperability between Java and COBOL, the convergence toward the EJB model, the delivery of existing COBOL business logic into that model, and utilizing Java classes from COBOL should be combined.

While such interoperability has long been possible, it has not necessarily been easy. The Java platform allows Java methods to call non-Java (or native) methods via the mechanism known as Java native interface (JNI). Yet COBOL programmers must still perform low-level API functions to make Java calls.

Accessing Legacy COBOL Assets from Java

The existing (or legacy) COBOL applications contained within enterprises represent the result of a huge investment over many years, embodying the core of the business practices within COBOL business logic. The last thing one wants to do is throw that all away and rewrite everything in Java.

If one has newer systems already written in Java, or wishes to take advantage of Java for less business orientated new development, the ability to call legacy COBOL programs from Java (and as we will see later from EJBs) provides a fast way to make existing COBOL business logic available to Java programs. One is not required to have any knowledge of object COBOL syntax. The support is provided through a special Java class (`mfcobol.runtime`) that provides functions to enable one to load, call, and cancel COBOL programs.

Calling Legacy COBOL from Java

If one understands COBOL jargon, here is an example of calling a legacy COBOL program from Java. This is a simple COBOL subroutine, named `subroutine.cbl`, consisting of a working-storage section, a linkage section, and procedure division.

```
working-storage section.
01 wsResult pic s9(9) comp-5.
linkage section.
01 wsOperand1 pic s9(9) comp-5.
01 wsOperand2 pic s9(9) comp-5.
01 wsOperation pic x.
procedure division using wsOperand1 wsOperand2 wsOperation.
evaluate wsOperation
when "a"
add wsOperand1 to wsOperand2 giving wsResult
when "s"
subtract wsOperand1 from wsOperand2 giving wsResult
end-evaluate
exit program returning wsResult.
```

Below is a Java program that calls this subroutine.

```
import mfcobol.* ;
class SimpleCall
{
  public static void main(String argv[])
  {
    Object theParams[] =   {new Integer (4),
                            new Integer(7),
                            new Byte((byte)'a')} ;
    int i = runtime.cobcall_int("subroutine", theParams) ;
    System.out.println(i) ;
    theParams[2] = new Character ('s') ;
    i = runtime.cobcall_int("subroutine", theParams) ;
    System.out.println(i) ;
  }
}
```

Java Considerations

To make COBOL support available to a Java program, include the following statement at the start of the Java source file: import mfcobol.*. Calling COBOL from Java is a straightforward process. In the case of legacy COBOL, this involves the use of static cobcall_ functions provided by the classes supplied and imported as shown in the example code above.

As discussed, parameters are converted between Java and COBOL data. In the example above, the COBOL program is returning a signed integer such as Pic S9(9) comp-5 that is equivalent to the Java data type int. Thus, one would call the COBOL program using the cobcall_int function.

COBOL Considerations

Java runtime systems are multi-threaded, so any COBOL program to be used with Java must be linked with the COBOL multi-threaded runtime system, whether or not the Java program calling it uses multi-threading. If the COBOL program is going to be called from a multi-threaded Java program, one needs to take care that the COBOL data accessed from one thread is not corrupted by another thread.

Calling Java from COBOL

Calling Java from COBOL translates to calling Java objects because Java is an object-oriented language. This does not, however, mean that one has to rewrite the entire COBOL application in Object COBOL or as an Object COBOL class, but one will be using some Object COBOL syntax to call (or invoke) Java. Add a Class-Control section to a COBOL program and use the INVOKE verb each time one wants to call a Java function — and it can be done without touching any business logic.

Java classes can easily be declared for use in a COBOL program with a single entry in Class-Control section.

```
class-control.
Rectangle is class "$java$java.awt.Rectangle"
```

The Java Rectangle class can be instantiated in several different ways, including the two shown below in Java code.

```
Rectangle r1 = new Rectangle ()
Rectangle r2 = new Rectangle(4, 5, 10, 20)
```

The equivalent COBOL code is shown below.

```
working-storage section.
01 r1 object reference.
01 r2 object reference.
...
procedure division.
...
invoke jRectangle "new" returning r1
invoke jRectangle "new" using 4, 5, 10, 20
returning r2
```

The Rectangle class has three different add() methods, which take different parameters. The Java code below shows three different ways one can call the add() method on a rectangle.

```
Rectangle r1 = new Rectangle(0,0,0,0) ;
Point pt = new Point(6,6) ;
Rectangle r2 = new Rectangle(3,4,9,9) ;
r1.add(4,5) ;
r1.add(pt) ;
r1.add(r2) ;
```

The equivalent code in COBOL looks like the following.

```
class-control.
jRectangle is class "$java$java.awt.Rectangle"
jPoint is class "$java$java.awt.Point"
    .
    .
    .
working-storage section.
01 r1 object reference.
01 r2 object reference.
01 pt object reference.
procedure division.
invoke jRectangle "new" returning r1
invoke jPoint "new" using 4 5 returning pt
invoke jRectangle "new" using 3 4 9 9 returning r2
invoke r1 "add" using 4 5
invoke r1 "add" using pt
invoke r1 "add" using r2
```

Calling COBOL Classes from Java

With Net Express one can write COBOL-wrapped Java classes. Essentially, these are classes in COBOL that can be called from Java programs as if they were Java classes. One does this by providing a simple Java wrapper class, which provides a function for each method in the COBOL class. The Net Express Class and Method Wizard generates the Java code at the same time as the COBOL code while creating a complete class infrastructure.

The most interesting part is an Object COBOL infrastructure into which one can slot COBOL business logic, either within the class itself or by calling out to existing COBOL applications. While the class generated by the wizard differs little from any other COBOL class, it inherits from javabase, the Java domain supplied in COBOL.

The following code fragments illustrate the definition of a class and method in COBOL.

```
*>--------------------------------------------------
*> Class description
*>--------------------------------------------------
class-id.JavaCalc
  inherits from javabase.
Object section.
Class-control.
  JavaCalc is class "javacalc"
*>--------------------------------------------------
working-storage section. *> Definition of global data
*>--------------------------------------------------
class-object. *> Definition of class data and methods
*>--------------------------------------------------
object-storage section.
```

```
01 currentRate pic 9(2).9(2) value 0.
01 currentRate-x pic x(5) redefines currentRate.
*>----------------------------------------
method-id. "setInterestRate".
Local-storage Section.
*>---USER-CODE. Add any local storage items needed below.
Linkage Section.
01 rate pic x(5).
Procedure division using by reference rate.
*>---USER-CODE. Add method implementation below.
Move rate to currentRate-x
exit method.
End method "setInterestRate".
```

The following Java code invokes the above COBOL code fragment.

```
Public static void setInterestRate (String rate) throws
Exception, COBOLExceptions
{
  // Parameters are passed to COBOL in an array
  Object[] params = {rate};
cobinvokestatic_void ("setInterestRate", params);
}
```

COBOL Enterprise JavaBeans

We have seen how to create COBOL-wrapped Java classes with Net Express. This same technology can be applied one step further, facilitating the creation of COBOL-wrapped EJBs. The Net Express class wizard enables one to create a COBOL class for use as an EJB.

EJBs are software components that run on application servers. The application server is responsible for all the services required by the bean, such as security, transaction integrity, and persistence, so that EJBs only need to implement business logic. By calling business logic within COBOL-wrapped EJBs, one can combine the benefits of an application server environment with the performance gain of compiled COBOL code.

For a COBOL-wrapped EJB, the Net Express class wizard will create the following files, as shown in Exhibit 1.

Exhibit 2 shows the main development steps.

Enterprise JavaBeans Deployment Descriptor

Each method added to the COBOL class must be added to the Java wrapper class, and also to the remote interface class. If using the Net Express method wizard, it automatically updates the wrapper and remote interface.

Now one has a COBOL EJB that can be tightly or loosely coupled with the legacy COBOL application. Maintaining the connectivity to a defined interface helps to deliver the same business logic to multiple component technologies.

Exhibit 1. COBOL-Wrapped EJB Files

COBOL file	Classname.cbl	
Methods	ejbCreate, ejbRemove, ejbActivate, ejbPassivate, setSessionContext	The COBOL file for each class includes required EJB methods; they are part of the SessionBean interface, which is implemented by all Enterprise JavaBeans
Class	Classname.java	The Java wrapper class corresponds to the COBOL class and contains the EJB methods
Class	*classname*Home.java	The home interface to the Java wrapper
Class	*classname*Remote.java	The remote interface to the Java wrapper
XML file	Ejb-jar.xml	

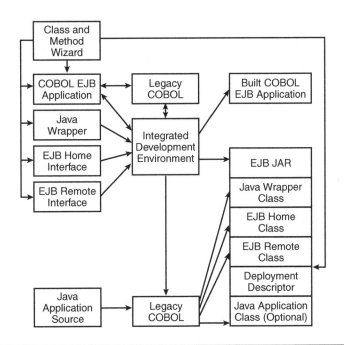

Exhibit 2. COBOL EJB Development Steps

Deploying COBOL Enterprise JavaBeans Application

At deployment time, COBOL-wrapped EJBs require the presence of the COBOL Runtime (also known as the application server). This server can be deployed either on Windows (with Net Express application server) or major UNIX platforms (with Server Express application server) as shown in Exhibit 3.

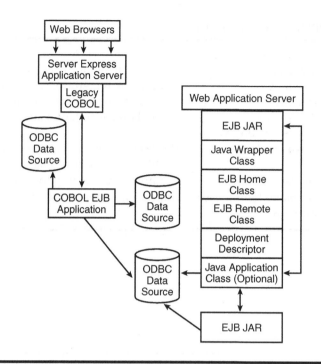

Exhibit 3.   COBOL EJB Application Deployment

Combination ActiveX/Java Classes

One can also create Object COBOL classes that can be used either by Java as Java classes or through OLE automation as ActiveX classes. The support that enables one to create combination ActiveX/Java classes is provided through an Object COBOL class called `componentbase`. ActiveX servers usually inherit from a class called `olebase`, and Java classes inherit from a class called `javabase`. If one changes the inheritance of one of these classes to `componentbase`, it can be used within either the Java or OLE automation domains. The domain to which the class is available depends on how it was first loaded within a process. The simplest way to create a class is to use the class wizard to create a class for OLE automation, and then create the Java wrapper class and methods manually.

This technology also enables one to create an Object COBOL class that can be used as a Microsoft Transaction Server (MTS) Object or as an EJB. It also allows one to call COBOL subroutines, middleware, ESQL, etc. as one would expect the COBOL EJB to do.

Wireless Access Protocol: Accessing Oracle

This section is based on the author's article "Accessing Oracle over the Air."

E-business users access two types of content from their cellular phones and personal digital assistants (PDAs): static content, such as stock quotes, news, and weather information; and transactional applications used to manipulate corporate data from various ERP and CRM systems. End users get them after requesting access to remote data and applications through the Oracle9*i* Application Server Wireless Edition.

This edition provides adapter/transformer pairs to allow content to go directly to a wireless device while permitting developers to skip intermediary steps of converting into XML documents. Adapters convert the content in its original format from a database table into XML documents, while transformers convert the XML documents into one of many formats, such as Wireless Markup Language (WML) or VoXML. The Wireless Edition ships with a set of preconfigured adapters for common data sources and markup languages and allows developers to build their own adapters.

WAP Application

Because Oracle does not provide wireless platforms, it has partnered with Motorola to collaborate on delivering WAP, VoXML, and Bluetooth applications to businesses with a mobile workforce. With a WAP-enabled phone, one can say certain words and hear the reply as the phone speaks. This process of interacting with the system is known as dialogue in the WAP world.

To begin, the user dials in a key number to make a connection and the system transparently refers the user to a database and opens it as specified in an Active Server Pages (ASP) script. The system then takes the user to the XML script in the same application. The XML script will not work if the ASP script fails to connect to and open the database. The user must include <?XML version = "1.0"?> to indicate the start of the script.

Depending on the number of dialogues between a user and the system, the application can have several ASP/XML scripts. A dialogue in one XML script may call another in a different XML script and get a returned value.

Dialogue Scenarios

Suppose the user is in the following dialogue, assuming all CIOs are located in Washington, D.C. The user goes through a series of steps to get the fax number needed to use with a fax machine in sending important documents to a CIO. Scanning bulky documents and e-mailing them are not cost-effective.

The following are three scenarios of simple interaction between a user and the system.

Scenario One

The user says a CIO's name that is already in the database.

System:	Welcome aboard my ship! How can I help you?
User:	CIO
System:	Which CIO?
User:	John Adams
System:	210 666-7878
System:	To hear fax number, say fax or another CIO's name
User:	Fax
System:	210 666-9090
User:	Bye
System:	Goodbye

Scenario Two

The user says a CIO's name that does not have a phone number in the database. (*Note:* Skip to bold lines to see the changes.)

System:	Welcome aboard my ship! How can I help you?
User:	CIO
System:	Which CIO?
User:	**Thomas Adams**
System:	**There are no current phone numbers for Thomas Adams**
User:	**Bye**
System:	**Goodbye**

Scenario Three

The user says a CIO's name that has only the phone number in the database. (*Note:* Skip to bold lines to see the changes.)

System:	Welcome aboard my ship! How can I help you?
User:	CIO
System:	Which CIO?
User:	**Robert Adams**
System:	**210 868 4678**
System:	**To hear fax number, say fax or another CIO's name**
User:	**Fax**
System:	**There are no fax numbers available for Robert Adams**
User:	**Bye**
System:	**Goodbye**

Database Table

Before writing a WAP-based application, create and open a database. The next step is to create a table: CIOlist containing CIO's name, organizational code, city, phone number, and fax number.

```
CREATE TABLE CIOlist (
  id integer INTEGER;
  Lastname VARCHAR2 (50),
  Firstname VARCHAR2 (25),
  Organizational_Code VARCHAR2 (5)
  City VARCHAR2 (10)
  Phone VARCHAR2 (15)
  Fax VARCHAR2 (15)
);
```

One can add variables to the database table and reassign primary, foreign, and alternate keys. One can also create other tables and relate the CIOlist table with another primary and other keys. For WAP-based applications, it is best to keep the database table concise, clear, and compact.

ASP Script: Connecting to Database

Before starting a dialogue, one must create an ASP script using VBScript as its language for each dialogue to make the connection to the database. All scripts begin with `Option Explicit`. One must make the connection (`objConnection`) private to one's application, not shared with others. This is also true for the other three variables — `rsCIOs`, `strCIO`, and `SQLQuery`. Private variables in the other two dialogues may be different. All other variables remain the same.

To connect to and open a database for the first dialog, use

```
Set objConnection = Server.CreateObject("ADODB.Connection")
ObjConnection Open "NavyCIO Database"
```

The following is a complete ASP script.

```
<%@ LANGUAGE = "VBSCRIPT" %>
<%
Option Explicit
Private objConnection, rsCIOs
Private strCity, SQLQuery
Set objConnection = Server.CreateObject("ADODB.Connection")
ObjConnection Open "NavyCIO Database"
%>
```

The other two dialogues are shown in the following listings.

```
<%
Option Explicit
Private objConnection, rsPhone, SQLQuery
Private strCIO, Valid
Set objConnection = Server.CreateObject("ADODB.Connection")
objConnection.Open "NavyCIO Database"
%>

<%
Option Explicit
Private objConnection, rsPhone, SQLQuery
Private strCIO, Valid
Set objConnection = Server.CreateObject("ADODB.Connection")
objConnection.Open "NavyCIO Database"
%>
```

To get the connection to work, establish an ODBC for Oracle. Under Windows 98, click the ODBC Data Sources icon in the Control Panel, and then the Add button in the Systems tab. One must have Oracle 7.3 or higher and networking components before selecting Micfrosoft ODBC for Oracle. If using Windows 2000, look for the ODBC Data Sources icon in the Administrator's Tools folder. Enter the Microsoft ODBC for Oracle into the System folder.

XML Syntax

As one can see in the complete WAP application in Appendix A, each dialogue part (dialog1.asp, dialog2.asp, dialog3.asp) has a beginning tag and an ending tag:

```
<DIALOG>.........</DIALOG>.
```

This block starts with a class name:

```
<Class Name = class name>
```

One can have as many class names as one wishes inside the block. If using

```
<OPTION NEXT = option name>...</OPTION>
```

as part of the option list

```
<INPUT TYPE = "OPTIONLIST">
  <OPTION NEXT = option name1>...</OPTION
  <OPTION NEXT = option name2>...</OPTION
  <OPTION NEXT = option name3>...</OPTION
</INPUT>
```

one needs a routine that an option name can call when needed. This routine has the following syntax:

```
<Step Name = name PARENT = parent name>
```

Note that PARENT is optional. It is needed when there is more than one class name within a dialogue.

XML Script

In the script, there are two class names: help_top and help_dialog1. The "init" step is the "help_top" class's child. This step gives a list of options, one of which can be activated by a spoken word to call a step whose parent is "help.dialog1." For example, if the user says "CIO," the "init" step will take the user to the "cio" step as the "help.dialog1" class's child.

Then, the application will prompt the user for a CIO name. When the user says "John Adams," the system gets all CIO names and then jumps to the second dialogue to list phone numbers that correspond to the CIO name requested. The system says the results and then gives the user a choice of speaking "FAX" or another CIO's name.

If the user chooses "fax," the system takes the user to another step named "next command," with "help.dialog1" as its parent. This step moves to the third dialogue to list fax numbers. If they do not exist, the system apologizes that these numbers are not available for a certain CIO.

To get an idea of how the system retrieves all CIO names from the CIOlist table and compares each one to the requested CIO's name, take a look at the INPUT block in the "CIO" STEP. This routine assigns

```
SELECT * FROM CIOlist
```

to SQLQuery. The system then sets rsCIOs records to SQLQuery that is executed when it connects to and opens a database.

As one can see,

```
<% DO UNTIL rsCIOs.EOF%>
            .
            .
            .
<% LOOP %>
```

allows the system to repeat the process of moving to the next record until it reaches the last one. During this process, the system calls the second dialogue to check if the CIO's name in the record matches the CIO's name the user wants. If they match and the corresponding phone number exists in the table, the system speaks it. On the other hand, if they match and the table does not have the phone number, the user gets a polite apology from the system.

Keep in mind that the "committee" and "airgram" steps in the first dialogue are not currently supported. The fourth step ends the dialogue when the user says "Bye." They are included for demonstration purposes.

Dialogues

Appendix A shows a complete program that has been adapted from the Motorola's scripts at http://www.mobileblueprint.com.

Conclusion

User-system interaction with a remote database is one big step forward for the mobile workforce. The only problem is that digital connection may not be available in certain areas. This type of connection is not as widespread as its analog counterpart. Other problems include bandwidth allocations, traffic bottlenecks, and quality of service. With the evolving and emerging technologies for mobile users, one would expect to see more and more developers putting out marketable mobile services.

XML: Its Role in TCP/IP Presentation Layer (Layer 6)

This section was previously published in Auerbach's *Data Communications Management,* (51-40-65), 2000.

Breaking the Barrier

Integration between applications should be viewed, at least, as a communication problem. Like the parties on the telephones, the applications should speak the same language to effectively communicate with one another. If the sending application uses one language, and the receiving application speaks in another language, they would need a translator, just like a human counterpart, to understand one another as long as both agree on the semantics and syntax of the language.

Once the applications speak the same language independently or through a translator, there should be a mechanism to support the exchange of messages in a standard way. One such instance is XML, which has become the *de facto* standard for communication between applications. Using XML allows human agents to send all messages of self-describing texts between applications. This makes it easier for both humans and machines to understand the messages on a common ground. While it nearly achieves the concept of human–machine interaction, it falls short in the packaging of these messages. XML scripts in text format can be quite a bit larger than their binary representation of the same information.

There are three aspects of inter-application communication:

- *Transport:* refers to how the information gets across the wire
- *Protocol:* refers to how to package the information sent across that wire
- *Message:* refers to the information itself

The transport is usually a lower-level network standard such as TCP/IP. On top of such transports are CORBA, DCE, and DCOM. This means each transport uses a different protocol to communicate. CORBA uses IIOP while electronic mail uses SMTP. One can package, for example, a message, specify a destination, and send the message to the destined location.

While XML does have SOAP as a lightweight XML protocol, it relies on other protocols as well. Using SOAP allows one to use various synchronous and asynchronous mechanisms to send messages based on whatever appropriate protocol one chooses. However, this protocol seems constrained and has not overcome the barrier imposed by the TCP/IP model scheme. What this means is that some protocols are not as easily extended as XML. Flexibility and extensibility are the norm for XML. They easily lead to standardization of definitions, semantics, schemas, and templates in the exchange of information between products, applications, and vendors.

XML documents contain meta-information about the information being transmitted and can easily be extended. One advantage of using XML is that both humans and computers can read the documents. A disadvantage is that XML is less efficient than transmitting information in binary format. This efficiency is overcome, in part, with the latency of Web-based applications so the overhead is not as large as it seems. Any protocol can be used to send XML messages.

To send or receive an XML message, one must enable an application to do so — independent of the protocol used. Once one gets applications or organizations to agree on the meanings of the XML message, one can send a package of these messages to its intended destination. The meanings must be exact and unambiguous. A data dictionary is suggested to list the XML vocabularies, their meanings, and their associated schemas that define document structure for specific industries. This allows industry-specific information to be exchanged as XML and would serve as input into the development of XML templates that organizations can use to send and receive messages.

For example, FPML defines an XML schema for the financial industry to exchange information about financial products. ebXML uses an XML schema for the electronic commerce to exchange information business-to-business and business-to-customer scenarios. adXML targets advertising agencies, while CIML (Customer Identity Markup Language) is useful for information on customer relationship management. More than 200 XML schemas for specific industries, groups, and programs are listed at www.xml.org.

These schemas, along with others, are the foundation for building reusable templates of schemas. More templates are on the way as organizations see the merits of standardizing meta-information contained in XML messages and applications.

To get a message to where it is supposed to go, HTTP is a natural choice. Because XML documents do not have the ability to listen to a port like HTTP does (port 80), they must be translated into HTML formats — via XSL, for example. This protocol generates HTTP requests/responses as an application (the other example is FTP) at the Application layer (the top) of the TCP/IP model.

Once translated, the application moves in the next layer down the TCP/IP road — the Presentation layer. Here, the layer formats the data so that it is recognizable or readable by the receiver. It provides services such as encryption, text compression, and reformatting to provide a standardized interface. It is also concerned with the data structures used by programs and therefore negotiates data transfer syntax for the receiving application layer. When the HHTP requests/responses get the data down to the wire, they take a ride on the highway, get off it, and enter the "welcome" door of a receiving host's TCP/IP tower.

Product Integration

One of the great benefits of XML is the ease of integration of products. A good example of the power of XML in this area comes from the CiscoWorks 2000 Service Level Management Solution that determines the impact on various enterprise resources and the degree of success in moving an application or its data from a failed server, node, cluster, or any other network component to an operational one.

By providing XML interfaces via an SDK, Cisco has allowed partner products to integrate more closely into CiscoWorks 2000. Extending the benefits of the Cisco Management Connection, the XML interface allows other products to access Cisco information at the Transport and Network layers of the OSI model and other information on remaining layers, including the Application and Presentation layers, and present the information to the user under one seamlessly integrated display.

XML integration also allows an XML partner's product to pass control information and data to CiscoWorks 2000. The interface allows CiscoWorks 2000 to perform actions to a group of routers, for example, thus providing a one-to-many capability for the partner's product. This is one of the ways XML standardizes the definitions between products — accomplished through the Presentation layer.

Translating for All Browsers

While various tools are available to translate XML documents into HTML using XSL, Microsoft's XSLISAPI lets users enable XML on all browsers. The transformation occurs entirely on the server and enables a browser to convert XML documents into HTML requests/responses for processing by the Presentation layer.

XSLISAPI is a self-extracting executable and one can obtain it from the MSDN Online Downloads Site. It currently works on Windows 2000 Server on Win2K Advanced Server if one installs SXLML 2.4 or higher. It comes with restrictions when it is used on the Windows NT 4.0 Server. XSLISAPI may change significantly to fit into the ASP+ and .NET architecture.

The tool automatically chooses different stylesheets based on a client's browser. Downloading the file will not complete the installation. One needs to take additional steps:

1. Enter at the command line prompt: regsvr32 `xslisapi2.dll`.
2. Right-click the Default Web Site node (if right-handed) in the IIS administration Control Panel applet.
3. Select Properties and then the ISAPI Filters tab.
4. Add the new filter to the list. After closing and reopening the Properties dialogue box, a green arrow will appear next to the new filter name.
5. Create a new virtual directory — Xslisapi. Do not forget to point this directory to the folder where xslisapi.exe was expanded.
6. Set the Run Script permissions on the virtual directory.

To associate an XSL file with an XML document, do the following in an XML processing instruction:

```
<?xml version="1.0"?>
<?xml-stylesheet type="text/xsl"
  server-coding="sampleA-Config.xml"
href="sampleA=IE5.xsl"?>
```

`href` takes precedence over `server-config`. If `href` is not included, the `server-config` attribute points to an XML file in the same folder as the XML document. The XML file contains information about which XSL stylesheet to use for a given browser. An example of a code snippet from a possible `server-config` file is:

```
<server-styles-config>
    <device browser="IE" version="5.0">
    </device>
    <device browser="Netscape" version="4.5">
      <stylesheet href\"NN45.xsl"/>
    </device>
</server-styles-config>
```

From the `server-config` file, the filter points to `NN45,xsl` as a XSL stylesheet to use and loads it. Next, the filter transforms the XML code into HTML, as illustrated in the following example:

```
OrigPath=Request.ServerVariables("HTTP_SSXSLSRCFILE:");
ServDoc.URL = origPath;
ServDoc.UserAgent = Request.ServerVariables("HTTP_USER_AGENT:");
ServDoc.Load(requestPath);
ServDoc.Transform(Response);
```

Dynamic XML Servers

Not all servers are the same. They are generally grouped into repository and dynamic. Repository servers have been around for a while. They hold XML documents — those documents that already have been encoded in XML. Too many, however, can consume enormous resources with the Presentation layer on their way over to an XML server and eat up precious disk space with such a server.

Enter dynamic XML servers as a partial solution. Rather than storing the source information as an XML document, they collect information in a traditional data source or in a live application. What this means is that one can pull data out of a traditional database on one server, pass its more streamlined format through the Presentation layers, and transform it into an XML document on another server.

One can also use the dynamic server as an XML interface for the existing acquisition tracking component of the much larger E-commerce system. One example function of this interface is to receive XML documents from prospective bidders at a Web site and extract the XML documents from those documents. After passing through the Presentation layer, the interface stores it in a database, gets it to generate XML documents of another kind, and then feeds it to the live acquisition tracking application on the receiving server. The dynamic interface can be accomplished through protocols such as CICS and JavaBeans.

One advantage of using the dynamic XML server is to make publicly available the XML parsers, Java, or a scripting language and make calls to a database given the appropriate access rights and privileges. A disadvantage is that one may not have the expertise to handle the load-balancing problems, database connection pooling, and to set the limits that the cache pages and memory can reach. One might be better off with a ready-made dynamic XML server. When considering a server, keep in mind that vendors offer different storage capabilities and methods, especially when they store and retrieve data from various sources, assign XML tags, and distribute them to applications.

XML Mapping

Mapping between XML and relational databases is more complicated than mapping between XML and objects. There are additional joins in SQL queries needed to create the XML, while the XML and the objects are very similar. In parsing XML, one will find a one-to-one relationship between each object and XML.

Recognizing the problems regarding XML mapping, Oracle offers a database with hybrid capabilities that can store XML natively. Its SQL syntax has been extended with XML Query Language. Because they provide a more natural XML mapping, some products are being marketed as XML databases created from the ground up (Tamino from Software AG) or redesigned (eXcelon Corp.). While each provides an XML Query Language, it has not been standardized. The World Wide Web Consortium (W3C) is currently working on a XML Query Language. By itself, this language will access XML files as if they were databases.

Natural Language Dialogue

In March 2000, voice forum (www.voicesml.org) released Voice XML 1.9. Two months later, W3C accepted it as the basis for developing a W3C dialogue markup language that could be used to provide voice interfaces on traditional interactive voice response platforms. Three initial versions of the language included support for basic state-based dialogue capabilities, using a design with simple form-based natural language capabilities that leave room to grow as the technology evolves.

While VoiceXML reuses many concepts and designs from HTML, the differences between visual and voice interactions should be noted. When an HTML document is fetched from a network resource specified by a uniform resource identifier, it is presented to the user all at once. A VoiceXML document, in contrast, contains a number of dialogue units (menus or forms) presented sequentially — only if the user is talking to or listening to one other person. This difference is due to the visual medium's ability to display a number of items in parallel, while the voice medium is inherently sequential.

The field of spoken interfaces is not nearly as mature as the field of visual interfaces; thus, standardizing an approach to natural dialogue is more difficult than designing a standard language for describing visual interfaces such as HTML. VoiceXML allows applications to give users some degree of control over the conversation — in a standard way. The data used in voice interfaces is negotiated in the Presentation layer for transfer to the receiving application.

Universal XML

When standards organizations ratify key standards for XML and implement them, one will see a new trend in the market. Within two years, XML is destined to be universally supported, so that separate XML products will not be necessary. When standards are in place, the market will offer general-purpose dynamic XML server products. The developers will no longer think in terms of low-level details of XML syntax and semantics when they develop applications. In addition, one may see an extension to the Presentation layer based on the powerful capabilities of XML. This extension would be the first attempt in associating the data transfer syntax with bits on the wire.

Conclusion

The powerful capabilities of XML when applied to TCP/IP applications appear to be unlimited. Universal XML will help make the move easier beyond the traditional TCP/IP model that has been constrained by lack of a standardized way of associating data with blobs and bits on the wire.

XML Schemas

On May 1, 2001, the W3C announced that the XML Schemas has been finally declared a formal recommendation — after more than two years of review and revision. W3C Recommendation status is the final step in the consortium's standards approval process. This indicates that the schema is a fully mature, stable standard backed by more than 500 W3C member organizations.

XML Document

```
<Book>>
    <Title>XML Schema</Title>
  <Author>John Doe</Author>
</Book>
```

DTD

```
<!ELEMENT Book (Title, Author)>
<!ELEMENT Title (#PCDATA)>
<!ELEMENT Author (#PCDATA)>
```

XML Schema

```
<element name='Book' type="BookType"/>
<complexType name='BookType'>
  <element name='Title' type='string'/>
  <element name='Author' type='string"/>
</complexType>
```

Exhibit 4. Comparing Complex Data Types

The finalized Schema solves the primary problem of B2B communication and interoperability that has held XML back from its full potential. The W3C expects XML Schemas to integrate data exchange across business and to facilitate and accelerate electronic business.

XML Schema was conceived to overcome shortcomings of Document Type Definitions (DTDs). It provides developers with:

- Strong typing for elements and attributes
- Key mechanism that is directly analogous to relational database foreign keys
- Standardized way to represent null values
- Defined as XML documents, making them programmatically accessible

This section focusses on the first two advantages, after a brief overview on comparing data types in DTD and XML Schema.

Comparing XML Schema and DTD

To give an idea why XML Schema is better than DTD, look at Exhibit 4, which compares complex data types in DTD and XML Schema. Although the XML code in Exhibit 4 conforms to both DTD and XML Schema fragments, there is a big difference between them. In a DTD, all elements are global. The XML Schema allows `Title` and `Author` to be defined locally within the element `Book`. To exactly duplicate the effect of the DTD declarations in XML Schema, the elements `Title` and `Author` must have a global scope as shown in the following table. The `ref` attribute of element `element` allows one to refer to previously declared elements.

```
<element name='Title' type='string'/>
<element name='Author' type='string'/>
```

```
<element name='Book' type='Booktype'/>
<complexType name='BookType'/>
  <element ref='Title'/>
  <element ref='Author'/>
</complexType>
```

In the examples in Exhibit 4 and in the code above, `BookType` is global and can be used to declare other elements. By contrast, the code below makes the type local to the definition of element `Book` and makes it anonymous. Note that the XML document fragment in Exhibit 4 matches all three schema fragments in Exhibit 4, in the code above, and in the following:

```
<element name='Title' type='string'/>
<element name='Author' type='string'/>
<element name='Book' />
<complexType name='BookType'/>
  <element ref='Title'/>
  <element ref='Author'/>
</complexType>
```

Strong Typing Advantage

In a DTD, there is not much choice in specifying constraints for elements and attributes. There is no way to specify that an element's text content must be a valid representation of an integer, or even that the content may not exceed a certain number of characters.

Unlike DTD, XML Schema offers greater flexibility for expressing constraints on the content model of elements. Like DTD, one can associate attributes at the simplest level with an element declaration and indicate that a sequence of one only (1), zero or more (*), or one or more (+) elements from a given set of elements can occur with it. With XML Schema, one can express additional constraints using, for example, `minOccurs` and `maxOccurs` attributes of element `element`, and the `choice`, group, and `all` elements.

```
<element name='Title' type='string'/>
<element name='Author' type='string'/>
<element name='Book' />
<complexType name='BookType'/>
  <element ref='Title' minOccurs='0'/>
  <element ref='Author' maxOccurs='2'/>
</complexType>
```

When one sets the minimum number of titles to zero, it means the occurrence of `Title` is optional in `Book`. When one sets the maximum number of authors to two, it means there must be at least one, but no more than two authors in the element `Book`. The default value of `minOccurs` and `maxOccurs` is 1 for `element`. Another element, `all`, expresses the constraint that all child elements in the group may appear once or not at all, and they may appear in any order. The following code expresses the constraint that both Title and Author must occur in Book in any order, or neither will. Such constraints are difficult to express in a DTD.

```
<xsd:element name='Title' type='string'/>
<xsd:element name='Author' type='string'/>
<xsd:element name='Book' />
<xsd: complexType name='BookType'/>
  <xsd:all>
    <xsd:element ref='Title'/>
    <xsd:element ref='Author'/>
  </xsd:all>
</xsd:complexType>
</xsd:element>
```

True Key Representation Advantage

If one has ever attempted to describe a relational database with a complex relationship map using a DTD, then one has likely had to use the ID-IDREF pointing mechanism. For example, in a structure where two entities are related in a many-to-many way through a relating table (borrowers and assets on a loan application, for example), the simple XML parent-child relationship is insufficient. However, IDs and IDREFs have their own weaknesses: IDs must be unique across an entire document, and IDREF declarations do not specify the type of element an instance of the IDREF attribute must reference. XML Schema provides a way to specify these pointing relationships in much the same way that foreign key relationships are declared in a relational database. For example, if one has a foreign key relationship that cannot be expressed using a simple parent-child relationship in the XML, one can declare the two related elements as in the following listing.

```
<xsd:element name="rootElement">
  <xsd:complexType>
    <xsd:sequence>
      <xsd:element name="elementOne" maxOccurs="unbounded">
        <xsd:complexType>
          <xsd:attribute name="elementOneKey" type="integer" />
          <xsd:attribute name="elementOneDesc" type="text" />
        </xsd:complexType>
        <xsd:key name="elementOnePK">
          <xsd:selector xpath=".//elementOne"/>
          <xsd:field xpath="@elementOneKey"/>
        </xsd:key>
      </xsd:element>
      <xsd:element name="elementTwo" maxOccurs="unbounded">
        <xsd:complexType>
          <xsd:attribute name="elementTwoKey" type="integer" />
          <xsd:attribute name="elementOneKey" type="integer" />
          <xsd:attribute name="elementTwoDesc" type="text" />
        </xsd:complexType>
        <xsd:keyref name="elementOneFK" refer="elementOnePK">
          <xsd:selector xpath=".//elementTwo"/>
```

```
         <xsd:field xpath="@elementOneKey"/>
       </xsd:keyref>
     </xsd:element>
   </xsd:sequence>
  </xsd:complexType>
 </xsd:element>
```

In this code, the `key` definition in the complex type for the `elementOne` element declares that the `elementOneKey` attribute must be present for all `elementOne` elements, and that it must be unique across all `elementOneKey` attributes on `elementOne` elements (note that this differs from IDs, which must be unique regardless of the element with which they are associated). The `keyref` definition in the complex type for the `elementTwo` element then states that the `elementOneKey` field must match one of the `elementOneKey` fields found on an `elementOne` element elsewhere in the document.

Another nice feature of this key mechanism is that the keys can be strongly typed — as opposed to ID and IDREFs, which must be XML name tokens — so one can use that automatically incremented primary key in a table without modification. It is also possible to define composite keys so that one can create primary keys (using the `key` element) and foreign keys (using the `keyref` element) that map directly to the keys found in one's existing relational database.

To get started with XML Schema, check out the W3C XML Schema primer (http://www.w3.org/TR/xmlschema-0/). For more details, refer to the structural reference at http://www.w3.org/TR/xmlschema-1/and data type reference at http://www.w3.org/TR/xmlschema-2/.

IBM has a robust XML Schema verification tool, XML Schema Quality Checker, at http://www.alphaworks.ibm.com/tech/xmlsqc. It is available as a free-trial download through alphaWorks. The Checker is a program that takes as input an XML Schema written in the W3C XML schema language and diagnoses improper uses of the schema language. For schemas composed of numerous schema documents connected via <include>, <import>, or <redefine> element information items, a full schema-wide checking is performed.

Appendix A: Complete WAP Script

```
<%@ LANGUAGE="VBSCRIPT" %>
<%
Option Explicit
Private objConnection, rsCIOs
Private strCIO, SQLQuery
Set objConnection = Server.CreateObject("ADODB.Connection")
objConnection.Open "NavyCIO Database"
%>
<?xml version="1.0"?>
<!--_____-->
<!-- dialog1.asp

_____-->
<DIALOG>
<CLASS NAME="help_top">
<HELP> You are at the top level menu. For NavyCIO information,
say CIO. </HELP>
</CLASS>
<STEP NAME="init" PARENT="help_top">
<PROMPT> Welcome aboard my ship!.<BREAK SIZE="large"/>
How may I help you? </PROMPT>
<INPUT TYPE="OPTIONLIST">
<OPTION NEXT="#NavyCIO"> CIO </OPTION>
<OPTION NEXT="#committee"> committee </OPTION>
<OPTION NEXT="#airgram"> airgram </OPTION>
<OPTION NEXT="#bye"> exit </OPTION>
</INPUT>
</STEP>
<CLASS NAME="help_dialog1">
<HELP> Your choices are <OPTIONS/>. </HELP>
</CLASS>
<STEP NAME="CIO" PARENT="help_dialog1">
<PROMPT> Which CIO? </PROMPT>
<INPUT TYPE="optionlist" NAME="CIO">
<% ' Get all CIO names. %>
<% SQLQuery = "SELECT * FROM CIOList" %>
<% Set rsCIOs = objConnection.Execute(SQLQuery) %>
<% Do Until rsCIOs.EOF %>
<% ' Create an OPTION element for each CIO. %>
<OPTION NEXT="dialog2.asp#getphone"
VALUE="<%= rsCIOs("CIO") %>">
<%= rsCIOs("CIO") %></OPTION>
<% rsCIOs.MoveNext %>
<% Loop %>
<OPTION NEXT="#bye"> exit </OPTION>
</INPUT>
</STEP>
<STEP NAME="nextcommand" PARENT="help_dialog1">
<% strCIO = Request.QueryString("CIO") %>
<PROMPT> To hear fax number <%=strCIO%>, say
fax, or say another CIO name. </PROMPT>
<INPUT TYPE="optionlist" NAME="CIO">
<% ' Get all CIO names. %>
```

```
<% SQLQuery = "SELECT * FROM CIOList" %>
<% Set rsCIOs = objConnection.Execute(SQLQuery) %>
<% Do Until rsCIOs.EOF %>
<% ' Create an OPTION element for each CIO. %>
<OPTION NEXT="dialog2.asp#getphone"
VALUE="<%= rsCIOs("CIO") %>">
<%= rsCIOs("CIO") %></OPTION>
<% rsCIOs.MoveNext %>
<% Loop %>
<OPTION NEXT="dialog3.asp#getfax"
VALUE="<%= strCIO %>"> fax </OPTION>
<OPTION NEXT="#bye"> exit </OPTION>
</INPUT>
</STEP>
<STEP NAME="committee">
<PROMPT> Committee update is currently not supported. </PROMPT>
<INPUT TYPE="NONE" NEXT="#init"/>
</STEP>
<STEP NAME="airgram">
<PROMPT> Airgram update is currently not supported. </PROMPT>
<INPUT TYPE="NONE" NEXT="#init"/>
</STEP>
<STEP NAME="bye" PARENT="help_top">
<PROMPT> Goodbye. </PROMPT>
<INPUT TYPE="NONE" NEXT="#end"/>
</STEP>
</DIALOG>
<!--_____End of Dialog1.asp_____-->
<%@ LANGUAGE="VBSCRIPT" %>
<%
Option Explicit
Private objConnection, rsPhone, SQLQuery
Private strCIO, Valid
Set objConnection = Server.CreateObject("ADODB.Connection")
objConnection.Open "NavyCIO Database"
%>
<?xml version="1.0"?>
<!--_____-->
<!-- dialog2.asp
_____-->
<DIALOG>
<CLASS NAME="help_dialog2">
<HELP> Your choices are <OPTIONS/>.</HELP>
</CLASS>
<STEP NAME="getphone">
<% strCIO = Request.QueryString("CIO") %>
<% Valid = "TRUE" %>
<% SQLQuery = "SELECT * FROM CIOlist WHERE( CIO='" & strCIO & "'
)" %>
<% Set rsPhone = objConnection.Execute(SQLQuery) %>
<% If rsPhone.EOF Then %>
<% Valid = "FALSE" %>
<PROMPT> Sorry, <BREAK/> There are no current phone
number available for <%=strCIO%>.<BREAK/></PROMPT>
<% Else %>
```

```
<% ' Speak current phone number %>
<PROMPT> <%=rsPhone("Current")%> </PROMPT>
<%End If %>
<INPUT TYPE = "Hidden" NAME="CIO" VALUE="<%=strCIO%>" >
</INPUT>
<% If ( Valid = "FALSE" ) Then %>
<INPUT TYPE="none" NEXT="dialog1.asp#init"</INPUT>
<% Else %>
<INPUT TYPE="none" NEXT="dialog1.asp#nextcommand"></INPUT>
<% End If %>
</STEP>
</DIALOG>
<!--_____End of Dialog2.asp_____-->
<%@ LANGUAGE="VBSCRIPT" %>
<%
Option Explicit
Private objConnection, rsPhone, SQLQuery
Private strCIO, Valid
Set objConnection = Server.CreateObject("ADODB.Connection")
objConnection.Open "NavyCIO Database"
%>
<?xml version="1.0"?>
<!--_____-->
<!-- dialog3.asp
-->
<!--_____-->
<DIALOG>
<CLASS NAME="help_dialog3">
<HELP> Your choices are <OPTIONS/>.</HELP>
</CLASS>
<STEP NAME="getfax">
<% strCIO = Request.QueryString("CIO") %>
<% Valid = "TRUE" %>
<% SQLQuery = "SELECT * FROM CIOlist WHERE( CIO='" & strCIO & "' )" %>
<% Set rsPhone = objConnection.Execute(SQLQuery) %>
<% If rsPhone.EOF Then%>
<% Valid = "FALSE" %>
<PROMPT> Sorry, <BREAK/> There is no fax number
available for <%=strCIO%>.<BREAK/></PROMPT>
<% Else %>
<% ' Speak fax number information %>
<PROMPT> <%=rsPhone("Fax")%> </PROMPT>
<% End If %>
<INPUT TYPE = "Hidden" NAME="CIO" VALUE="<%=strCIO%>" > </INPUT>
<% If ( Valid = "FALSE" ) Then%>
<INPUT TYPE="none" NEXT="dialog1.asp#init"</INPUT>
<% Else %>
<INPUT TYPE="none" NEXT="dialog1.asp#nextcommand"></INPUT>
<% End If %>
</STEP>
</DIALOG>
<!--_____End
```

Chapter 8

Middleware Performance

This chapter discusses various performance considerations as they apply to middleware and its associated technologies. They include traffic performance, service levels, communications middleware paradigms, performance tools, and middleware selection.

Introduction

Integration broker middleware is the largest segment in the middleware market and the fastest growing. Risks abound for vendors and users due to rapid changes in technology, standards, and product packaging. Such risks include degraded performance, network (or rather middleware) bottlenecks, poor caching schemes, and defective service level agreements, among others.

Various performance solutions and standards have been debated, tried, and offered — both proprietary and open source — yet we have not seen a Middleware Performance Service Provider for Enterprise Application Integration (EAI) systems although other provider types[1] have been around for a while that aim to free time that enterprise management requires to make important strategic decisions. Should this type of provider emerge by the time this book hits the market, time has caught up with us.

This chapter focuses on the various performance issues and considerations regarding the design, deployment, use, and maintenance of middleware products. While it is not possible to address all performance issues, the chapter does look at middleware products that act as a translator, converter, or integrator — or all three simultaneously as the glue between applications.

IP Traffic Performance

The biggest problem is that thousands of users, devices, routers, and applications could tie up IP traffic when they look for the same information or

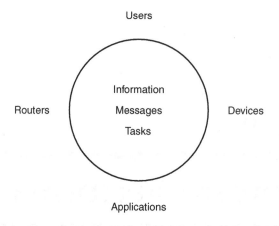

Exhibit 1.   Information, Messages, and Tasks

Exhibit 2.   Network Bandwidths

messages or performing similar tasks over the Internet simultaneously — with the middleware products of all sorts standing between them (see Exhibit 1). One possible outcome is a blank screen or a page greeting the users with "Page is not available" or even a shaky cursor during, for example, extreme network traffic fluctuations.

Web sites with heavy network traffic or rich multimedia, particularly those containing a large gallery of heavy-duty images and Java applets of computer voices, sometimes experience slow loading pages or even outages, even when they are using data, voice, and image streaming technology. In addition, the quality of packetized voices is sometimes below "toll-grade" PSTN calls, partly due to the inability of a network to reserve enough bandwidth or achieve the quality of service (QoS) at acceptable levels.

The amount of bandwidth can affect how the fragmented packets arrive at a destination for reassembling of the fragments in their proper sequence. If the bandwidth is insufficient, the system will either retransmit too many times or completely lose packets. When this happens, a computer voice or screen will stutter, causing a user to quickly move to another Web site that offers faster and more appealing loading pages and better voice quality.

In the network world, there are thousands and thousands of gateway destinations through which the packets must pass data to a maze of middleware products. Not all destinations, however, have the same types of gateways. Some can restrict the amount of bandwidth they can accept. The bandwidth, for example, is more limited for a WAN than for a LAN (see Exhibit 2); and the pipes, in turn, are narrower for a LAN than for a T1 line. Things can get a bit complicated with thousands of LANs connected to several WANs, and then to a T1 line.

When there is not enough bandwidth, some companies tend to limit throughput as a way of stretching bandwidth resources and cut backbone traffic to manageable levels. This technique is not a good idea because it can dramatically reduce QoS.

One way of increasing the quality is to include a service level agreement (SLA) that specifies guaranteed bandwidths[2] and network tools to manage bandwidths, delivery contents, and Web caches, and shape network traffic at acceptable levels. This agreement must specify uptime availability, service availability and quality, and should also include what the scope of service is, how it can be applied to applications development services, security services, feasibility study, system design and specifications, and what the special requirements are.

Whatever the methods or techniques a company will choose for an SLA, periodic throughput and other performance tests should be part of the service contracts. Without them, there will be no way of knowing whether the performance will decline or improve in regard to bandwidth, traffic patterns, caching schemes, and network contents.

For a bandwidth manager to work, one must divide traffic into classes, typically by IP address or TCP/IP application-level port number, although the classification schemes vary widely from product to product. Then tell the bandwidth manager, for example, how much of the WAN traffic each class gets. Each product has different capabilities, ranging from assigning a simple raw number to more complex rules involving setting priorities and minimum and maximum amounts of traffic the device can pass.

Without a bandwidth management device, managing bandwidths can be quite complex. Throttling back applications efficiently requires in-depth knowledge of the entire protocol stack being used. An application running over TCP may have internal retransmissions if packets are lost or delayed. TCP has an entire series of internal timers and buffer interactions that vary from implementation to implementation, and IP and Ethernet have their own sensitivities. Taken together, the simple-minded approach of "drop packets when limits are reached" can have the effect of wasting WAN bandwidth, as well as skyrocketing LAN traffic and protocol stack CPU time.

Before going any further, take a look at the following case study.

Case Study

About five years ago, transmitting EAI files through intermediary systems at three states was a headache. Every time the files arrived late at a destination, a system engineer would get a phone call asking him or her to explain why certain systems along the way failed to accept them at specific times or why a file update screen appeared to stutter.

The engineer was fully aware that an operating system running at each intermediary point was different from another (Exhibit 3). They included

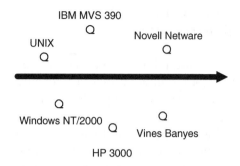

Exhibit 3.   Heterogeneous Network

UNIX, Windows NT, Honeywell, IBM MVS/390, HP 3000, Novell Netware, and Vines Banyes, and quite a few others. On top of them was a maze of LANs, WANs, and routers, each with a different network topology as well messaging and middleware products, enterprise servers, databases, and firewall/network products.

The engineer knew about the problems of sending packetized files to the network and associated gateways, each with a different maximum bandwidth it could carry. The engineer also suspected that some original applications — front-end middleware and back-end — were consuming bandwidth more than usual.

After many meetings and phone calls, the engineer got the files at the final destination — his or her office. If the engineer's staff had bandwidth managers, traffic shapers, content network delivery, and caching schemes, as well as other tools to better manage network traffic fluctuations and the resulting middleware performance, the files would arrive during normal hours, as scheduled.

So, take a look at some tools that monitor and improve middleware performance and consider the downsides and advantages of each.

Bandwidth Managers

Among the causes of network bottlenecks are the applications that consume an unusual amount of bandwidth allocated to network traffic. If the applications do not get enough bandwidth, they will drop out of the network or be subject to excessive delays or retransmission. Compounding the problem is packet queuing in routers that are vulnerable to delay, dropped packets, and frequent retransmission. Even when this vulnerability is not exploited, the packets can travel at uneven rates through multiple networks in a heterogeneous environment, taking somewhat longer to reassemble the fragmented packets in the proper sequence.

All happen because business, engineering, and EAI applications do not know anything about network flows and may request more bandwidth than is available. Without proper monitoring tools, the network does not know when the loads are coming, how long they will last, or how and what the user demand is going to be. These tools, however, do not always make good predictions on the bandwidth behavior of some applications.

An average user can wait no more than eight seconds for a Web page to load onto a PC desktop. Otherwise, the user will grow impatient and go to another site that takes much less time to download pictures, sound, and text. As a partial solution, the SLAs focus on maximum upload availability and guaranteed bandwidth. Consistent response time for latency-sensitive applications, however, are not guaranteed.

Due to the complexity and heterogeneous environment of networks, bandwidth management can be quite complex, requiring full-time attention from a network manager. For example, throttling back applications efficiently involves an in-depth knowledge of the entire protocol stack being used.

Then come the bandwidth managers to help network administrators attend to other tasks while managing bandwidths. They work exclusively on TCP/IP traffic, dropping or passing through non-IP traffic and can look at a customer's bandwidth utilization. Because they can throttle the link, they give service providers the capability to limit the bandwidth a customer can consume.

No two managers are alike. Some can slow down the lower-priority applications and deliver more bandwidth to those with higher priority, while others can reject any new connections or accept new ones with lower prioritized rates. Yet another can provide brokering of bandwidth between server providers or other domains.

More advanced bandwidth managers allow customers to request bandwidth on demand. Customers can use this feature to alert the service providers that more bandwidth is needed for certain times. Another advanced feature is the capability to signal the network of the desired QoS. Some bandwidth managers are of a proprietary nature and may require a networking expert to make them interoperable with others in another category.

To give the enterprise an easier way to enforce its policies across its networks, the Internet Engineering Task Force (IETF) adopted Intel's open source version of the Common Open Policy Service (COPS) technology in January 2001. This provides network equipment vendors with a standard technology that they can use with bandwidth managers and other network devices, such as routers, switches, and load-balancing devices. While open source products aim at network interoperability, some have features that others do not.

Whatever features a bandwidth manager offers, it is far cheaper than leasing T1 line to get more bandwidth. ASPs that are unable to contain costs of bandwidth among others, regardless of various network tools, are on their way out. Web services are seen as an alternative way of controlling bandwidth costs by allowing customers to rent components from various sources rather than all software components from one place. Time will tell if this meets customers' overall expectations in the long run.

Traffic Shapers

Traffic shapers permit one to control the traffic going out of an interface in order to match its flow to the speed of the remote, target interface. Some traffic shapers can peek at the application riding inside every packet, while others can determine who is using what bandwidth and when. Others use traffic policies to set maximum bandwidths and rate parameters, allowing packets that exceed the acceptable amount of traffic to drop out of sight or transmit with a different priority.

In general, traffic shapers come in two groups:

- Changing traffic rates
- Moving higher-priority applications

Changing Rates

A traffic shaper can change the rate at which traffic generated from an application can flow. It takes advantage of certain QoS capabilities that allow applications to request a certain level of bandwidth from the network. This allows for more important applications the service they need to run efficiently, thus preventing a single application from becoming a bandwidth hog in a congested network. QoS, however, should be specified in an SLA so that it will be available to the applications when needed.

Moving Applications

This second type of traffic shaper can move high-priority applications more quickly and more efficiently than the lower-priority ones in a heavy traffic. Controlling flows can be accomplished through TCP rate control and FIFO Queue bucket.

TCP rate control is a technique that smoothes out the IP flow by detecting a remote user's access speed, factoring in network latency, and correlating this data with other traffic for information. It is designed to distribute packet transmissions by controlling TCP acknowledgments to the sender. When there is insufficient bandwidth, the sender can throttle back to avoid packet loss.

FIFO Queue bucket collects varying incoming flows and controls how they flow out of the bucket. It comes in two flavors: leaky bucket (see Exhibit 4) and token type. A leaky bucket uses a fixed transmit rate mechanism to smooth out the traffic, while the token type gets a fixed number of tokens with burst capability.

More and more office workers are turning to mobile devices while on the road or roaming from one office to another in the same building. Under certain conditions, these workers are prone to sudden bouts of LAN contention. For example, in an enterprise in which decision makers bring wireless laptops to a meeting, lecturers may ask them to access a particular Web site all at once — from the wireless segment of a corporate enterprise network (see Exhibit 5). Tens or hundreds of simultaneous Web page downloads from a confined area will overload the available access points. It turns out that this wireless segment is a strong candidate to benefit from traffic-shaping technologies and equipment. The New York Stock Exchange (NYSE), for example, which runs wireless LANs used by brokers with handheld terminals, must be

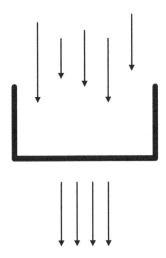

Exhibit 4.   Leaky Bucket

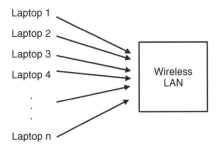

Exhibit 5.   Simultaneous Access

sure that bandwidth is allocated equally and fairly among all traders. A one-second delay could give an overt advantage to one broker over another.

The NYSE installed the Packeteer PacketShaper, a LAN-side bandwidth manager, to allocate equal amounts of LAN bandwidth (using a capability called dynamic subscriber partitioning) to the several hundred NYSE members registered to use wireless computers on its trading floor.

One way of utilizing a traffic-shaping technique is to cluster bandwidth management devices to function as a traffic shaper (see Exhibit 6). Sitara allows large companies (and service provider users) to cluster, for example, two Sitara QoSWorks bandwidth management devices to function as one in managing application traffic. They divide traffic into four schemes: class-based queuing (CBQ), TCP rate shaping, packet-size optimization, and an algorithm for fair allocation of bandwidth by connection.

CBQ classifies traffic and queues based on that classification, while TCP rate shaping bypasses queuing by applying flow-control policies to individual traffic flows and classes of flows. Packet-size optimization manages latency by reducing packet size. Fair bandwidth allocation doles out an equitable

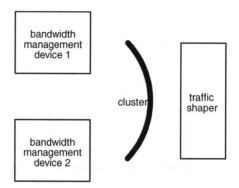

Exhibit 6.   Clustering into Traffic Shaper

share of bandwidth for connections within a class, so that individual connections do not timeout.

Content Delivery Networks

One good definition is that a content delivery network (CDN) is a network that delivers specific content, such as static Web pages, transaction-based Web sites, streaming media, or even real-time video or audio — through communications, database, and system middleware.

There are two general approaches to building CDNs: the overlay approach and the network approach. In the overlay approach, application servers or caches at various points in the network distribute Web graphics, streaming video, or other likes. It does not consider the core network infrastructure needed in content delivery. Good examples of the overlay model are the CDNs deployed by companies such as Akamai, Digital Island, and Speedera, which replicate content to thousands of servers worldwide. These CDNs aim to improve Web site response time by redirecting user requests for Web content to the nearest CDN server.

The network approach, on the other hand, deploys code to routers and switches so that they can recognize specific application types. Examples of this approach include devices that redirect content requests to local caches or switch traffic coming into data centers to specific content delivery servers. In some cases, both the network and overlay approaches are used, for example, when a switch at a server farm's front end redirects a hypertext transfer protocol (HTTP) request to an Akamai server located closer to the end user. IP Multicast is a good example of the combined network–overlay approach.

How fast a user's content request travels to its final destination (server) depends on how heavy the traffic is at any given time. There is, however, one drawback: some CDNs are of a proprietary nature, and thus are not compatible with others. Another drawback is that many CDNs do not integrate with associated technologies such as application deployment, content edge delivery, content switching, and intelligent network devices. A third concern is that Web servers can be bogged down with the heavy use of non-content applications.

One way of speeding the performance of Web sites with large amounts of data, images, and other multimedia content is to combine content delivery with traffic management. Another way is to distribute the content traffic between multiple sites. To free space to handle multiple content requests, a Web server should offload non-content requests such as Secure Sockets Layer (SSL) security processing functions.

Some products offer service providers with capabilities to control network bandwidth availability and original server scalability, and handle distance or latency obstacles and cope with network bottlenecks. Others are more limited in their scope.

Whatever the products offer, they are useful to the application service providers (ASPs) that specialize in producing digital video and audio Web site acceleration, streaming media, distance learning, and media-enriched E-commerce. There is one drawback, however, in that many CDNs do not integrate content technologies such as application deployment, content edge delivery, content switching, and intelligent network services.

In September 2000, The Content Alliance was formed by service providers to support content peering that would allow smaller enterprises and service providers to create CDNs and peer these networks to provide global content distribution coverage. This group endorsed a content peering standard and submitted the draft standard to the IETF. In April 2000, the Wireless Multimedia Forum (WMF) was formed to help content creators deliver rich media to any IP-ready wireless device.

Recently, CDN services have focused on helping companies make streaming media a reality, but Web-enabled, corporate, and E-commerce applications also benefit from CDNs. They make the content available to users when they want it.

Caching

Everyone knows that a cache is a place where it can temporarily hold downloaded pages when one is in a browser mode. One can go back to the pages by having the browser quickly fetch them from the cache. The cache comes in handy when it takes too long to download them over the lines or when the lines are experiencing network congestion.

Not all cache mechanisms, however, are alike. Some have features not available in others. Elegant features do not always guarantee high cache performance; some may bog down performance during peak times. If the cache for Web pages is insufficient, the cache is not performing well. The PC either automatically reboots itself or greets the user with an exiting message.

To determine how well a cache is performing, the following criteria should be used: peak throughput, hit ratio, cache age, response time, and downtime. What each criteria measures is shown in Exhibit 7.

Peak throughout measures the maximum number of HTTP requests per second that the cache can handle at peak load. The results are presented in

Exhibit 7.   Cache Criteria

Criteria	Measures
Peak throughput	Maximum HTTP request
Hit ratio	Number of times a cache produces a hit
Cache age	Age of oldest object
Response time	Delay time during peak times
Downtime	Recovery time

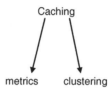

Exhibit 8.   Caching Performance

a price/performance metric that shows how much throughput can be purchased for a certain value.

Hit ratio measures the number of times a cache produces a hit vs. the times it passes the request to the Web. This amounts to the percentage of times the cache successfully finds a requested Web page. For example, if one is in the second-last page instead of the immediate last page when the BACK button on the browser is hit, one would know if a cache misses it. A higher cache hit ratio can cut down the bandwidth required.

Cache age measures the average age of the oldest object stored in a cache. The hit rate is higher when a product stores an object the longest before it is dumped from the cache. Caches have a finite amount of storage space and are programmed in different ways to allow for new storage.

Response time is the time it takes for a packet to be delivered under peak load conditions. As mentioned in the section on bandwidth managers, packets are sometimes retransmitted or travel at uneven rates on their way over to the destinations due to insufficient bandwidth.

The average user can only stand to wait a maximum of eight seconds for a Web page to load onto a PC desktop. If the user waits too long, he or she grows impatient and then moves to another Web site that gives better cache response time in delivering a packet or so under peak load. Consistent response time for latency-sensitive applications, however, are not guaranteed.

Downtime is the time it takes for the cache to recover from an unexpected condition such as a power outage or emergency maintenance shutdown. It is important to periodically back up the cache if it is not recoverable. It is common sense to place backup tapes and drives off-site rather than in a library next to a computer/network room in the same building.

Caching metrics are not the only means of measuring how well caching schemes are performing (see Exhibit 8). Another way is to cluster caches into a single function. Cache device maker Stratacache, for example, offers Super-liner, an enterprise cache system that lets users direct traffic to a single cache by scaling up to 16 Intel processors in a single box. This system provides an alternative to clustered cache offerings where, for example, a news site might have cached content about weather on one cache device and requests for feature stories about health issues might be handled by another cache.

According to Oracle, Oracle9*i* lets dynamic Java applications serve up to 85 times more users than it would running on the same hardware without Edge Side Includes (ESI)-enabled caching. ESI is a proposed open industry standard for dynamic Web content caching.

Load Balancing

Load balancing is traditionally associated with four traditional tiers: browsers, Web servers, transaction servers, and database servers. Now a fifth one is added: middleware servers. Load balancing means having any number of these servers working on one application — middleware, front end, and back end.

Load balancing allows for even distribution of processing and communications activity across a computer network so that no single device is over-whelmed. It is especially important for networks where it is difficult to predict the number of requests that will be issued to a server. Busy Web sites typically employ two or more Web servers in a load-balancing scheme. If one server starts to get swamped, requests are forwarded to another server with more capacity. Load balancing can also refer to the communications channels themselves.

SolidSpeed Networks offers open-source software products that let enterprises or service providers implement load balancing and measure the speed and availability of their Web sites. One example is FEZ-Director, a software for load balancing across distributed Web servers. It allows mirroring, caching, and multi-homing. Multi-homing is the ability to put Web software on more than one site and balance traffic between them. In addition, FEZ-Director measures latency and packet loss in DNS and sites that use HTTP redirection and reroutes users to the sites that are capable of handling the traffic.

Service Level Management

Corporations all over the world have turned to enterprise resource planning (ERP) applications to provide comprehensive business and information management tools that fully integrate business processes on a global basis. To ensure optimal utilization of this ERP environment, organizations seek to minimize downtime, optimize application performance, monitor availability, establish application control, predict problems or constraints, and control user experience.

Complicating this situation is the fact that the middleware technology has grown in many different directions, which results in many trade-offs when considering middleware performance. Typically, software development project leaders select middleware without considering performance. This kind of impetuosity can lead to disaster, including failed projects, upset users, or both.

One way of improving performance is to establish a policy on service level management (SLM) solutions, such as those offered by BMC Software. They offer maximum availability, performance, and recovery of ERP applications such as SAP R/3 Suite, PeopleSoft, Oracle Applications, and Microsoft Commerce Server 2000 (the follow-on release to Site Server Commerce Edition), along with their underlying databases and technologies.

In particular, BMC Software's PATROL for EAI solutions provides capabilities for end-to-end service level management. These solutions support the widest variety of applications, databases, middleware, and Web technologies across an array of operating systems. They work with MQSeries Integrator, Tuxedo, as well as BEA WebLogic and IBM WebSphere Application Server Advanced Edition.

BMC Software also offers online self-assessment and permits one to rate SML competency on factors, such as minimizing connection delays among the middleware, front-end, and back-end applications, lowering operating system outages downtime, and reducing the chances of getting human error factors into system outages. Also included are the amount of customer rebates when SLAs are not fulfilled, and determining if the company's stock price is directly tied to the availability of its Web site.

Communications Paradigms and Tools

For the purposes here, communications paradigms can be divided into synchronous, asynchronous, direct or queued.[3] Some middleware products may use one, two, or all of these communications paradigms. After a short discussion on the paradigms, this section compares some middle products and then provides a brief discussion of XML-RPC.

Comparing Paradigms

A remote procedure call (RPC), such as the one that exists within products such as the Open Software Foundation's Distributed Computing Environment (DCE), is the best example of a synchronous middleware layer. The RPC is the calling program (see Exhibit 9) that sends a request to a remote program and waits for the response. The calling program, however, must stop processing or is blocked from proceeding until the remote procedure produces a response.

In contrast, asynchronous communications are unblocked or do not block the program from proceeding. The program can make the request and continue processing before a response occurs; it does not stop processing to wait for a response. Most message-oriented middleware (MOM) layers support asynchronous communications through the point-to-point-messaging[4] or message queue models.

In direct communications, the middleware layer accepts the message from the calling program and passes it directly to the remote program. One can

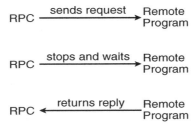

Exhibit 9. Remote Procedure Call

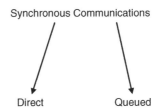

Exhibit 10. Synchronous Communications

use either direct or queued communications with synchronous processing (see Exhibit 10); however, the direct type is usually synchronous in nature, and the queued type is usually asynchronous.

When using queued communications, the calling process (typically a queue manager) places a message in a queue. The remote application retrieves the message at any time after it has been sent. If the calling application requires a response, such as a verification message or data, the information flows back through the queuing mechanism.

The advantage of the queuing model over direct communications is that the remote program does not need to be active for the calling program to send a message to it. Because it is asynchronous in nature, queuing communications middleware typically does not block either the calling or the remote programs from proceeding with message processing.

Trade-Offs

One should review what middleware is before discussing trade-offs among the products. Middleware is the software that connects two or more separate applications. For example, there are a number of middleware products linking a database system to one or more Web servers. These products enable users to employ Web-based forms to dynamically request data from and enter them into the database, and get a reply from a Web server.

In particular, middleware serves as the "glue" between two or more applications and is often referred as the "plumbing" through which applications transfer data among them. Middleware has been traditionally grouped into transaction processing (TP) monitors,[5] DCE environment,[6] RPC systems, object request brokers (ORBs), database access systems, and message passing. Database access systems are discussed in Chapter 6. For information on other middleware types, see the section entitled "Middleware Selection" in this chapter.

The primary advantage of using RPCs (remote procedure calls) is their simplicity. The major issue with RPCs is that they require a lot more processing power. In addition, many exchanges must take place across a network to carry out the request. For example, a typical RPC might require 20 distinct steps to complete the requests, as well as several calls across the network.

The overhead of RPCs can be high. RPCs may require 10,000 to 15,000 instructions to process a remote request. They may make requests to three services: security, naming, and translation. They do not scale well unless combined with other middleware mechanisms such as a transaction processing (TP) monitor or message queuing middleware.

Another problem is that RPCs are bundled into so many products and technologies. For example, if RPCs exist within DCE products, they also make requests to directory, time, threads, and distributed file services. All add to the overhead of RPCs.

While RPCs are slow, their blocking nature provides the best data integrity control. For example, if using an asynchronous layer to access data, one would not know that the update occurs in a timely manner. An update to a customer database could be sitting in a queue waiting for the database to free up while the data entry clerk is creating a sales transaction using the older data. When using RPCs, updates are always applied in the correct order. Thus, if data integrity is more important than performance, consider RPCs.

Another example would be the CORBA-compliant distributed objects that sit on top of an RPC and thus rely on synchronous connections to communicate object-to-object. The additional layer means additional overhead when processing a request between two or more distributed objects. Both CORBA and DCOM provide similar types of capabilities as traditional RPCs. This is one of the reasons that there has been so much discussion of and presentation on scalability issues of CORBA and (to a lesser extent) DCOM.

MOM (message-oriented middleware) has some performance advantages over traditional RPCs. There are two models supported by MOM: point-to-point and message queuing (MQ). Unlike RPC, MQ lets each participating program proceed at its own pace without interruption from the middleware layer. The calling program can post a message to a queue and leave it there. If a response is required, it can get the message from the queue later.

Because the MQ software (e.g., IBM's MQ Series, Microsoft's MSMQ, FioranoMQ,[7] SonicMQ, TIBCO,[8] and Talarian) manages the distribution of the message from one program to the next, the queue manager can take steps to optimize performance. Messages are stored in queues that can be buffered (reside in memory) or persistent (reside on a permanent device). The MQ software's asynchronous communications style provides a loosely coupled exchange across multiple operating systems.

There are many performance enhancements that come with these products, including prioritization, load balancing, and thread pooling. Some features in one messaging product may be better than others in another, depending on the organizational requirements.

All implement key requirements for messaging server, including clustering and load balancing, key security features, integration with application servers, and Lightweight Directory Access Protocol (LDAP) servers. Additionally important are scalability and latency factors. There is a maximum limit to the number of users that a server can handle concurrently. These are strict requirements governing the delay between the time a message is published and the time it is received by one or more subscribers. Latency is a critical factor for measuring performance with overall throughput of the system.

As of August 2001, the American Stock Exchange (AMEX) decided to install Talarian's SmartSockets to replace TIBCO and take advantage of the scalability features as a way of coping with ever-increasing quote traffic. For a while, both Talarian and TIBCO will co-exist until such time that all key exchange applications are fully into Talarian's messaging architecture. The rising quote volume trend is partially attributed to volatility and product expansion.

TP monitors provide the greatest performance advantage over both MQ and RPCs. Several features of TP monitors, such as BEA's Tuxedo, IBM's CICS, and Microsoft Transaction Server (MTS), enhance performance as well as provide the ultimate in scalability.

TP monitors also provide message queuing, routing, and other features, which let distributed application developers bypass the TP monitor's transactional features. One can assign priorities to classes of messages, letting the higher priority messages receive server resources first.

XML-RPC

XML-RPC is a way of overcoming the limitations of traditional RPCs that are restricted to a few operating systems. This specification is a set of implementations that allow software running on disparate operating systems and in different environments to make procedure calls over the Internet. As a remote procedure, XML-RPC makes the calls using HTTP as the transport and XML as the encoding. It is designed to permit complex data structures to be transmitted, processed, and returned — synchronously.

XML-RPC works by encoding the RPC requests into XML and sending them over a standard HTTP connection to a server (or *listener* piece). The listener decodes the XML, executes the requested procedure, and then packages the results in XML and sends them back over the wire to the client. The client decodes the XML, converts the results into standard language datatypes, and continues executing. Exhibit 11 is a diagram showing an actual XML-RPC conversation between a client (requesting customer information) and a listener who is returning the results of that procedure.

There are two important aspects of this protocol that one should keep in mind when building middleware. XML-RPC is built on HTTP and, like ordinary Web traffic, its stateless conversations are of the request and response variety. There is no built-in support for transactions or encryption.

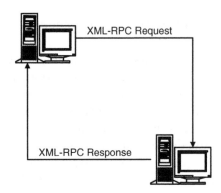

Exhibit 11.   XML-RPC Conversation

Other Performance Tools

This section looks at some tools to improve Java database and enterprise performance. It also briefly discusses the merits of the Microsoft Operations Manager 2000 and the Internet and Security Acceleration (ISA) Server 2000.

Managing EJB and Java Performance

Computer Associates Athena not only monitors Java 2 Enterprise Edition (J2EE) application servers, but also examines and tests the performance of large, complex E-business applications based on Enterprise JavaBeans (EJBs). It looks at how the beans interact with one another and reports potential performance bottlenecks at the bean level. The product reduces the operational overhead of ensuring performance and availability of EJB components and J2EE-compliant application servers such as BEA WebLogic, IBM WebSphere, Silverstream, as well as J2EE-compliant Web servers.

Straka JProbe Profiler, a part of the JProbe ServerSide Suite, pinpoints Java performance problems (EJB or Java Server Pages (JSPs)) with server-side profiling. The ServerSide Edition provides the the ability to work with Java applications running remotely in a networked, heterogenous environment; for example, profiling one's server-side applications as they run on a Solaris or NT/2000 server.

JProbe Profiler provides detailed code performance information: looping, memory usage (heap, stack, and garbage collection). It lets one monitor interdependencies between methods, prevent deadlock, overflow, etc.

Database

The Transaction Processing Performance Council (TPC) divides database performance into three categories: online transaction processing (OLTP), ad hoc queries, and Web E-commerce transactions. Based on the council's criteria, the best performers in the first category went to Microsoft SQL Server 2000 running Windows 2000 Datacenter Server on an IBM xSeries 370 machine.

Topping the list in the second category were IBM DB2 UDB 7.2 running Linux on an SGI 1450 Server, and Microsoft SQL Server running Windows 2000. Only SQL/Windows 2000 received best scores for the third category.

Microsoft Operations Manager 2000

Microsoft Operations Manager 2000 incorporates event and performance management tools for Windows 2000 Server and the family of .NET Enterprise Servers, as well as a variety of third-party enterprise and data-center software. It primarily collects and views event information to monitor servers and applications. The software consolidates events, compressing repetitive events into one single event (which logs the number of repeated attempts) to prevent event log overflow. The same happens with event notices when a server fails. Network administrators are notified once, although the event notification logs the number of users affected.

Microsoft has collaborated closely with NetIQ in the development of the Microsoft Operations Manager, as NetIQ licensed the Operations Manager technology to Microsoft. NetIQ plans to develop XMPs (Extended Management Packs) that integrate the Microsoft Operations Manager with a variety of other platforms and environments, including Linux, UNIX, Novell, Lotus Notes, Oracle, and SAP.

Internet Security and Acceleration Server 2000

The ISA Server 2000 integrates an extensible, multi-player enterprise firewall and a scalable high-performance Web cache. It builds on Microsoft Windows 2000 security and directory for policy-based security, acceleration, and management of internetworking.

ISA Server comes in two editions: Standard Edition and Enterprise Edition. Both have the same feature sets, although the Standard Edition is a stand-alone server supporting a maximum of four processors. For large-scale deployments, server array support, multi-level policy, and computers with more than four processors, one will need ISA Server Enterprise Edition.

ISA Server protects networks from unauthorized access, inspects traffic, and alerts network administrators to attacks. It includes an extensible, multi-player enterprise firewall featuring security with packet-, circuit-, and application-level traffic screening, stateful inspection, broad application support, integrated virtual private networking (VPN), system hardening, integrated intrusion detection, smart application filters, transparency for all clients, advanced authentication, secure server publishing, etc.

Middleware Selection

According to Exhibit 12, ten basic requirements should be ranked when selecting middleware.

Exhibit 12.   Middleware Selection Criteria

Security	Access to Legacy Data
24×7 Availability	99.9 percent uptime availability in SLAs
Scalability	Fault tolerance
Remote management	Load balancing
Protocol support	Performance

While performance is among the most important selection criteria, other criteria that should be considered include:

- How middleware is defined
- How a middleware hierarchy is developed
- What are the desired types of middleware products
- What performance levels are acceptable
- What roles the middleware products will play in an EAI system
- What are the organization's future plans

All are related to performance criteria in one way or another. The following are examples of answers to two questions: middleware definition and hierarchy.

Definition: middleware is an integrator, converter, and translator — all facilitating the communication between two applications. It provides an API through which applications invoke services over the network. If one divides middleware products into management and development, management middleware connects existing applications, while development middleware provides management tools and a development platform. Management middleware can be further grouped into communications middleware, database middleware, systems middleware, E-commerce middleware, and Java-based middleware (see Exhibit 13).

In particular, communications middleware allows one to connect applications based on communication styles such as message queuing, ORBs, and publish/subscribe, while database middleware allows clients to invoke SQL-based services across multi-vendor databases via de facto standards such as JDBC, ODBC, DRDA, and RDA.[9] System middleware, on the other hand, provides inter-program communications regarding the use of local facilities to access remote resources. An example is TP monitors that are required to control local resources and also cooperate with other resource managers to access remote resources.

Communications Middleware

Communications is further broken down into object middleware and message-oriented middleware (see Exhibit 14). Object middleware permits clients to invoke methods or objects that reside on a remote server. This middleware revolves around OMG's CORBA and Microsoft's DCOM.

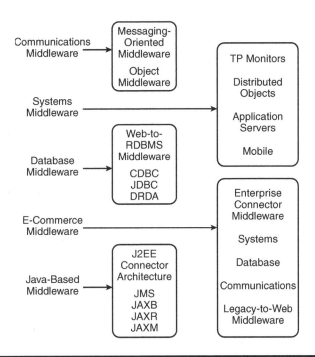

Exhibit 13.   Management Middleware Hierarchy

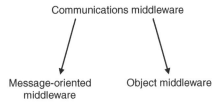

Exhibit 14.   Communications Middleware

MOM is a set of products that lets users run applications remotely on different systems by sending and receiving application data as messages. It provides an interface between client and server applications, allowing them to send data back and forth. Examples include RPC, CPI-C, and message queuing. CPI-C (an acronym for Common Programming Interface Communications) refers to IBM's SNA peer-to-peer API that can run over SNA and TCP/IP. Message queuing allows one to store messages in queues in memory (buffered queue) or on a disk or other permanent storage device (persistent queue). It runs in an asynchronous communications style and provides a loosely-coupled exchange across multiple operating systems.

Database Middleware

Applications such as databases or spreadsheets are used by individuals to create, store, and manage raw data on one or more local or remote databases.

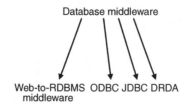

Exhibit 15.   Database Middleware

But people who need to see this data may be using different operating systems and applications. Database middleware bridges this gap for users (see Exhibit 15); it does not, however, transfer calls or objects.

In addition, database middleware does not allow for two-way communication between servers and clients. Unlike messaging middleware, servers cannot initiate contact with clients; they can only respond when asked. One uses a standard browser to get data via Web middleware or send data to a database via Web-to-RDBMS middleware.

This middleware employs Structured Query Language (SQL) services for multi-vendor databases through standards such as ODBC, DRDA, RDA, and JDBC. DRDA stands for IBM's Distributed Relational Database Architecture while RDA is spelled out as Remote Data Access, usually to an RDBMS via SQL. ODBC is short for Open Database Connectivity, a Windows standard API for SQL communication. It is based on the Call-Level Interface (CLI) specifications from X/Open and ISO/IEC for database APIs.

JDBC is a trademarked name, not an acronym, although it can be thought of as "Java Database Connectivity." It is a technology that enables universal data access for the Java Programming Language. With Java and the JDBC API, it is possible to publish a Web page containing an applet that uses information obtained from remote databases running on different operating systems, including Windows and UNIX.

Systems Middleware

Systems middleware, on the other hand, provides inter-program communications regarding the use of local facilities to access remote resources (see Exhibit 16). An example is a TP monitor that is required to control local resources and also cooperate with other resource managers to access remote resources. It can sit between a requesting client program and databases, ensuring that all databases are updated properly. This middleware is a control program that manages the transfer of data between multi-terminals (or smart desktop computers and laptops) and the application programs that serve them.

Other examples include distributed object middleware, mobile middleware, and application server middleware. Distributed object middleware manages the real-time execution of processes on remote systems while mobile middleware involves the use of mobile agents to add a layer of mobility services on top of distributed object middleware. Ideally, these services support wireless

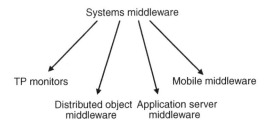

Exhibit 16.   Systems Middleware Hierarchy

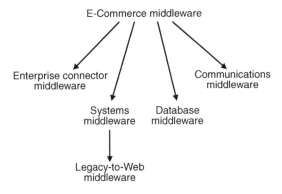

Exhibit 17.   E-Commerce Middleware

user mobility and mobile access to remote resources, such as those offered by IBM's MQSeries Everywhere. Application server middleware is a Web-based application server that provides interfaces to a broad range of applications and can be used as middleware between browser and legacy systems.

E-Commerce Middleware

E-commerce middleware connects back-end enterprise software and data to users over the Internet or through direct connections via the Web. It comes in three layers: enterprise connector middleware, application servers, and messaging middleware (see Exhibit 17). Legacy-to-Web middleware aims at unifying browser client interfaces to multiple applications. B2B integration of EAI applications is an ongoing process.

Enterprise Connector Middleware

If one wants to connect legacy applications to application servers (e.g., the Web), one should consider enterprise connector middleware. Connector middleware tools are generally used for translating mainframe application data into a form usable by Web applications. Examples include Information Builders' EDA and J2EE.

Application Servers

When one needs to translate data into many forms for use by many different types of E-commerce applications, one needs one or more application servers. They provide a layer of business logic that handles incoming requests and converts back-end data into an appropriate form for transfer outside a firewall. Application servers include both prepackaged applications and application development platforms. Outsourced E-commerce solutions such as online marketplaces rely heavily on application server infrastructure.

Some application servers are built with a specific type of E-commerce in mind. Microsoft's BizTalk Server 2000 is designed for server-to-server connections between organizations, using XML-based messages to perform Internet transactions. Other application servers rely on custom-built or packaged components to provide business services within their application framework.

Many of these servers use the EJB component framework for application logic components. Microsoft's Commerce Server 2000 relies on Microsoft's enhanced Component Object Model, known as COM+, while other products offer a blend of the Java and COM worlds.

Messaging Middleware

When E-commerce applications integrate from server to server instead of using a Web interface, one will likely require messaging middleware. These messaging products are generally used to guarantee that transactions are delivered and acted upon in a specific order, and to ensure that more sophisticated applications with complex transaction rules do not fail because of a lack of network bandwidth or a client disconnect.

An E-commerce application can use any or all types of middleware, depending on the type of application. A wireless supply requisitioning application, for example, could consist of a wireless application server, multiple types of connector middleware to hook into legacy accounting systems, and messaging middleware — possibly with additional application servers — to handle transaction routing and guarantee secure delivery to an appropriate vendor.

Java-Based Middleware

An infrastructure can be built to integrate B2B with Java-based middleware products in addition to other middleware types covered in this section. Java-based middleware uses standards such as J2EE Connector Architecture (J2EE CA), Java Messaging Service (JMS), JAXB, JAXR,[10] and Simple Object Access Protocol (SOAP) as well as Web services.

To understand how Java-based middleware can be used, one can start with a standard Web browser. When one sends a request, it goes to a J2EE server that interfaces with Web services[11] (for details, see Chapter 5). In response to the request, Web services looks up a wholesale customer in a Universal Description, Description and Integration (UDDI) directory that catalogs services, mostly

Exhibit 18. Java APIs

Java API for XML (JAX)	Send messages and exchange data
Java Architecture for XML Binding (JAXB)	Map elements in the XML documents to Java classes
Java API for XML Registries (JAXR)	Update the UDDI Registry
Java API for XML Messaging (JAXM)	Integrate a back-end legacy system with a company's supply chain via a B2B private exchange; enable a system to send SOAP messages

with Web Services Description Language (WSDL) describing the services' locations and protocols. These services are then accessed over SOAP that supports RPCs over the applications protocol that binds the Web with the HTTP. See the section on RPC trade-offs.

To complete the integration of this online with the Web services, one requires several Java APIs, as shown in Exhibit 18. Note that Web services platforms like Microsoft's .NET initiative are built on XML, the SOAP, WSDL, and UDDI. Some platforms, notably BEA System's WebLogic, iPlanet, and IBM's WebSphere, support both J2EE and SOAP.

Web Services Technology

Web services technology can be thought of as an evolution of CORBA. Its major advantage over CORBA is that Web services do not require integration of an ORB. The underlying transport protocol behind Web services is based on XML over the HTTP.

There is one drawback. For Web services for application integration to work properly, several extensions must be added to the collection of Web services specifications. Web services currently lack a mechanism to encapsulate a user interface. This encapsulation allows packaging of an application and embedding it into another application.

As a partial solution, the Web Services User Interface (WSUI) Initiative was drawn up in June 2001 and defines the concept of what views the developers should use to display a Web service on a screen. It specifies that views employ eXtensible Stylesheet Language Transformation (XSLT) to transform into a Hypertext Markup Language (HTML) or Wireless Markup Language (WML) script.

Another drawback is that Web services lack security facilities. The application of Web services for business-to-business integration (B2Bi) will be limited if services for authentication, encryption, access control, and data integrity are not available.

A third problem is that Web services cannot certify the identity of the publisher or consumer of a Web service. There are no facilities to restrict access to a Web service to a group of authorized users. As a partial solution, the XML-Based Security Services Technical Committee from the Organization for the Advancement of Structured Information Standards (OASIS) is working on a specification for Security Assertion Markup Language (SAML). OASIS is also working on XACML (eXtensible Access Control Markup Language), which would allow organizations to limit access to services to authenticated, authorized users.

Among other system standards being developed regarding the implementation of low-level security services is the XML Key Management Specification (XKMS) proposed by Microsoft, VeriSign, and WebMethods. This specification aims at reducing the complexity of creating products that support public key infrastructure (PKI).

Middleware Interoperability

Another performance criteria to consider is the interoperability of some middleware products. On August 15, 2001, IONA, a leading E-business platform provider, announced that Web services created in Microsoft .NET can be utilized in Sun Micrososystem's J2EE environments, and vice versa, using the IONA XMLBus technology. This software allows developers to build Web services from J2EE applications running on the IONA iPortal, BEA WebLogic, or IBM WebSphere application servers. Available free of charge, it provides support for industry standards such as SOAP, WSDL, and the XML Schema. In addition, JMX instrumentation ensures that customers can administer and manage Web services in the same way that they manage their existing systems.

Development Middleware

One good example of a middleware development platform is Computer Associates' Jasmine ii — the ii stands for intelligent infrastructure. Jasmine ii is an object-oriented development environment that provides database support, e-mail management and middleware services through a single interface. It also supports a mix of CORBA and EJB components.

At the core of Jasmine are reusable objects based on the Jasmine object database. To control the objects in an application using Jasmine, the objects must be identified as fitting one of the Jasmine providers. Among the providers that Computer Associates has created so far are ones for COM, CORBA, JavaBeans, the Microsoft Messaging Application Programming Interface (MAPI), Microsoft Object Linking and Embedding (OLE), XML, LDAP, Computer Associates' Neugents technology, as well as database management and enterprise resource planning systems.

Notes

1. Examples include management services provider (MSP), Internet service provider (ISP), and application service provider (ASP).
2. Guaranteed bandwidths are not prioritized bandwidths.

3. Other paradigms include connectionless communications and connection-oriented communications. For the former paradigm, the calling program does not enter into a connection with the target process. The receiving application acts on the request and responds if required. For the latter paradigm, the two parties first connect, exchange messages, and then disconnect.

4. The most common messaging models are publish-subscribe messaging, point-to-point messaging, and request–reply messaging. Not all MOM providers support each model. When multiple applications need to receive the same messages, publish–subscribe Messaging is used. With this model, it is possible to have multiple senders and multiple receivers. When one process needs to send a message to another process, point-to-point messaging can be used. It can take either a one- or two-way direction. The first type of point-to-point messaging systems involve a client that directly sends a message to another client. The second type is based on the concept of a message queue. For either type, there may be multiple senders of messages and only a single receiver. When an application sends a message and expects to receive a reply, request–reply messaging, the standard synchronous object-messaging format, can be used. Unlike the other two messaging models, Java Message Service (JMS) does not explicitly support request–reply messaging.

5. TP monitor is a program that monitors a transaction as it passes from one stage in a process to another. The TP monitor's purpose is to ensure that the transaction processes completely or, if an error occurs, to take appropriate actions.

6. DCE is a suite of technology services developed by The Open Group for creating distributed applications that run on different platforms. DCE services include:
   a. RPC
   b. Security service
   c. Directory service
   d. Time service
   e. Threads service
   f. Distributed file service

7. Fiorano is the first vendor to implement the JMS specification.

8. TIBCO Software is a leading integration middleware provider.

9. See the "Database Middleware" section regarding these four acronyms.

10. See Exhibit 18 on explanations of Java APIs.

11. The concept has existed for several years, first in component-based computing frameworks such as Forte's and more recently in platforms such as Java 2 Enterprise Edition (J2EE).

Chapter 9

What Lies Ahead?

This chapter discusses what lies ahead for middleware technologies. It looks at evolutionary paths the technologies have taken and at competing paradigms between the .NET initiative and J2EE platform. The chapter then proceeds to a middleware hierarchy that can be expanded to incorporate new technologies. Also included are the emerging Internet standards, innovative interoperability technologies, better performance tools, and improved service levels.

Introduction

Renting components is not really new. One can rent a vendor's visitor monitoring control as a component of one's Web page to assist in tracking the visitors coming to the site — by client operating system, hour, day, and country. It takes much less time to rent the component (a few minutes) than to code, program, test, and implement it (from a few days to several months), and make it part of one's Web page.

What is really new is the concept of Web services. This concept goes a little further than ASPs in allowing companies to rent an entire software package — enterprise resource planning (ERP),[1] supply chain management (SCM), customer relationship management (CRM), and other aspects of the enterprise application integration (EAI) paradigm. Customers can rent components from various sources on the Internet, and mix and match them to create new Web services, such as:

- Currency conversion
- Credit authorization
- Translation
- Hotel reservation
- Airline reservation
- Local weather report

any of which the customers could link to a vendor's database service. By changing the mix of components, they can determine which applications show the best performance on an overall basis.

When a customer mixes and matches components, it means that the Web services are reconfigurable or, in a more formal sense, loosely coupled. Although tasks are reconfigurable, a change in the implementation of one function does not require a change to the invoking function.

The problem here is that Web services have different meanings for the following groups of users:

- Consumers
- Service providers
- Independent software vendors
- Managed service providers
- Corporate application developers

Each group has a different perception of what Web services are and what they should do. (See Chapter 5 for a list of various definitions.) Unlike Internet standards, a common definition for Web services does not exist.

Web services include gateways into back-end systems. They can be used in banking, insurance, brokerage, telecommunications services, retailing, manufacturing and supply chain management, and many other industries to expose existing systems via either the public Internet or private intranets and extranets within service-oriented architectures.

Evolutionary Paths

Microsoft's .NET platform represents an evolution of the Component Object Model (COM) because it is used to create software components that are completely object-based. The "COM.NET" is the next step in COM evolution. Microsoft replaced ActiveX Data Objects (ADO) with ADO.NET and ASP with ASP.NET, and launched Web services when .NET became available in late 2001.

Web services technology can also be thought of as taking an evolutionary path from Common Object Request Broker Architecture (CORBA). Its major advantage over CORBA is that Web services do not require integration of an ORB. In the Java world, Web services are encapsulated as Enterprise JavaBeans (EJBs).

All three object models — the COM, CORBA/IIOP, and EJB — are tools that allow the creation of reusable software components. The underlying transport protocol behind Web services is based on eXtensible Markup Language (XML) over the Hypertext Transport Protocol (HTTP). All use SOAP to transmit services (and messages, as well). Most vendors — including Microsoft, IBM, Oracle, and Sun — are now providing SOAP-enabled products, services, and toolkits. The open-source community has also released SOAP modules for the Apache server and Perl.

Web services have entered into the third wave of the Internet, allowing companies to connect their systems and business processes with those of their partners and customers. As such, the third wave has evolved from the second wave whereby the Web sites are connected to people, and, in turn, from the first wave in which e-mail is used to connect with people.

Competing Paradigms

Currently, two competing paradigms are clamoring for the Web services spotlight: Microsoft's product strategy (.NET initiative) and a standard called Java 2 Enterprise Edition (J2EE) created by Sun Microsystems.

The great thing about the J2EE standard and .NET initiative is that they are very compatible with each other. The main reason is that both entities are complying with Internet standards. The key standards thus far include Universal Description, Discovery and Integration (UDDI) for describing and locating services; XML for handling data in a uniform way, Simple Object Access Protocol (SOAP) for defining the interface and how to send the services; HTML; and Web Services Description Language (WSDL) for accessing the components comprising a Web service.

Although all provide the means by which software modules can work with and find one another on the Web, Web services have drawbacks, particularly in security and user interface. As a partial solution, new Internet standards have emerged or are in the development to make Web services more interoperable, more user-friendly and more secure. A short discussion on these standards is covered in the section entitled "Emerging Internet Standards."

Middleware Hierarchy

In the first attempts to define comprehensive software platforms for distributed applications 25 years ago, researchers created basic middleware elements such as remote procedure call (RPC), file service, and directory service based on dramatic advances (in those days) in hardware technology and fast networking and workstation systems. In the industrial world, RPC has evolved into XML-RPC to enable RPC to work with a wider range of operating systems. File service took two evolutionary directions (database management systems and network file services) while directory service has blossomed into more sophisticated directory networking services.

It is believed that the history of "industrial" middleware began when it was necessary to connect front-end client applications with back-end databases, using RPC and directory services to send messages and data between applications. Middleware allows independent applications to access and share functions and data stored in heterogeneous databases. In a large bank, hundreds of application subsystems must be integrated. These applications access data stores ranging from relational databases to external information providers (e.g., credit validation service).

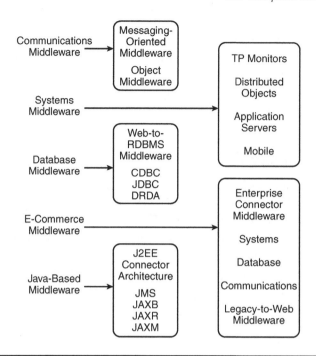

Exhibit 1. Middleware Hierarchy

The scope of middleware is now much broader, incorporating other types of middleware that include:

- Database middleware
- Communications middleware
- Systems middleware
- E-commerce middleware
- Java-based middleware

All address the issues of quality-of-service (QoS) management and information security to varying degrees. Exhibit 1 shows how each is grouped into sub-levels where appropriate in an arbitrary middleware hierarchy (for details, see Chapter 8).

The middleware hierarchy's big picture will change, including new middleware types not yet dreamed of. Whatever the hierarchy will be, one must consider the many trade-offs of various middleware products when considering how well these products will perform and interoperate with protocols and diverse platforms in a distributed environment of applications and systems over the Internet.

This section looks at database middleware, Web services, and workflow systems.

Database Middleware

SQL/relational databases evolved from the Indexed Sequential Access Method (ISAM), which is dependent primarily on COBOL to index records and is not yet formalized as a data model. Today, almost all major databases are XML enabled. They include two from IBM (DB2 XML Extender and Informix), two from Microsoft (SQL Server 2000 and Microsoft Access 2002), and one from Oracle (Oracle8i/9i Application Servers). In particular, Access 2002 imports XML documents into Access (Jet) or an SQL server database and exports XML from Access into other formats. It can both upload tables to corporate-level, back-end SQL Server and access information from it.

With Microsoft SQL Server, one can use ADO as a tool to process XML directly, without having to make conversions between XML and some other format. As of September 2001, Microsoft released XQuery Demo on the Web. XQuery is an SQL equivalent for use with XML data, based on the World Wide Web Consortium's (W3C's) XQuery working draft released on June 7, 2001. It allows developers to manipulate sets of XML data and combine it with other XML data. It is much better than using XPath query language to locate and process items in an XML document and the Extensible Stylesheet Language Transformation engine (XSLT) to filter the information. For a list of issues that need to be resolved, go to http://131.107.228.20/xquerydemo/demo.aspx.

Web Services

One possible addition to the middleware hierarchy is Web services, when the market for them reaches its full potential by 2002 or 2003. Some third-party vendors already offer tools to compose, test, and deploy Web services. Salcentral.com, for example, provides a short tutorial on how to create a Web service with Visual Basic (Versions 5 and 6). At a future date, it will provide tutorials on using other languages to create Web services. This brokerage also offers various utilities that convert schemas to the WSDL format.

One major vendor — Microsoft — launched its first commercial Web services (currently known by the code name "HailStorm") at the beginning of 2002, a few months after the .NET platform, which came out in November 2001. Included in the 14 services scheduled for the HailStorm release are:

- myProfile (name, nickname, special dates, picture)
- myContacts (electronic relationships/address book)
- myNotifications (notification subscription, management, and routing)
- myCalendar (time and task management)
- myDocuments (raw document storage)
- myWallet (receipts, payment instruments, coupons, and other transaction records)
- myDevices (device settings, capabilities)

They are for personal use. One can build "business" Web services with .NET platform, J2EE platform, or third-party tools or servers, such as Shinka Technologies's Integration Server 1.2, a Web services platform. One can also get information from Dun and Bradstreet's Web services. Mobile users can look forward to Java 2 Micro Edition (J2ME) for micro services.

According to Gartner, Web services are already having "an impact on commerce strategies." Examples include E-commerce services for providing payment, logistics, fulfillment, tracking, and rating services; E-syndicated services for incorporating reservation services on a travel site or rate quote services on an insurance site; Bow Street for providing the Business Web Factory to create interactive Web services that can be mass-customized and assembled at runtime; and Web Collage Syndicator for providing the capability to assemble interactive Web services, customize them, and place them in the partner's site.

Emerging Internet Standards

Internet standards have emerged to rectify some of the drawbacks of Web services in areas where CORBA, EJB, and COM object models shine, and to make workflow processes more open, more standardized, and more flexible. This section covers standards for user interface, security, and workflow processes.

User Interface

The Web Services User Interface (WSUI) Initiative was drawn up in June 2001; it defines the concept of what views the developers should use to display a Web service on a screen. It specifies that views employ XSLT to transform into a Hypertext Markup Language (HTML) or Wireless Markup Language (WML) script.

This initiative provides Web services with a mechanism to encapsulate a user interface. This encapsulation allows packaging of an application and embedding it into another application. It is not necessary to add several extensions to a collection of Web services, as one must do so when not using the user interface standard.

Security

The XML-Based Security Services Technical Committee from the Organization for the Advancement of Structured Information Standards (OASIS) is working on a specification for the Security Assertion Markup Language (SAML). This standard lets Web services certify the identity of the publisher or consumer of a Web service. Without it, there are no facilities to restrict access to a Web service to a group of authorized users.

OASIS is also working on eXtensible Access Control Markup Language (XACML), which would allow organizations to limit access to services to authenticated, authorized users. The application of Web services for business-to-business integration (B2Bi) will be limited if services for authentication, encryption, access control, and data integrity are unavailable.

Related to these security initiatives are the system standards being developed regarding the implementation of low-level security services. They include the XML Key Management Specification (XKMS) proposed by Microsoft, VeriSign, and WebMethods. This specification aims to reduce the complexity of creating products that support public key infrastructure (PKI).

Workflow Standard

The problem is that a company can only call one set of Web services from another company. Suppose a drapery contractor interacts with a fabric materials provider to supply the material, a drapery manufacturing company to make the draperies for an industrial plant, a drapery fixture company to set up the rods and other fixtures above the windows, and a utility company to map where the rods can or cannot be. The drapery contractor needs to find a way to order the fabric materials and send them to the drapery manufacturer and have this process coordinated with the windows fixture company to actually set up the draperies. On top of that, the drapery contractor needs all these services rolled back if the utility company says that the current blueprint for the draperies crosses essential utility lines. Currently in this system, there is no standard way of aggregating all these services together to act as one transaction and have them automatically stop or change in some way based on the responses from each or all of the mentioned services. This is where IBM's Web Services Flow Language (WSFL), introduced in May 2001, comes into play.

What the WSFL (described as an XML document) does is allow a company to:

- Define all its external services that it routinely deploys in a WDSL format.
- Map connections between its business processes so that the services are aggregated.
- Finish the process if and when services are successfully executed as planned.
- Coordinate the canceling of some or all of the services if things go wrong.

What was demonstrated above is from the industrial drapery contractor's side. Now suppose that the other companies that do business with the contractor also support the WSFL standard. Like the contractor, they would know how to coordinate the services requested from them with the contractor's other needed services. For example, the fabric provider can coordinate with the contractor's packaging company of choice to send fabrics to the drapery manufacturing company. And using that one document, the drapery manufacturing company can do the exact same thing when it has to ship the draperies to the drapery fixture company.

After the WSFL has been standardized, it is more likely that it will be used more widely as the market for Web services reaches full scale in 2002. Do not confuse this workflow standard with the creation and deployment of Web services in workflow processes (briefly discussed below).

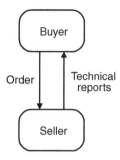

Exhibit 2.   Simple Workflow

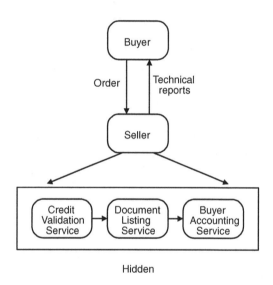

Hidden

Exhibit 3.   Complex Workflow (Hidden)

A Web service can serve both as an activity in one workflow and a series of sequenced activities in another workflow, and can be composed out of a workflow.

Start with a simple Web service workflow: a seller service (publisher) and a buyer service (author or technical report user), as shown in Exhibit 2. The seller service interface is defined using WSDL. The buyer service is invoking the technical report order on the seller service using SOAP and WSDL. It knows what the SOAP reply message looks like as defined in WSDL.

As shown in Exhibit 3, the seller service is a workflow encapsulated as a single Web service. The seller service consists of a credit validation activity, a document listing activity, and a buyer accounting service. The system uses WSDL to interface the seller service with the buyer interface. The seller service does not expose the details of this service to public applications and services that seek to use the seller service.

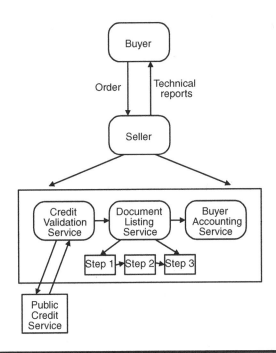

Exhibit 4.　Complex Workflow (Public Credit Service)

Now expand the workflow to include several activity steps for the Document Listing Web Service (see Exhibit 4). The Credit Validation Service hidden from public view uses a Pubic Credit Service over the Internet from a UDDI registry.

Now assume that the Buyer Accounting Service is an encapsulated EJB and replace the activities in the Document Listing Service as EJBs (see Exhibit 5). Also add an encapsulated EJB to serve as a Web service client application between the Credit Validation Service and the Public Credit Service. This workflow also calls out middleware products that currently support or will support WSFL.

Interoperability

We need more than open middleware as provided by Java APIs, standards, and platforms. What is needed is to increase the scope of interoperability using SOAP protocols and among platforms such as J2EE and .NET. Although CORBA 3.0 can be used with Java, EJBs, and SOAP, third-party tools for interoperability among the "big three" — J2EE, .NET, and CORBA — are yet to be seen and may become available by the time, or shortly after, this book is published.

SOAP Protocol

This protocol comes in three primary flavors: Microsoft (the original contributor), Perl, and Apache. Differences among them have been noted when, for

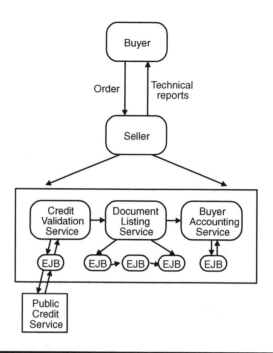

Exhibit 5.   EJB-Based Workflows

example, the developers change from a Microsoft operating system to a non-Microsoft one, and vice versa.

Using the WSDL description for a Web service listed in a UDDI registry, one can create a SOAP message that binds an application to the described Web service and then sends that message over HTTP to invoke the service itself. A SOAP-enabled interface on the service side translates the SOAP message and directly invokes the service, sending the response message (through SOAP) back. One can then translate the SOAP response message for one's own uses.

HTTP is not the only transport protocol over which one can send SOAP messages. One can e-mail a SOAP message by binding the application to the Web service and then send the message over Simple Mail Transport Protocol (SMTP) that a service has been invoked or will be invoked pending a user prompt.

Whatever transport protocol is used, SOAP is a tool for developing Web services on both .NET and J2EE platforms. While the former platform for Web services was discussed earlier in this chapter, BEA Systems' rationale for using SOAP to develop Web services on the J2EE platform is briefly discussed here.

First, BEA chose this platform because of the ability of the EJBs to encapsulate Web services. Second, BEA has taken advantage of using J2EE applications to expose EJBs and Java Messaging Service (JMS) destinations as Web services. Exposed services use WSDL as the service description language and provide access to components.

Third, it can use the J2EE Connector Architecture (CA) to integrate with partners' service by some applications of the EAI paradigms via private and public registries. BEA Systems' future J2EE products will eventually support and possibly standardize how Web services will work as part of complex business processes participating in business transactions.

J2EE and .NET Platform

The main benefits and disadvantages of J2EE and .NET involve how they link into legacy systems, which platforms they can run on, which languages they use, how portable the systems are, how much they cost, and their performance and scalability metrics. The ability to interoperate is possible because both platforms have continually incorporated support for XML. In the near future, one will see .NET on non-Microsoft operating systems as a result of Microsoft's ongoing efforts to make its Web services available to non-Microsoft users in all five categories: consumers, service providers, independent software vendors, managed service providers, and corporate application developers.

In late 2000, Microsoft submitted key parts of the technology for standardization to the ECMA,[2] an international standardization body. The elements still under discussion include the common language runtime (CLR), Common Language Specification (CLS), Microsoft Intermediate Language (MSIL), C#, and more than 1000 components from the basic libraries. Microsoft is actively pushing to complete the work much faster than the usual time it takes for such standards processes.

When Microsoft's .NET platform was released in November 2001, many users worked with or used both the .NET and J2EE platforms. The latter platform had an earlier start in achieving interoperability among diverse operating systems.

To take advantage of Web services in both environments, IONA developed XMLBus technology to allow one to create Web services in .NET and utilize them in J2EE environments. What this means is that developers can build Web services created in .NET from J2EE applications running on the IONA iPortal, BEA WebLogic, or IBM WebSphere application servers. Sun's Java Management Extensions (JMX) instrumentation ensures that customers can administer and manage Web services in the same way that they manage their existing systems.

XMLBus provides tools and a runtime environment to turn existing Java and J2EE applications into Web services without having to write code. Java classes and EJBs can be exposed as standard Web services. IONA XMLBus generates Java code for the appropriate Web server container, and enlists the Web service to the specified UDDI registry.

This technology provides a portable Web services container that can be installed on top of an existing J2EE environment or run as a stand-alone application. Web services are deployed into the container with automatic connection to back-end resources, via dispatchers. The container is available on most application server platforms or as a XMLBus stand-alone.

Dispatchers are provided for Java classes and EJBs. No programming is required to bind new Web services to preexisting application functionality supported by these dispatchers. Future dispatchers will include support for

IONA Enterprise Integrator, IONA B2B Integrator, CORBA 2.3,[3] JMS, and MQSeries.

The XMLBus technology, in addition, provides support for SOAP with Attachments (SwA) to permit the development of Web services based on document passing style. Multi-part MIME attachments within a SOAP message can transmit XML documents, images, arbitrary binary data, and encrypted messages across the wire. This implementation demonstrates IONA's commitment to ebXML.

Used in conjunction with IONA's EAI and business-to-business integration (B2Bi) technologies, IONA XMLBus contributes to IONA's support for end-to-end E-business integration. For example, coupled with IONA Enterprise Integrator, IONA XMLBus provides a platform for building service-oriented architectures. When coupled with IONA B2B Integrator, IONA XMLBus provides a platform for business process collaboration among trading partners.

Performance Tools

This section discusses various performance issues and considerations regarding the design, deployment, use, and maintenance of middleware products. While it is not possible to address all performance issues, this section looks at middleware products that act as a translator, converter, or integrator — or all three simultaneously as the glue between applications.

Among others, performance data is important criteria in middleware selection. If software development project leaders select middleware without considering performance, it can lead to budget overruns, frequent rescheduling, high staff turnover, and even disaster, including failed projects. When dealing with third-party vendors, it is important to determine if their SLAs are adequate.

Integration broker middleware is the largest segment in the middleware market, as well as the fastest growing. It is slightly larger than the transaction processing (TP) segment. Risks[4] abound for vendors and users due to frequent changes in technology, standards, and product packaging, among other factors such as middleware technology bugs and incomplete ERP packages. They include degraded performance, network (or rather middleware) bottlenecks, poor caching schemes, and defective service level agreements.

Another problem is that business, engineering, and EAI applications via integration broker middleware do not know anything about network flows and may request more bandwidth than is available. Without proper monitoring tools, the network does not know when the loads are coming, how long they will last, or how and what the user demand is going to be.

Various performance solutions and standards have been debated, tried, and offered — both proprietary and open source. As monitoring tools, they do not always guarantee that they can make good predictions on traffic behavior of some applications. They instead provide good estimates on traffic patterns that could occur based on statistical and qualitative analysis of historical data collected over a period of time.

Among the causes of network bottlenecks are the applications that consume an unusual amount of bandwidth allocated to network traffic. If the applications do not get sufficient bandwidth, they will drop out of the network or be subject to excessive delays or retransmission. Compounding the problem is packet queuing in routers that are vulnerable to delay, dropped packets, and frequent retransmission. Even when this vulnerability is not exploited, the packets can travel at uneven rates through multiple networks in a heterogeneous environment, taking somewhat longer to reassemble the fragmented packets in their proper sequence.

An average user can usually wait no more than eight seconds for a Web page to load onto a PC desktop. Otherwise, the user will grow impatient and go to another site that takes much less time to download pictures, sounds, and text. As a partial solution, the SLAs focus on maximum upload availability and guaranteed bandwidths. Consistent response times for latency-sensitive applications, however, are not guaranteed.

Due to heterogeneous environment of open, distributed networks, bandwidth management can be quite complex, requiring full-time attention from a network manager. For example, throttling back applications efficiently involves an in-depth knowledge of the entire protocol stack being used.

Bandwidth managers came to help network administrators attend to other tasks while managing bandwidths. They work exclusively on TCP/IP traffic, dropping or passing through non-IP traffic and can look at a customer's bandwidth utilization. Because they can throttle the link, they give service providers the capability to limit the bandwidth a customer can consume.

No two managers are alike. Some can slow down the lower-priority applications and deliver more bandwidth to those with higher priority, while others can reject any new connections or accept new ones with lower prioritized rates. Another provides brokering of bandwidth between server providers or other domains.

More advanced bandwidth managers allow customers to request bandwidth on-demand. Customers can use this feature to alert service providers that more bandwidth is needed for certain times. Another advanced feature is the capability to signal the network of the desired QoS. Some bandwidth managers are of a proprietary nature and may require a networking expert to make them interoperable with others in another category.

Whatever features a bandwidth manager offers, it is far cheaper than leasing a T1 line to get more bandwidth. ASPs that are unable to contain the costs of bandwidth among others, regardless of various network tools, are on their way out. Web services are seen as an alternative way of controlling bandwidth costs by allowing customers to rent certain components from various sources rather than renting all components of a software package from one place. Time will tell if it meets customers' overall expectations in the long run.

To give the enterprise an easier way to enforce its policies across its networks, the Internet Engineering Task Force (IETF) adopted Intel's open-source version of the Common Open Policy Service (COPS) technology in January 2001. This gives network equipment vendors a standard technology that they can use with bandwidth managers and other network devices, such as routers, switches, and load-balancing devices. While open-source products aim at network interoperability, some have features that others do not have.

For information on other performance tools, see Chapter 8.

Service Levels

Corporations all over the world have turned to enterprise resource planning (ERP) applications to provide comprehensive business and information management tools that fully integrate business processes on a global basis. To ensure optimal utilization of this ERP environment, organizations seek to minimize downtime, optimize application performance, monitor availability, establish application control, predict problems or constraints, and control user experience.

One way of improving performance is to establish a policy on service level agreements (SLAs) and service level management (SLM) solutions. The SLAs focus on maximum upload availability and guaranteed bandwidth, while the SLM solutions, such as those offered by BMC Software, offer maximum availability, performance, and recovery of ERP applications[5] along with their underlying databases and technologies.

In particular, BMC Software's PATROL for EAI solutions provide capabilities for end-to-end service level management. These solutions support the widest variety of applications, databases, middleware, and Web technologies across an array of operating systems. They work with MQSeries Integrator, Tuxedo, as well as BEA WebLogic and IBM WebSphere Server Advanced Edition.

BMC Software also offers online self-assessment and permits one to rate one's SML competency on factors such as minimizing connection delays among the middleware, front-end, and back-end applications; lowering operating system outages downtime; and reducing the chances of getting human error factors into system outages. Also included are the amount of customer rebates when SLAs are not fulfilled and determining if a company's stock price is directly tied to the availability of its Web site.

For either service level type, consistent response times for latency-sensitive applications, however, are not guaranteed. The minimum acceptable level of latency between an event and the response can be specified as long as the effects of latency, such as voice, cursor, or screen, do not appear to stutter.

Notes

1. PeopleSoft began by specializing in back-office systems and then expanded into the ERP's front office. Oracle specialized in relational database management systems, went into data warehousing, and then moved into ERP. SAP started by specializing in manufacturing automation before expanding into other ERP areas.
2. The ECMA is an international industry association founded in 1961 and dedicated to the standardization of information and communication systems.
3. See Chapter 2 on CORBA 3.0.

4. Risks also occur from management, user, and other technical problems such as middleware technology bugs, incomplete ERP packages, complex and undefined ERP-to-legacy-system interfaces, and poor system performance.
5. SAP R/3 Suite, PeopleSoft, Oracle Applications, and Microsoft Commerce Server 2000 (the follow-on release to Site Server Commerce Edition).

Chapter 10

Glossary

A2A: Application-to-Application.

ACL: Access Control List.

ActiveX: A Microsoft Corp. architecture that lets components interact in a networked environment, regardless of the language used to create them.

AD: Active Directory.

ADO: ActiveX Data Objects.

ADS: Windows Active Directory Service.

AMEX: American Stock Exchange.

AMI: Application Messaging Interface.

API: Application Programming Interface.

APPC: Advanced Program-to-Program Communication.

Application server middleware: Software that lets users access legacy programs either locally or remotely via a browser.

ASP: Active Server Pages.

ASP: Application Service Provider.

Asynchronous Communications: A form of communication by which applications can operate independently, so that they do not have to be running or available simultaneously; a process sends a request and may or may not wait for a response; a non-blocking communications style.

ATMI: Application-to-Transaction Monitor Interface.

Automatic Binding: Describes the action when an *RPC* client stub locates a specific server on a list of servers.

AVI: Audio-Visual Interleaved.

B2B: Business-to-Business, in reference to commerce conducted between companies rather than between companies and private individuals or consumers.

B2Bi: Business-to-Business integration.

B2C: Business to Consumer; this refers to commerce conducted between companies and individuals or consumers, in contrast to B2B.

B2E: Business-to-Enterprise.

Bandwidth: The amount of data that can be sent through a connection; usually measured in bits per second.

Binding: The association of a client and a server.

Blocking Communications: A synchronous messaging process whereby the requestor of a service must wait until a response is received.

BMP: Bean-Managed Persistence.

BOA: Basic Object Adapter.

BTP: Business Transaction Protocol.

Buffered Queue: A message queue that resides in memory.

CAE: Common Application Environment.

CBQ: Class-Based Queuing.

CCF: Common Connector Framework (CICS).

CCI: Common Client Interface.

CCM: CORBA Component Model.

CDN: Content Delivery Network.

CGI: Common Gateway Interface.

CIAS: Clinical Image Access Service.

CIDL: Component Implementation Definition Language.

CIML: Customer Identity Markup Language.

CLI: Call Level Interface.

CLR: Common Language Runtime.

CLS: Common Language Specification.

CMI: Common Messaging Interface.

CMP: Container-Managed Persistence.

COM+: An extension to COM that makes it easier to use C++ and avoids the complexities of the Interface Definition Language.

COM: Component Object Model.

Connectionless: The calling program does not enter into a connection with the target process; the receiving application acts on the request and responds if required.

Connection Oriented: The two parties first connect, exchange messages, and then disconnect.

COPS: Common Open Policy Service.

CORBA: Common Object Request Broker Architecture.

CPI: Container-Provided Interface.

CRM: Customer Relationship Management.

CTG: CICS Transaction Gateway.

CVS: Concurrent Versions Systems.

CWM: Component Warehouse Modeling.

cXML: Commerce XML. A meta-language that defines the necessary information about a product. It is a set of document type definitions (DTD) for the XML specification. Eventually, it will be used to define the exchange of transaction data for secure electronic transaction over the Internet..

DAD: Document Access Definition.

Data Level Integration: A form of *EAI* that integrates different data stores to allow the sharing of information among applications. It requires the loading of data directly into the database via its native interface and does not involve the changing of business logic.

Data Transformation: A key requirement of *EAI* and *message brokers*. There are two basic kinds: syntactic translation changes one data set into another (such as different date or number formats), while semantic transformation changes data based on the underlying data definitions or meaning.

Database Middleware: Software used to integrate database contents across an enterprise.

DCE: Distributed Computing Environment.

DCOM: Distributed COM.

DDL: Data Definition Language.

Development Middleware: Software that adds routines to make applications network-cognizant.

DII: Dynamic Invocation Interface.

Distributed Object Middleware: Software that makes applications on one part of a system available everywhere on the network.

DLL: Dynamic Link Library.

DMTF: Distributed Management Task Force.

DNS: Domain Name System.

DOM: Document Object Model.

DRDA: IBM's Distributed Relational Database Architecture.

DSI: Dynamic Skeleton Interface.

DTD: Data Type Definition.

DTP: Distributed Transaction Processing.

E2e: E-business to enterprise.

EAI: Enterprise Application Integration.

EAR: J2EE Archive.

ECI: External Call Interface (IBM).

EDI: Electronic Data Interchange.

EDOC: Enterprise Distributed Object Computing.

EIS: Enterprise Integration System.

EJB: Enterprise JavaBean.

EMA: Enterprise Memory Architecture.

ERP: Enterprise Resource Planning.

ESI: Edge Side Includes.

Extranet: A network that links an enterprise to its various divisions and business partners and uses secured Internet links.

FTP: File Transfer Protocol.

Gateway: A hardware/software setup that performs translations between disparate protocols.

GBR: Global Business Registry.

GIOP: General Inter-ORB Protocol.

Groupware: A collection of technologies that allows the representation of complex processes that center around collaborative human activities.

GUI: Graphical User Interface.

HCL: Hardware Compatibility List.

HMP: Heterogeneous Multi-Processing.

HTL: X/Open High-level Transaction Language.

HTML: Hypertext Markup Language.

HTTP: Hypertext Transfer Transport Protocol.

HTTPR: Reliable HTTP.

IDL: Interface Definition Language.

IETF: Internet Engineering Task Force.

IIOP: Internet Inter-ORB Protocol.

IIS: Internet Information Server.

Invasive Integration: An implementation approach that requires changes or additions to existing applications; opposite of *non-invasive integration*.

IPX: Internetwork Packet Exchange.

ISA: Internet Security and Acceleration Server 2000.

ISAM: Indexed Sequential Access Method.

ISAPI: Internet Server API.

ISO: International Standards Organization.

J2EE CA: J2EE Connector Architecture.

J2EE: Sun Microsystems' Java 2 platform, Enterprise Edition.

JAAS: Java Authentication and Authorization Support.

JAR: EJB Java Archive.

JavaBeans: Modules written in Java.

JavaScript: A Web scripting language derived from Java.

Java: Sun Microsystems' universal platform language, which is replacing C++ for many applications on the Web.

JAX/RPC: The Java APIs for XML-based RPC.

JAXB: Java API for XML Data Binding.

JAX: Java API for XML.

JAXM: Java API for XML Messaging.

JAXP: Java API for XML Parsing; Java API for XML Processing.

JAXR: Java API for XML Registries.

JCE: Java Cryptography Extensions.

JCP: Java Community Program.

JDBC: Java Database Connectivity.

JDK: Java Developer's Toolkit.

JDNI: Java Naming and Directory Interface.

JMF: Java Media Framework.

JMS: Java Message Service.

JMX: Java Management Extensions.

JNI: Java Native Interface.

JSP: Java Server Page.

JSSE: Java Secure Socket Extension.

JTA: Java Transaction API.

JVM: Java Virtual Machine.

LDAP: Lightweight Directory Access Protocol.

Legacy-to-Web Middleware: Unifies browser interfaces with multiple applications.

Load Balancing: Automatic balancing of requests among replicated servers to ensure that no server is overloaded; distributing work to avoid overloading a system.

Management Middleware: Complex software that manages data moving between disparate elements.

MAPI: Microsoft Messaging Application Interface.

MDA: Model-Driven Architecture.

MDC: Meta-Data Coalition.

Message Broker: A key component of *EAI*, a message broker is an intelligent intermediary that directs the flow of messages between applications, which become sources and consumers of information. Message brokers provide a very flexible communications backbone and provide services such as *data transformation, message routing,* and *message warehousing.*

Middleware: Software that connects disparate computers, operating systems, and protocols.

MIDL: Microsoft Interface Description Language.

MIP: Meta-Interchange Patterns.

MMC: Microsoft Management Console.

MOF: Meta-Object Facility.

MOM: Message-Oriented Middleware.

MPEG: Motion Picture Experts Group.

MQI: Messaging Queuing Interface.

MQ: Message Queuing.

MSIL: Microsoft Intermediate Language.

MSMQ: Microsoft Message Queuing.

MSP: Management Services Provider.

MTS: Microsoft Transaction Server.

MTR/MTU: Maximum Transmission Unit Rate.

NDR: Network Data Representation.

NDS: NetWare Directory Service.

NIS+: Network Information Services.

NLB: Network Load Balancing.

Non-Blocking Communications: An asynchronous messaging process whereby the requestor of a service does not have to wait until a response is received from another application.

Non-Invasive Integration: An implementation approach that does not require changes or additions to existing applications.

NOS: Network Operating System.

NSAPI: Netscape API.

NYSE: New York Stock Exchange.

O/R: Object/relational.

OAG: Open Applications Group. An industry consortium formed to promote the easy and cost-effective integration of key business application software components.

OAMAS: Open Applications Group as its Open Application Middleware API Specification.
OASIS: Organization for the Advancement of Structured Information Standards.
OC4J: Oracle9i/AS Container for J2EE.
ODBC: Open Database Connectivity, a Windows standard *API* for *SQL* communication.
ODBMS: Object Database Management System.
OID: Oracle Internet Directory.
OLAP: Online Analytical Processing.
OLE: Object Linking and Embedding.
OLTP: Online Transaction Processing.
OMG: Object Management Group. A consortium of object vendors and the founders of the **CORBA** standard.
ONC: Open Network Computing.
ORB: Object Request Broker.
OSF: Open Software Foundation.
OSI: Open Standard Interconnect.
PAE: Physical Address Extension.
PDA: Personal Data Assistant.
PDL: Persistent Definition Language.
Perl: Practical Extraction Report Language.
Persistent Queue: Queues stored on a permanent device (e.g., disk).
PIM: Platform-Independent Model.
PIPs: Partner Interface Processes.
PKI: Public key infrastructure.
POA: Portable Object Adapter.
PSM: Platform-Specific Model.
PSS: Persistent State Service.
PTP: Point-to-Point.
Publish/Subscribe: Publishers broadcast data to subscribers that have issued the type of information to receive; an application or user can be both a publisher and subscriber.
QC: Microsoft Queued Components.
QoS: Quality of Service.
RDA: Remote Data Access.
RDBMS: Relational DBMS.
RDF: Resource Description Framework.
RDO: Remote Data Object.
RDS: Remote Data Service.
RMF: Rich Media Format.
RMI: Remote Method Invocation.
ROF: Relational Object Framework.
Router: A special-purpose computer or software package that handles the connection of two or more networks; routers check the destination address of the packets and decide the route to send them.
RPC: Remote Procedure Call (network services via TCP port 80).
RSS: Rich Site Summary.

RTP: Real-Time Transport Protocol.

RTSP: Real-Time Streaming Protocol.

SAML: Security Assertion Markup Language.

SAN: System Area Network.

SAX: Simple API for XML.

SCI: Server Container Interface.

SCL: Service Contract Language.

SCM: Supply Chain Management.

SCSL: Sun Community Service Licensing.

SLA: Service Level Agreement.

SLM: Service Level Management.

SMP: Symmetric Multi-Processing.

SMTP: Standard Mail Transfer Protocol.

SNA: System Network Architecture, a network architecture from IBM.

SNMP: Simple Network Management Protocol.

SOAP: Simple Object Access Protocol.

Sockets: A portable standard for network application providers on TCP/IP networks.

SPI: Service Provider Interface.

SQLJ: Embedded SQL in Java.

SQL: Structured Query Language.

SRMP: SOAP Reliable Messaging Protocol.

SSL: Secure Sockets Layer.

Stateful: An entity or object keeps track of the state of interaction.

Stateless: There is no record of previous interactions and each interaction request has to be handled based entirely on information that comes with it.

STDL: Structured Transaction Definition Language.

Stored Procedure: A program that creates a named collection of SQL or other procedural statements and logic that is compiled, verified, and stored in a server database.

STP: Straight Through Processing occurs when a transaction, once entered into a system, passes through its entire life cycle without any manual intervention; STP is an example of a *Zero Latency Process*, but one specific to the finance industry which has many proprietary networks and messaging formats.

SwA: SOAP with Attachments.

Synchronous Communications: A form of communication that requires applications to run concurrently; a process issues a call until it receives a response.

TCP/IP: Transmission Control Protocol/Internet Protocol (RPC and Web services network services via TCP ports 111 and 80).

TDS: Tabular Data Screen.

TP Monitor: Transaction processing monitor.

TPC: Transaction Processing Performance Council.

TP: Transaction Processing.

Trigger: A stored procedure that is automatically invoked on the basis of data-related events.

Two-Phase Commit: A mechanism to synchronize updates on different machines or platforms so that they all fail or all succeed together. The decision to commit is centralized, but each participant has the right to veto. This is a key process in real-time transaction-based environments..

UDDI: Universal Description, Discovery and Integration.

UDP: User Datagram Protocol.

UDS: Universal Data System.

UML: Unified Modeling Language.

UMS: Utility Management System.

UN/CEFACT: United Nations Centre for Trade Facilities and Electronic Businesses.

VBScript: An extension of Visual Basic used to create scripts.

VoXML: Voice over XML.

VPN: Virtual Private Network.

W3C: World Wide Web Consortium.

WAP: Wireless Access Protocol.

WAR: Web Component Archive.

WBEM: Web-Based Enterprise Management.

WebDAV: Web Distributed Authoring and Versioning.

Web-to-RDBMS Middleware: Software that can be used to publish data on the Web.

WinSock: Windows Sockets.

WMF: Wireless Multimedia Forum.

WMI: Windows Management Instrumentation.

WML: Wireless Markup Language.

WSCL: Web Service Conversational Language.

WSDL: Web Services Description Language.

WSFL: Web Services Flow Language.

WSH: Windows Script Host.

WSUI: Web Services User Interface.

X/Open: An independent open systems organization. Its strategy is to combine various standards into a comprehensive integrated systems environment called Common Applications Environment, which contains an evolving portfolio of practical *APIs*.

XACML: eXtensible Access Control Markup Language.

XAMTI: X/Open ATMI.

XDR: External Data Representation.

XHTML: eXtensible HTML.

XKMS: XML Key Management Specification.

XLANG: Cross language (Microsoft).

XMI: XML Meta Interchange.

XML: eXtensible Markup Language.

XMLP: XML Protocol.

XMP: Extended Management Pack.

XSD: XML Schema Datatypes.

XSLT: eXtensible Stylesheet Language Transformation.

Zero Latency: No delay between an event and the response.

Zero Latency Enterprise: An enterprise in which all parts of the organization can respond to events as they occur elsewhere in the organization, using an integrated IT infrastructure that can immediately exchange information across technical and organizational boundaries.

Zero Latency Process: An automated process with no time delays (i.e., no manual re-entry of data) at the interfaces of different information systems. STP is an example.

About the Author

Judith M. Myerson is a systems engineer/architect with a Master's degree in engineering. A noted columnist and writer with over 150 articles/reports published, she is the editor of Auerbach's *Enterprise Systems Integration, 2nd edition,* handbook covering a broad range of technologies relevant to an enterprise. They include middleware, enterprisewide systems, databases, enabling technologies, application development, network management, distributed systems, component-based technologies, and project management.

She is also the author of the following articles for Auerbach:

- "XML: Its Role in TCP/IP Presentation Layer (Layer 6)"
- "Designing a Capacity Database Server"
- "Web-Enabling a Capacity Database Server"
- "Virtual Server Overview"
- "Managing ERP Systems in a Heterogeneous Environment"
- "Oracle in Wireless Offices"
- "Performance Tuning: SQL Query (Indexes, Joining Process, Fragmentation, and Other Stuff)"
- "Web-Enabling Image and Sound Objects in Database Tables"

About the Author

Index

A

Access Control List (ACL), 99
ACL, see Access Control List
Active Server Pages (ASP), 8, 199
Adapter Offering, 22
ADO, see Microsoft ActiveX Data Object
Akamai server, 224
AlphaBean examples, 91
alphaWorks, 213
American Stock Exchange (AMEX), 231
AMEX, see American Stock Exchange
AMI, see Application Messaging Interface
Analysis and Design platform task force, 49
API, see Application programming interface
Application(s)
  back-end, 93, 256
  business-to-business, 35
  business-to-consumer, 35–36
  cluster-aware, 81
  E-mail newsletter, 102
  J2EE, 96, 97
  line-of-business, 81
  memory tuning, enabling of, 78
  Message Queuing, 76
  Messaging Interface (AMI), 20
  Microsoft Component Object Model, 14
  mining, 192
  model, Publish/Subscribe, 102
  objects, 30
  programs, 22
  security, 25
  servers, 95, 238
  service providers, 225
  telephony client, 187
  WAP, 202
  Web-based, 115
  workflow, 16
Application programming interface (API), 11
  flows, Java, 93
  Java, 108, 239
    for data binding, 109
    for XML parsing, 109
  MQSeries, 19, 20
  types

  container, 39
  external, 39
Ardent Software, Inc. JRB–Java Relational
    Binding, 178
Ariba, 131
ASP, see Active Server Pages
AST.NET
  authorization services, 68
  handler, 67
Asynchronous invocations, 34
Asynchronous messaging, 22, 100
Attunity Connect, 167
Authentication, 67
Authorization, 67
AVI format, see Microsoft Audio-Video
    Interleaved format

B

Back-end
  applications, 93, 256
  systems, gateways into, 244
Back-office environments, 163
Bandwidth
  allocations, 204
  management, 221
  manager, 220, 255
Basic Object Adapter (BOA), 30
Batching calls, 3
BB, see Bulletin Board
B2B, see Business-to-business (B2B)
B2C applications, see Business-to-consumer
    applications
BDI Systems, Inc. DB/XML Vision and xPower
    Transform, 168
Bean(s)
  class, 86
  deployment descriptor, 94
  entity, 90
  -managed components, 94
  -managed persistence (BMP), 90
  message-driven, 88, 90, 102, 103
  session, 89
  source code, 98

stateful session, 89
stateless session, 90
BEA Systems, 107
    jdbcKona, 177–178
    Tuxedo, 15
    Tuxedo/Q component, 18
    WebLogic, 192, 256
    Web services, 124
Beatnik Rich Media Format (RMF), 108
BeOS, 92, 103
BizTalk.org, 118, 127
Black & White Software, Inc. PRO/Enable, 180
Blue Matrix, 134
BMP, see Bean-managed persistence
BOA, see Basic Object Adapter
Borland
    Delphi, 168
    Web services, 125
Bowstreet, 131
BPM, see Business process management
Broadcasting calls, 3, 4
Broker Web service description, 138
Browsers, translating for all, 206
BTP, see Business Transaction Protocol
Bulletin Board (BB), 15
Business
    process management (BPM), 21
    software, 67
    Transaction Protocol (BTP), 124
Business-to-business (B2B)
    applications, 35
    communication, primary problem of, 210
    integration, 163, 239, 248, 254
        brokers, 94
        technologies, 136, 254
Business-to-consumer (B2C) applications, 35–36

C

Cache, 225
    age, 226
    criteria, 226
    performance, 226
CAE, see Common Application Environment
Callback procedures, 3
Call-Level Interface (CLI), 236
Cape Clear Software, 134
CapeConnect architecture, 136
Caribou Lake Software, Inc.
    JdbCache, 177
    JSQL, 178
    Jsvr, 178–179
CBQ, see Class-based queuing
CCF, see Common Connector Framework
CCI, see Common Client Interface
CCM, see Common Object Request Broker
        Architecture Component Model
CDN, see Content delivery network
C4I Domain task force, 49
Cell phones, 110
Channel security, 25
CIAS, see Clinical Image Access Service
CICS offerings, 27
CIDL, see Component Implementation
        Definition Language

CIML, see Customer Identity Markup
        Language
CiscoWorks 2000, 206
Class-based queuing (CBQ), 223
ClearPath Servers, 14
CLI, see Call-Level Interface
Client
    CORBA, 30
    RPC runtime library, 7
Clinical Image Access Service (CIAS), 53
CLR, see Common language runtime
CLS, see Common Language Specification
Clustering, 98, 99
    -aware applications, 81
    services, 74, 80, 81
    technology, 79
CMI, see Common Messaging Interface
CMP, see Container-managed persistence
COBOL, 60
    business logic, 191
    calling Java from, 194
    code fragment, 196
    Enterprise JavaBeans, 196, 197, 198
    language environment, 170
    legacy, 193
    programmers, subroutine linkage
        mechanisms familiar to, 18
    subroutine, 192
    support, 193
Code
    bean source, 98
    fragment, COBOL, 196
    JMF source, 108
    managed, verified, 65
    unmanaged, 59, 66
Collection service, 40
COM, see Component Object Model
Commercial messaging, 24
Common Application Environment (CAE), 13
Common Client Interface (CCI), 95
Common Connector Framework (CCF), 26
Common Enterprise Models Domain task
        force, 49
Common frameworks, 29
Common language runtime (CLR), 59, 253
Common Language Specification (CLS), 59,
        253
Common Messaging Interface (CMI), 20
Common Object Request Broker Architecture
        (CORBA), 29, 113, see also CORBA 3
    -based notification service, 42
    basic metatype in, 37
    client, 30
    /COM, .NET vs., 60
    Component Model (CCM), 32, 36, 90
        component categories, 38
        development stages, 37
        event model, 38
    fault-tolerant, 35
    Firewall Traversal specification, 34
    messaging, 35
    minimum, 31, 35
    object services, 40, 41
    organizational structure, 31
    Portable Object Adapter, 90
    Real-Time, 31, 35, 36
    release summary, 30, 31
    RMI and, 104

Services and Extensions, 43
Common object services, 29
Common Open Policy Service (COPS), 221, 255
Common Programming Interface Communications (CPI-C), 235
Communications(s)
  B2B, primary problem of, 210
  connectionless, 139
  inter-application, 204
  middleware, 217, 234, 235, 246
  synchronous, 229
COM.NET, 58
Component(s)
  assembly, 37
  bean-managed, 94
  CCM, 38
  declaration, 37
  deployment and installation, 37
  developers, 86
  EJB, 86
  entity, 39
  Implementation Definition Language (CIDL), 36
  instance activation, 37
  Object Model (COM), 10, 57, 244
  packaging, 37
  process, 39
  reusable, 116
  service, 38
  session, 38
  usage patterns, 38
  Warehouse Modeling (CWM), 50
  Web, 97
Concurrency service, 41
Concurrent Versions Systems (CVS), 92
Configuration management, 15
Connectionless communications, 139
Connect Software, FastForward, 174–175
Container
  API types, 39
  -managed persistence (CMP), 90
  programming model, 39
  -provided services, 39
  Provider Interface (CPI), 91
Content delivery network (CDN), 224
COPS, see Common Open Policy Service
CORBA, see Common Object Request Broker Architecture
CORBA 3, 29–56
  CORBA object services, 40–44
    accessing object services, 40–43
    OpenORB, 43–44
  CORBA release summary, 30–31
  modeling specifications, 46–56
    additional specifications, 55
    bridging platforms, 56
    extensions to IDL, 56
    IDL specified models, 55
    MDA inner core, 51–52
    MDA middle core, 52–53
    MDA outer core, 53–54
    UML profiles, PIM, and PSMs, 54
  OMG Technology Committee, 44–46
  organizational structure, 31–32
  other supporting facilities, 44
  what is new, 32–40
    CCM development stages, 37

CCM extensions to OMG IDL, 37–38
component usage patterns, 38–39
container programming model, 39
CORBA component model, 36
improved integration with Java and Internet, 33–35
integration with Enterprise JavaBeans, 39–40
quality of service control, 35–36
work-in-progress status, 46
CPI, see Container Provider Interface
CPI-C, see Common Programming Interface Communications
Credit card
  payments, processing of, 61
  transactions, authorizing, 113
Credit Validation Service, 131, 132
CRM, see Customer relationship management
CryptoBeans, 91
Cryptographic objects, 68
Currency exchange rate, 130
Customer
  Identity Markup Language (CIML), 206
  relationship management (CRM), 73, 85, 113, 158, 243
CVS, see Concurrent Versions Systems
CWM, see Component Warehouse Modeling

D

Data
  binding, Java API for, 109
  Junction Suite, 169
  transfer syntax, 206
  type(s)
    comparison of complex, 210
    definition (DTD), 34, 130
  warehouse standards, OMG, 52
Database(s)
  access
    interfaces, 96
    systems, 230
  multi-vendor, 234
  SQL/relational, 246
  table, 201
  Universal Data System, 14
  updates, 24
  XML-enabled, 182
Database middleware, 157–189, 234, 235, 236, 246
  data-level integration, 157–164
    iWay Software B2B integration, 163
    iWay Software EAI Solutions, 160
    iWay Software E-business integration, 160–162
    iWay Software E-commerce integration, 163–164
    iWay Software mobile E-business integration, 162–163
    WebFOCUS business intelligence suite, 158–160
  DBMS/SQL middleware, 164–165
    MERANT data connectivity, 165
    Pervasive.SQL middleware, 164–165
  flavors of, 157
  HTTPR, 188

Java-based database middleware, 171–182
  Business Sight Framework, 172
  CoCoBase, 172–173
  DataDirect SequeLink, 173
  dbANYWHERE Server, 173–174
  DbGen Professional Edition, 174
  DB2 Universal Database, 173
  Enterprise Component Broker, 174
  ExpressLane, 174
  FastForward, 174–175
  Fresco, 175
  HiT JDBC/400, 175
  HiT JDBC/DB2, 175–176
  IDS Server, 176
  Jaguar CTS, 176
  Javabase/400, 176
  jConnect for JDBC, 176–177
  JdbCache, 177
  JDBC Developer, 177
  jdbcKona, 177–178
  JDBC Lite, 177
  JDX, 178
  JRB–Java Relational Binding, 178
  JSQL, 178
  Jsvr, 178–179
  JYD Object Database, 179
  ObjectStore DBMS, 179
  ObjectStore PSE for Java, 179
  OpenLink Data Access Drivers for JDBC,
    179–180
  Oracle Lite, 180
  POET Object Server Suite, 180
  PRO/Enable, 180
  Relational Object Framework, 180–181
  Rmijdbc, 181
  SCO SQL-Retriever, 181
  SOLID JDBC Driver, 181
  SOLID Server, 181
  Versant ODBMS, 182
  VisiChannel, 182
Web services-enabled database
    middleware, 185
Windows telephony with TAPI, 185
XML database middleware, 165–171
  commercial products, 166–170
  evaluation-only products, 170–171
XML-enabled databases, 182–185
  DB2 XML Extender and DB2 Text
    Extender, 183
  Informix, 183
  Microsoft Access 2002, 184
  Microsoft SQL Server, 183–184
  Oracle8i/9i application servers, 184–185
Data-center software, 233
DataSnap, 125
DBMS/SQL middleware, 164
DCE, see Distributed Computing Environment
DCOM, see Distributed COM
Delphi 6 DataSnap feature matrix, 186–187
Deployment descriptors
  bean, 94
  XML-based, 56
Dequeuing, user-defined, 17
Development middleware, 240
Dialogue scenarios, 199
Digital signatures, 68
DII, see Dynamic invocation interface
DirContext, 106, 107

Directory
  EJB, 91
  package, 106
  services
    enterprise-level, 104
    JNDI, 105
Discovery Stack, 121
Distributed COM (DCOM), 58
Distributed Computing Environment (DCE),
    5, 228
Distributed Management Task Force (DMTF),
    83
Distributed object middleware, 236
Distributed transaction and messaging mid-
    dleware, 1–28
  distributed processing middleware, 12–19
    BEA Tuxedo, 15–18
    BEA Tuxedo/Q component, 18–19
    Unisys' Distributed Processing
      Middleware, 13–15
  IBM MQSeries, 19–27
    application programs and messaging,
      22
    CICS and MQSeries, 26
    commercial messaging, 24–25
    MQSeries family, 20–22
    MQSeries Internet Pass-Thru, 25–26
    MQSeries JMS support, 26–27
    queue managers, 23–24
  Microsoft Messaging Queuing, 8–12
    Microsoft queued components, 10–12
    MSMQ features, 9–10
    when network goes down, 12
    writing applications, 8–9
  Remote Procedure Call, 1–8
    Microsoft RPC components, 7–8
    Microsoft RPC facility, 5–6
    OSF standards for RPC, 7
    port mapper, 2
    RPC features, 3–4
    RPC layers, 2–3
    RPC model, 1–2
    stubs, 6–7
    XML-RPC, 4–5
Distributed Transaction Processing (DTP),
    12
Distribution lists, 75
DLLs, see Dynamic link libraries
DMTF, see Distributed Management Task
    Force
Document Listing Web service, 131
Domain
  objects, 29
  specifications, 44
  technology
    FTFs, 46
    RTFs, 46
    SIGs, 46
    task force, 47
Downtime, 226
DSI, see Dynamic skeleton interface
DTD, see Data type definition
DTP, see Distributed Transaction
    Processing
Dynamic content delivery, 65
Dynamic invocation interface (DII), 31
Dynamic link libraries (DLLs), 6, 58
Dynamic skeleton interface (DSI), 32

E

EAI, see Enterprise Application Integration
E-business
  integration, 93, 161, 162
  partnerships, 126
ebXML, 118
ECI, see External Call Interface
E-commerce
  middleware, 234, 237, 246
  suite, 164
  transactions, integration of Web services and, 126
E-conomy, 95
EDA/SQL middleware products, 157
EDGAR search, 130
EDI, see Electronic data interchange
EDOC, see Enterprise Distributed Object Computing
Eiffel, 60
EIS, see Enterprise Integration Systems
EJB, see Enterprise JavaBeans
EJBObject proxies, 88
Electricity Web service description, 138
Electronic Commerce Domain task force, 49
Electronic data interchange (EDI), 169
EMA, see Enterprise Memory Architecture
E-mail, 102, 130
Encapsulation, 116
Encryption, 68, 84
Endpoint supply service, 7
Enterprise
  Application Integration (EAI), 85, 118, 217, 243
  bean types, 88, 89
  connector middleware, 237
  Distributed Object Computing (EDOC), 53
  Integration Systems (EIS), 1
  Memory Architecture (EMA), 77
  network protocols, 160
  resource planning (ERP), 76, 85, 133, 227, 243, 256
    -to-legacy-system interfaces, 257
    packages, 159
  servers, 220
  Web sites, rapid time-to-market, 65
Enterprise JavaBeans (EJB), 34, 39, 85, 114, 158, 191
  application, deployment of COBOL, 197
  -based workflows, 133, 252
  built-in passivation and activation support, 90
  Component Model, 56
  deployment descriptor, 196
  directory, 91
  E-business applications based on, 232
  files, COBOL-wrapped, 197
  interoperability between CORBA components and, 40
  Java Archive (JAR), 96
  servers, 87
  three-tier architecture, 86
  vendor, 87
Enterprisewide system, bridging of gap in, 191–216
  bridging COBOL to Enterprise Java Beans, 191–198

accessing legacy COBOL assets from Java, 192
application mining, 192
calling COBOL classes from Java, 195–196
calling Java from COBOL, 194–195
calling legacy COBOL from Java, 192–194
COBOL Exterprise JavaBeans, 196
combination ActiveX/Java classes, 198
deploying COBOL Enterprise JavaBeans application, 197
Enterprise JavaBeans deployment descriptor, 196
complete WAP script, 214–216
role of XML in TCP/IP presentation layer, 204–209
  breaking of barrier, 204–206
  dynamic XML servers, 207–208
  natural language dialogue, 208–209
  product integration, 206
  translating for all browsers, 206–207
  universal XML, 209
  XML mapping, 208
Wireless Access Protocol, 198–204
  ASP script, 201–202
  database table, 201
  dialogue scenarios, 199–200
  WAP application, 199
  XML script, 203
  XML syntax, 202–203
XML schemas, 209–213
  comparing XML schema and DTD, 210–211
  strong typing advantage, 211–212
  true key representation advantage, 212–213
Entity
  beans, 90
  components, 39
ERP, see Enterprise resource planning
Error
  handling, 73
  -recovery programming, 12
E-Services Village, 118, 127
e-Speak business services, 127
E-transaction processing model, 13
Evaluation-only products, 170
Event service, 41
Evidence-based security, 66
eXtensible Access Control Markup Language (XACML), 125, 240, 248
eXtensible Markup Language (XML), 19, 113, 158, 244
  application servers, 182
  -based data model, 127
  -based deployment descriptors, 56
  configuration file, 87
  database middleware, 165
  deployment descriptor, 90
  documents, 205, 249
  -enabled databases, 182–185
  Junction, 169
  Key Management Specification (XKMS), 125, 240
  mapping, 208
  messaging, 108, 115
  Meta Interchange (XMI), 46
  parent-child relationship, 212

parsing, Java API for, 109
Protocol (XMLP), 122
Query Language, 208
-RPC, 4, 5, 231, 232
Schema Datatypes (XSD), 122
Schema Quality Checker, 213
Schema verification tool, 213
script, 203
servers, dynamic, 206
syntax, 202
universal, 209
eXtensible Stylesheet Language Transforma-
    tion (XSLT), 126, 239, 247
External API types, 39
External Call Interface (ECI), 94
Externalization service, 41

F

Fault-tolerant CORBA, 35
FIFO Queue bucket, 222
File Transfer Protocol (FTP), 119
Finance Web service description, 138
Financial Domain task force, 49
Financial software, 67
FioranoMQ, 230
Firewall(s), 10
    configuration, 34
    tunneling, 99
Fortran, 60
Forwarding server, 17, 18
FoxPro, 185
FTP, see File Transfer Protocol

G

GBR, see ResolveNet Global Business Registry
GIE Dyade RmiJdbc, 181
goto statements, 1
Grand Central Network, 134, 135
Group Policy, 82

H

Hailstorm, 122, 247
Hashing, 68
Haskell, 60
Healthcare Domain task force, 49
help.dialog1, 203
Heterogeneous multi-processing (HMP) envi-
    ronments, 14
Hewlett-Packard, 124, 127
HiT Software, Inc.
    Allora, 166
    HiT JDBC/400, 175
    HiT JDBC/DB2, 175–176
HMP environments, see Heterogeneous
    multi-processing environments
Honeywell, 220
HP-UX, 22
HTML, see HyperText Markup Language
HTTP, see Hypertext Transport Protocol
HTTPR, see Reliable HTTP

Human–machine interaction, 204
HyperText Markup Language (HTML), 126,
    160, 239, 248
Hypertext Transport Protocol (HTTP), 4, 5,
    113, 119, 224, 244
    transaction, 98
    transport, ways of using, 60
    tunneling, 99

I

IBM, 131
    Data Access Bean, 170
    DataCraft, 171
    DB2 Universal Database, 173
    DB2 XML Extender and DB2 Text Extender,
        183
    External Call Interface, 94
    Informix, 183
    middleware product portfolio, 28
    MQSeries, 19, 230
        Everywhere, 237
        Integrator, 162
    Net.Data, 170
    Network Dispatcher, 26
    Web Service Flow Language, 249
    Web Services ToolKit (WSTK), 120
    WebSphere, 192, 256
IDL, see Interface Definition Language
IDS Server, 176
IETF, see Internet Engineering Task Force
IFS, see Internet File System
IIOP, see Internet Inter-ORB Protocol
IIS, see Microsoft Internet Information
        Services
Indexed Sequential Access Method (ISAM),
        246
Information Builders, Inc.
    Enterprise Component Broker, 174
    FOCUS, 157
Informix, 96, 185
Infoscape, Inc. Fresco, 175
infoShark, XMLShark, 169
InitialContext, 106
Inter-application communication, 204
Interface Definition Language (IDL), 8, 30, 60
    compiler, 55
    extensions to, 56
    specified models, 55
    templates, 33
Internet
    Engineering Task Force (IETF), 68, 221, 255
    File System (IFS), 185
    integration with Java and, 33
    Inter-ORB Protocol (IIOP), 29, 119
    standards, emerging, 248
Internetwork Packet Exchange (IPX), 12
Interoperability of implementations, 55
Intrusion detection, 233
IONA Technologies, 136
IP traffic
    load-balancing of, 82
    performance, 217
IPX, see Internetwork Packet Exchange
ISAM, see Indexed Sequential Access Method
ISO 9000 certification, 159

Isolated storage, 68
iWay Software
   B2B integration, 163
   EAI solutions, 160
   E-business integration, 160
   E-commerce integration, 163
   Enterprise Integrator, 161
   mobile E-business integration, 162

J

JAAS, see Java Authentication and Authorization Support
JAR, see EJB Java Archive
Java, 19
   APIs, 108, 239
      for XML Messaging (JAXM), 92
      for XML parsing, 109
   Application Server, 162
   Authentication and Authorization Support (JAAS), 91
   -based connectivity, 165
   -based database middleware, 171
   -based middleware, 234, 238, 246
   calling COBOL classes from, 195
   CICS applications written in, 111
   classes, 194, 253
   clients, factory methods used by, 86
   Community Program (JCP), 108
   Cryptography Extension (JCE), 91
   Database Connectivity (JDBC), 92, 236
   -to-IDL mapping, 34
   integration with Internet and, 33
   Media Framework (JMF), 85, 107
   Messaging Service (JMS), 27, 85, 100, 169, 238, 252
   Naming and Directory Interface (JNDI), 85, 103
      architecture, 105
      -compatible naming service, 87
      directory services, 105
      1.2 features, 107
      federated naming facilities, 106
   Native Interface (JNI), 27, 192
   runtime systems, 193
   Secure Socket Extension (JSSE), 91
   Security Tools, 91
   Server Pages (JSP), 92, 136, 232
   technologies, 123
   Transaction Service (JTS), 189
   Virtual Machine (JVM), 95
   wrapper class, 197
   XML SQL utility for, 169
Java 2 Micro Edition (J2ME), 248
Java 2 Platform Enterprise Edition (J2EE), 85, 92, 189, 232, 241, 245
   application(s)
      configuring of, 96
      contents of, 97
   CA, see J2EE Connector Architecture
   Connector Architecture (J2EE CA), 124, 252
   enterprise servlets with, 98
   Java API flows in, 93
   security model, 99
JavaSpaces technology, 110
Java world, ever-expanding, 85–111

Enterprise JavaBeans, 85–92
   AlphaBean examples, 91
   container, 87–88
   CORBA Component Model, 90–91
   enterprise bean types, 88–90
   inside enterprise beans, 86–87
   OpenEJB and CVS, 91–92
   passivation and activation, 90
Java APIs, 108–109
   for data binding, 109
   for XML messaging, 108–109
   for XML parsing, 109
Java 2 Enterprise Edition, 92–100
   configuring and assembling J2EE applications, 96–98
   enterprise servlets with J2EE, 98–99
   integration with legacy, ERP, CRM, and SCM applications, 92–95
   J2EE security model for OC4J, 99
   Oracle9i AS Containers for J2EE, 95–96
   RMI and tunneling services, 100
Java Media Framework, 107–108
Java messaging service, 100–103
   EJB 2.0, 102–103
   messaging domains, 100–102
   OpenJMS, 103
Java naming and directory interface, 103–107
   directory package, 106–107
   JNDI 1.2, 107
   JNDI architecture, 105–106
   naming package, 106
   naming systems and services, 104–105
javax.naming.Reference class, 106
JAXM, see Java APIs for XML Messaging
JCE, see Java Cryptography Extension
JCP, see Java Community Program
JDBC, see Java Database Connectivity
J2EE, see Java 2 Platform Enterprise Edition
Jini technology, 110
J2ME, see Java 2 Micro Edition
JMF, see Java Media Framework
JMS, see Java Messaging Service
JMX, see Sun Java Management Extensions
JNDI, see Java Naming and Directory Interface
JNI, see Java Native Interface
JSP, see Java Server Pages
JSSE, see Java Secure Socket Extension
JTA/XA transaction, 97
JTS, see Java Transaction Service
JVM, see Java Virtual Machine
JXTA Project, 109
JYD Software Engineering Pty Ltd. JYD Object Database, 179

K

Kerberos security model, 16

L

Language mappings, 55

Laptops, 110
LDAP, see Lightweight Directory Access
    Protocol
Leaky bucket, 223
Legacy–Web–ERP integration, 159
Legacy-to-Web middleware, 237
Licensing service, 41
Life cycle service, 41
Lifescience Domain task force, 49
Lightweight Directory Access Protocol
    (LDAP), 104, 105, 124, 231
Line-of-business applications, 81
2Link Consulting, Inc. DbGen Professional
    Edition, 174
Linux, 22, 92, 103, 165
Listener piece, 231
Load balancing, 15, 16, 227
Local procedure call model, 1
Lotus software suite, 120

M

Macintosh, 92, 103
Managed code, verified, 65
Management
    middleware hierarchy, 235
    services, 82
Manufacturing Domain task force, 49
MAPI, see Microsoft Messaging Application
    Programming Interface
Mapping(s)
    Java-to-IDL, 34
    language, 55
    URL, 75
    XML, 208
Maximum transfer unit (MTU), 4
MDA, see Model-Driven Architecture
MDC, see Meta-Data Coalition
Memory management, advanced, 79
MERANT
    AssetMiner, 192
    DataDirect SequeLink, 173
Message(s)
    -driven beans, 88, 90, 102, 103
    journaling, automatic, 9
    once-only delivery of, 22
    -oriented middleware (MOM), 230
    passing, 230
    queuing (MQ), 12, 230
        application, 76
        asynchronous nature of, 25
        server, 17
    routing, 15
Messaging
    agent, 188
    asynchronous, 22, 100
    commercial, 24
    CORBA, 35
    domains, 100
    middleware, see Distributed transaction
        and messaging middleware
    multicast, real-time, 75
    patterns, 72
    point-to-point, 241
    priority-based, 74
    publish-subscribe, 241

Queuing Interface (MQI), 20
    request–reply, 241
    XML, 108, 115
Meta-Data Coalition (MDC), 52
Metadata Interchange Patterns (MIP), 52
Meta-Object Facility (MOF) extensions, 36
Microsoft, 131
    Access 2002, 184
    ActiveX Data Object (ADO), 166, 244
    Audio-Video Interleaved (AVI) format, 108
    Component Object Model, 14
    Content Management Server 2001, 63
    Exchange Server, 187
    Exchange Server 2000, 81
    Interface Description Language (MIDL), 6
    Intermediate Language (MSIL), 59, 253
    Internet Explorer, 57
    Internet Information Services (IIS), 8, 125
    Management Console (MMC), 83
    management strategy, 83
    Message Queuing (MSMQ), 8
        application programming interface, 11
        distribution lists, 75
        Exchange connector, 76
        features, 9
        network support, 13
        in processing client order, 9
        servers, 12
        Triggers, 76
        in Windows XP, 74
    Messaging Application Programming
        Interface (MAPI), 240
    MSMQ, 230
    Object Linking and Embedding (OLE), 240
    Online Analytical Processing (OLAP), 158
    Operations Manager 2000, 233
    Queued Components (QC), 10
    RPC, 6
        components, 7
        facility, 5
    SQL Server, 96
    SQL Server 2000, 183–184
    -supported languages, 60
    Transaction Server (MTS), 14, 58, 73, 198,
        231
    Visual Basic, 8
    Visual J++, 59
Microsoft stuff, 57–84
    Microsoft management strategy, 83
    Microsoft Transaction Server, 73–74
    MSMQ in Windows XP, 74–76
    .NET architecture, 58–69
        advantages, 60
        building .NET platform, 62–63
        Microsoft Content Management Server
            2001, 63–65
        multi-platform development, 59
        .NET architecture, 61–62
        .NET Enterprise Servers, 63
        .NET Framework Security policy, 65–69
        Web services, 61
        what .NET is not, 59–60
    Open.NET, 69
    SOAP, 69–73
    Windows 2000 Advanced Server, 78–82
        increasing server availability, 79
        increasing server performance, 79

SMP and advanced memory manage-
ment, 79–80
Windows 2000 clustering technologies,
80–82
Windows 2000 Datacenter, 76–78
Enterprise Memory Architecture, 77–78
Windows Clustering, 76–77
Winsock Direct, 78
Windows 2000 family management
services, 82–83
Middle-tier application server, 95
Middleware
communications, 217, 234, 235, 246
database, 234, 235, 236, 246
flavors of, 157
Java-based, 171
XML, 165
DBMS/SQL, 164
definition of, 234
development, 240
distributed object, 236
E-commerce, 234, 237, 246
enterprise connector, 237
hierarchy, 245, 246
Java-based, 234, 238, 246
Legacy-to-Web, 237
message-oriented, 230
messaging, 236, 238
products, EDA/SQL, 157
selection criteria, 234
systems, 234, 246
Middleware performance, 217–241
communications paradigms and tools,
228–231
comparing paradigms, 228–229
trade-offs, 229–231
XML-RPC, 231
IP traffic performance, 217–227
bandwidth managers, 220–221
caching, 225–227
case study, 219–220
content delivery networks, 224–225
load balancing, 227
traffic shapers, 221–224
middleware selection, 233–240
communications middleware, 234–235
database middleware, 235–236
development middleware, 240
E-commerce middleware, 237–238
Java-based middleware, 238–239
middleware interoperability, 240
systems middleware, 236–237
Web services technology, 239–240
other performance tools, 232–233
database, 232–233
Internet Security and Acceleration Server
2000, 233
managing ELB and Java performance,
232
Microsoft Operations Manager 2000, 233
service level management, 227–228
Middleware technologies, what lies ahead for,
243–257
competing paradigms, 245
emerging Internet standards, 248–251
security, 248–249
user interface, 248
workflow standard, 249–251

evolutionary paths, 244–245
interoperability, 251–254
J2EE and .NET platform, 253–254
SOAP protocol, 251–253
middleware hierarchy, 245–248
database middleware, 246–247
Web services, 247–248
performance tools, 254–256
service levels, 256
MIDL, see Microsoft Interface Description
Language
Minimum CORBA, 31
MIP, see Metadata Interchange Patterns
MMC, see Microsoft Management Console
Model(s)
CCM
event, 38
programming, 10
Component Object, 57
container programming, 39
CORBA Component, 32, 36, 90
-Driven Architecture (MDA), 46, 51
inner core, 51
middle core, 52
outer core, 53
DTP, 13
EJB Component, 56
E-transaction processing, 13
IDL specified, 55
Kerberos security, 16
local procedure call, 1
Microsoft Component Object, 14
OLTP, 13
Platform-Independent, 54
point-to-point, 101
Publish/Subscribe application, 102
queuing, advantage of, 229
RPC, 28
security, J2EE, 99
specifications, 46
XML-based data, 127
MOF extensions, see Meta-Object Facility
extensions
MOM, see Message-oriented middleware
Motion Picture Experts Group-1 (MPEG-1),
108
MPEG-1, see Motion Picture Experts
Group-1
MQ, see Message queuing
MQI, see Messaging Queuing Interface
MQIPT, see MQSeries Internet Pass-Thru
MQSeries
APIs, 19, 20
CICS and, 26
Everyplace for MultiPlatforms, 22
family, 20, 21
integration example, 21
Integrator, 21, 256
Internet Pass-Thru (MQIPT), 25
JMS support, 26
Workflow, 21
MSIL, see Microsoft Intermediate Language
MSMQ, see Microsoft Message Queuing
MTS, see Microsoft Transaction Server
MTU, see Maximum transfer unit
Multi-homing, 227
Multi-platform development, 59
MyBase, 185

N

Name-object bindings, 105
Name service provider, 7
Naming
    package, 106
    service, 35, 42, 87
    systems, 104
Natural language dialogue, 208
NDR, see Network data representation
.NET
    architecture, 58
    Enterprise Servers, 63, 64
    Framework Security policy, 65
    layer, description of, 62
    platform, building of, 62, 63
Netscape, 107
Netscape Navigator, 57, 85
NetWare, 165
Network(s)
    bandwidths, 218
    bottlenecks, 217, 255
    data representation (NDR), 6
    file services, 245
    heterogeneous, 220
    Load Balancing (NLB), 76, 79, 81
        cluster service and, 81
        incoming IP traffic load-balanced by, 82
    OLE, 58
    operating system (NOS), 76
    protocol independence, 9
    traffic fluctuations, extreme, 218
    wireless, 19
New York Stock Exchange (NYSE), 222
NLB, see Network Load Balancing
NOS, see Network operating system
Notification service, CORBA-based, 42
Novell, 107
Novell NetWare, 104
NYSE, see New York Stock Exchange

O

OAMAS, see Open Application Middleware
    API Specification
OASIS, see Organization for the Advancement
    of Structured Information Standards
Oberon, 60
Object(s)
    cryptographic, 68
    Database Connectivity, 165
    implementation, client sending request to,
        31
    Linking and Embedding Database data
        source (OLE DB), 165
    -oriented middleware, see CORBA 3
    -oriented programming languages, 32
    query language, 42
    Request Broker (ORB), 29, 43, 229–230
        examples, 33
        and Object Services platform task force,
            48
    request interfaces, structure of, 32
    Services Platform Task Force, 36
Object Design, Inc.
    ObjectStore DBMS, 179

ObjectStore PSE for Java, 179
Objectmatter Business Sight Framework, 172
OC4J, see Oracle9i Application Server Con-
    tainers for J2EE
ODBC, see Open Database Connectivity
OID, see Oracle Internet Directory
OLAP, see Microsoft Online Analytical
    Processing
OLE, see Microsoft Object Linking and
    Embedding
OLE DB, see Object Linking and Embedding
    Database data source
OLTP, see Online transaction processing
OMG Technology Committee, 44
Online transaction processing (OLTP), 76, 232
Open Application Middleware API Specifica-
    tion (OAMAS), 20
Open Database Connectivity (ODBC), 73
OpenJMS, 103
OpenLink Software, Inc. OpenLink Data
    Access Drivers for JDBC, 179–180
Open.NET, 69
OpenORB Enterprise Suite, 43
Open Software Foundation (OSF), 7
    -DCE remote procedure, 7
    standards, for RPC, 7
Oracle Corporation, 185
    Internet Directory (OID), 124
    Message broker, 188
    Oracle Lite, 180
    Web services architecture, 123
Oracle8i/9i application servers, 184–185
Oracle9i Application Server Containers for
    J2EE (OC4J), 95
ORB, see Object Request Broker
Order–shipping scenario, 10
Organization for the Advancement of
    Structured Information Standards
    (OASIS), 109, 117, 239–240, 248
Origin verification, 69
OS/2, 92, 103
OSF, see Open Software Foundation

P

Package Wizard, 74
Packeteer PacketShaper, 223
Packet-size optimization, 223
PAE, see Physical Address Extension
Pagers, 110
Partner Interface Processes (PIPs), 128
PDAs, see Personal data assistants
Peer
    groups, 110
    monitoring, 110
    -to-peer transaction, 111
    pipes, 110
PeopleSoft Component Interfaces, 95
PerCurrence PerXML Smart Transformation
    System, 168
Performance tools, 254
Perl, 60
Permission mechanisms, fine-grained, 69
Persistence state service, 42
Persistent Definition Language (PSDL), 37
Persistent State Service (PSS), 37

Personal data assistants (PDAs), 110, 116, 199
Pervasive Software, 164
Physical Address Extension (PAE), 76, 78
PIM, see Platform-Independent Model
PIPs, see Partner Interface Processes
PKI, see Public key infrastructure
Platform-Independent Model (PIM), 54
Platform Specific Models (PSMs), 54
Platform technology
    FTFs, 45
    RTFs, 45
    SIGs, 45
    task force, 45
Platform Technology Committee (PTC), 48, 70
POA, see Portable Object Adapter
POET Software Corporation POET Object
       Server Suite, 180
Point-to-point (P2P), 101
    domain, 101
    messaging, 241
    model, 101
Portability of implementations, 55
Portability of specifications, 55
Portable Object Adapter (POA), 30, 90
Port mapper server, 2
P2P, see Point-to-point
Process components, 39
Product integration, 206
Programming errors, 66
Property service, 42
Protocol stack CPU time, 219
PSDL, see Persistent Definition Language
PSMs, see Platform Specific Models
PSS, see Persistent State Service
PSTN, see Public switched telephone network
PTC, see Platform Technology Committee
Public Credit Service, 131, 132
Public key infrastructure (PKI), 126, 240
Public switched telephone network (PSTN),
       185, 218
Publish-subscribe
    application model, 102
    messaging, 241
Python, 60

Q

QC, see Microsoft Queued Components
QoS, see Quality of Service
Quality of Service (QoS), 31, 117, 218
    control, 35
    management, 246
Query
    manager(s), 23
        objects, access to, 25
        programs connected to different, 24
    service, 42
Queue, programs connected to same, 23
Queuing model, advantage of, 229
Quicktime, 108

R

RAD, see Resource Access Decision

Random number generation, 68
RDF Site Summary (RSS), 129
RDS, see Remote Data Service
Real-Time CORBA, 31, 35, 36
Real-time messaging multicast, 75
Real-Time PSIG, 49
Real-time Streaming Protocol (RTSP), 108
Real-Time Transport Protocol (RTP), 108
Recital Corporation, JDBC Developer, 177
Relationship service, 42
Reliable HTTP (HTTPR), 188
Remote Data Service (RDS), 166
Remote Method Invocation (RMI), 33
Remote procedure call (RPC), 1, 117, 230, 245
    components, 6
    features, 3
    layers, 2
    model, 28
    OSF standards for, 7
    requests, encoding of, 231
    runtime library, client, 7
Request prioritization, 16
Request–reply messaging, 241
Research languages, 60
ResolveNet Global Business Registry (GBR),
       129
Resource Access Decision (RAD), 44
Reusable components, 116
RMF, see Beatnik Rich Media Format
RMI, see Remote Method Invocation
RM/local transaction, 97
Rogue Wave Software XML-DB Link, 168
Role-based security, 66, 67
RPC, see Remote procedure call
RSS, see RDF Site Summary
RTP, see Real-Time Transport Protocol
RTSP, see Real-time Streaming Protocol
Runtime libraries, 7

S

Salesforce.com, 134
SAML, see Security Assertion Markup Lan-
       guage
SANs, see System area networks
SCI, see Server/container interface
SCL, see Service Contract Language
SCM, see supply chain management
SCO SQL-Retriever, 181
SCSL, see Sun Community Source Licensing
Secure Sockets Layer (SSL), 99, 225
Security, 72, 110
    application, 25
    Assertion Markup Language (SAML), 125,
        240, 248
    channel, 25
    evidence-based, 66
    Kerberos, 16
    model, J2EE, 99
    .NET Framework, 65
    role-based, 66, 67
    service, 42
Seller service, 250
Serialization support, 72
Server(s)
    Akamai, 224

application, 238
availability, increasing of, 79
ClearPath, 14
/container interface (SCI), 91
dynamic XML, 207
EJB, 87
enterprise, 220
forwarding, 17, 18
Java Application, 162
Lightweight Directory Access Protocol, 231
message queuing, 17
Microsoft Exchange, 187
Microsoft SQL, 96
Microsoft Transaction, 14, 58, 73, 198
middle-tier application, 95
MSMQ, 12
.NET Enterprise, 63, 64
performance, increasing of, 79
port mapper, 2
single view of multiple, 80
Tuxedo queue
Unix, 14
UNIXWare
WebSphere Application, 120
Windows 2000 Advanced, 78
Windows 2000 Datacenter, 76, 77
Windows NT, 14
wireless application, 238
XML application, 182
Service
components, 38
Contract Language (SCL), 122
level agreement (SLA), 130, 219
defective, 254
focus of on maximum upload availability
and guaranteed bandwidths, 255
policy on, 256
level management (SLM), 228, 256
package, 115
/provider interface (SPI), 91
Servlet distribution, 98
Session
bean, 89
components, 38
Shared Property Manager, 74
SIGs
domain technology, 46
platform technology, 45
SilverStream Software, 135
Simple Network Management Protocol
(SNMP), 83
Simple Object Access Protocol (SOAP), 57, 69,
117, 283
-based Web services, 70
implementations, 71–73, 137, 138
as lightweight XML protocol, 205
protocol, 251
with Attachments (SwA), 254
XML block, 61
SLA, see Service level agreement
SLM, see Service level management
Smalltalk, 32, 60
Smart transducers, 36
SMP, see Symmetric multi-processing
SMTP, see Standard Mail Transport Protocol
SNMP, see Simple Network Management
Protocol
SOAP, see Simple Object Access Protocol

Software, see also specific application
business, 67
data-center, 233
elements, various roles assumed by, 69
enterprise resource planning, 76
financial, 67
Solaris, 165
Solid Information Technology Ltd.
SOLID JDBC Driver, 181
SOLID Server, 181
SolidSpeed Networks, 227
SonicMQ, 230
SPI, see Service/provider interface
SQL, see Structured Query Language
SSL, see Secure Sockets Layer
Stack layers, emerging, 125
Standard Mail Transport Protocol (SMTP), 119,
252
Stateful session bean, 89
Stateless session bean, 90
STDL, see Structured Transaction Definition
Language
Stonebroom ASP2XML, 167
Strong name, 67
Structured Query Language (SQL), 157, 236
object derivatives of, 42
/relational databases, 246
statements, predefined, 169
Structured Transaction Definition Language
(STDL), 13
Stub procedure, local, 6
Sun, 107
Community Source Licensing (SCSL), 108
Java Management Extensions (JMX), 136,
253
J2EE environment, 240
ONE Web services, 122
Solaris, 21, 104
Super Distributed Objects DSIG, 49
Supplier Web service description, 138
Supply chain management (SCM), 85, 158,
243
SwA, see SOAP with Attachments
Swift, Inc. DB-X, 167
Sybase, Inc., 96
Jaguar CTS, 176
jConnect for JDBC, 176–177
Symantec dbANYWHERE Server, 173–174
Symmetric multi-processing (SMP), 76
Synchronous/asynchronous calls, 89
System(s)
area networks (SANs), 78
hardening, 233
middleware, 234, 246

T

Tabular Data Stream (TDS), 177
Talarian, 230
Tamino X-Bridge, 73
TAPI, see Windows Telephony Applications
Programming Interface
Tarantella, 107
Tarrific, 134
TCP/IP, see Transmission Control
Protocol/Internet Protocol

TDS, see Tabular Data Stream
Telasoft Data Corporation Javabase/400, 176
Telecommunications Domain task force, 49
Telephony client application, 187
Thought, Inc. CoCoBase, 172–173
TIBCO, 230
Time service, 42
Tivoli Web Services Manager, 120
TP, see Transaction processing
TPC, see Transaction Processing Performance
    Council
Trading object service, 43
Traffic
    bottlenecks, 204
    performance, 217
    rates, changing, 222
    shapers, 221, 222
Transaction(s)
    E-commerce, 126
    HTTP, 98
    management, 15
    Manager, 15, 16
    peer-to-peer, 111
    processing (TP), 14, 85, 229, 230, 254
    service, 43
    Web E-commerce, 232
Transaction Processing Performance Council
    (TPC), 232
Transmission Control Protocol/Internet
    Protocol (TCP/IP), 2
    application-level port number, 219
    MQSeries client using, 27
    networking protocols, 12
    presentation layer, role of XML in, 204
    tower, 206
    traffic, 255
Transportation Domain task force, 49
Transport interface modules, 7
Trigger monitor, 25
Tunneling
    firewall, 99
    HTTP, 99
    services, 100
Tuxedo queue servers, 17
Type verification, 69

U

UDDI, see Universal Description, Discovery
    and Integration
UDP, see User Datagram Protocol
UDS, see Universal Data System
UML, see Unified Modeling Language
UN/CEFACT, see United Nations Centre for
    Trade Facilitation and Electronic
    Business
Unified Modeling Language (UML), 37
    editor programs, 55
    profiles, 54
UNISYS, 15
Unisys e-@ction Distributed Processing
    Middleware, 13
United Nations Centre for Trade Facilitation
    and Electronic Business
    (UN/CEFACT), 109
United States Postal Service (USPS), 138

Units of work, 24
Universal Data System (UDS), 14
Universal Description, Discovery and Integra-
    tion (UDDI), 61, 113, 124, 238, 245
    Business Registry, 126, 127, 128
    information, organization of, 128
    Registry, 118, 252
    repositories, 135
Universal XML, 209
UNIX, 92, 103
    password file, 99
    server, 14
UNIXWare server, 14
Unmanaged code, 59, 66
URL mapping, external–internal, 75
U.S. Department of Commerce, 84
User
    Datagram Protocol (UDP), 2
    -defined dequeuing, 17
    interface, 248
USPS, see United States Postal Service

V

Verisign, 134, 240
Versant Object Technology Versant ODBMS,
    182
Virtual private networking (VPN), 233
Visigenic Software, Inc. VisiChannel, 182
Visual Basic, 247
VMS, 92, 103
VoiceXML document, 209
VPN, see Virtual private networking

W

WAN
    bandwidth, wasting of, 219
    traffic, 219
WAP, see Wireless Access Protocol
Watershed Technologies Relational Object
    Framework, 180–181
WBEM, see Web-Based Enterprise
    Management
W3C, see World Wide Web Consortium
Web
    -based applications, 115
    -Based Enterprise Management (WBEM),
        83
    Collage Syndicator, 248
    components, 97
    -connected device, 116
    description languages, 117
    E-commerce transactions, 232
    -enabling services, 14
    sites, Enterprise, rapid time-to-market, 65
WebFOCUS, 158
WebMethods, 240
Web service(s), 61, 113–156
    Anaconda WSDL example, 144–146
    architecture, Oracle, 123
    BEA, 124
    Borland, 125
    brokerages, 133

broker WSDL example, 148–149
container, portable, 137, 253
custom-developed, 115
definition of, 114
description of, 114
directory, specialized, 130
document listing, 131
electricity Web service WSDL example,
    155–156
FarmsandRegal WSDL example, 146–148
features of, 137
finance Web service WSDL example,
    151–154
Hewlett-Packard, 124
integration of E-commerce transactions
    and, 126
interoperability test WDSL example,
    140–144
listing of in UDDI registry, 252
management of, 64
postal rate calculator Web service WSDL,
    150–151
revolution, 70
SOAP-based, 70
stack, 114
Sun ONE, 122
third-party tools, 134–138
    Cape Clear, 134–135
    Grand Central, 134
    IONA technologies, 136–138
    Silverstream, 135–136
Web services stack, 114–133
    comparing definitions or descriptions,
      116–117
    defining or describing Web services,
      114–116
    emerging stack layers, 125–126
    UDDI registrars and services, 129
    UDDI registration, 126–128
    versioning of Web services, 133
    Web services architecture, 122–125
    Web services brokerage, 129–131
    workflow processes, 131–132
workflow, 250
Web Service(s)
    Broker, 123
    Conversational Language (WSCL), 119
    Description Language (WSDL), 61, 119, 239,
      245
    Flow Language (WSFL), 118, 132
    User Interface (WSUI), 125, 239
Web Services Description Language example
    Anaconda, 144–146
    broker, 148–149
    electricity Web service, 155–156
    FarmsandRegal, 146–148
    finance Web service, 151–154
    interoperability test, 140–144
    postal rate calculator Web service, 150–151
WebServices.org, 116
WebSnap, 125
WebSphere
    Adapters, 22
    Application Server, 120
    Business Integrator, 22
    Partner Agreement Manager, 22
Wily Technologies, 114

Windows, see also Microsoft
    Clustering, 76
    Management Instrumentation (WMI), 82, 83
    NT, 14, 92, 103, 220
    Script Host (WSH), 83
    Sockets, 78
    Telephony Applications Programming
      Interface (TAPI), 185
    Telephony with TAPI, 157
Windows 2000
    Advanced Server, 78
    clustering
      services, 74
      technologies, 80
    Datacenter Server, 76, 77
    Family Management Services, 82
    Messaging Queuing 2.0 for, 11
Windows XP
    Message Queuing 3.0 for, 10
    MSMQ in, 74
Winsock Direct, 78, 79
Wireless Access Protocol (WAP), 198
    application, 202
    -based applications, 201
    script, complete, 214–216
Wireless application server, 238
Wireless Markup Language (WML), 199, 239,
    248
Wireless Multimedia Forum (WMF), 225
Wireless networks, 19
WMF, see Wireless Multimedia Forum
WMI, see Windows Management
    Instrumentation
WML, see Wireless Markup Language
Workflow(s)
    applications, 16
    complex, 132, 250, 251
    EJB-based, 133, 252
    Management, 44
    processes, 131
    simple, 131, 250
    standard, 249
    Web service, 250
Work-in-progress status, 46, 48–50
World Wide Web Consortium (W3C), 68, 69,
    117, 208
    Web Services
      architecture stack, 121
      description stack, 121
      discovery stack, 121
    Web Services Workshop, 120
    XQuery working draft, 247
WSCL, see Web Service Conversational
    Language
WSDL, see Web Services Description
    Language
WSFL, see Web Services Flow Language
WSH, see Windows Script Host
WSTK, see IBM Web Services ToolKit
WSUI, see Web Services User Interface

X

XACML, see eXtensible Access Control
    Markup Language
XATMI, 17

XDb Systems ExpressLane, 174
XKMS, see XML Key Management
     Specification
XMI, see eXtensible Markup Language Meta
     Interchange
XML, see eXtensible Markup Language

xml.org, 118, 127
XMLP, see eXtensible Markup Language
     Protocol
XSD, see XML Schema Datatypes
XSLT, see eXtensible Stylesheet Language
     Transformation

T - #0639 - 101024 - C0 - 254/178/16 - PB - 9780849312724 - Gloss Lamination